Paragraph

A Journal of Modern Critical Theory

Volume 40, Number 3, November 2017

Literature and Psychoanalysis: Open Questions

Edited by Elissa Marder

Contents

Preface (To Reopen the Question) SHOSHANA FELMAN	iii
Introduction: Open Questions, Opaque Transmissions ELISSA MARDER	257
The Body's Testimony: Dramatic Witness in the Eichmann Trial CATHY CARUTH	259
The Transfer of Complaint: A Narcissistic Time-Share AVITAL RONELL	279
Nothing to Say: The Negative Phrase of Affect CLAIRE NOUVET	294
What Are the Chances? Psychoanalysis, Telepathy, and the Accident ELIZABETH ROTTENBERG	310
SF FORBES MORLOCK	329
Freud's Fictions: Fixation, Femininity, Photography ELISSA MARDER	349

The Function and Field of Scansion in Jacques Lacan's
Poetics of Speech
ISABELLE ALFANDARY   368

Small Experimental Action
SARAH WOOD   383

Dream Treatment: On Sitting Down to Read a Letter
from Freud
NICHOLAS ROYLE   399

Notes on Contributors   406

Preface (To Reopen the Question)

SHOSHANA FELMAN

In memory of Barbara Johnson and Neil Gordon

The year 1977 was an exciting time at Yale, a time of innovation and creative fermentation. When the volume I initiated as a special editor of *Yale French Studies* Nos 55/56, *Literature and Psychoanalysis: The Question of Reading: Otherwise*, was published in that year, I had been teaching at the university for seven years.

I.

Life encounters: Freud, Lacan

Previously, in my own younger days as a college student, I remember how (quite early on) I chanced to read a work by Freud, by accident, without anybody's guidance, and how this accidental reading soon became a passion, a desire to read more, to delve in further depth into this transformative visionary opening of the nuances, the complexity and the emerging riddles of the world around me. This first accidental reading and this chance encounter with Freud's work left on me a striking impact that almost instantly, in one blow, revolutionized my thinking, and marked, in my own eyes, something like the crossing of a threshold into critical adulthood. The psychoanalytic mode of understanding things became for me a second nature, and henceforth, an essential part of my intuitive perception of the world and of my conscious and unconscious, almost visceral or carnal intellectual 'luggage'.

Having done my PhD in France, I had become familiar later with the teachings of Lacan, whose seminars I had attended in the years in which I wrote my dissertation (in Geneva and in France), and whose books I read without ever attempting to understand them right away, and without seeking to master them (as dogma or as academic property): I merely breathed them into my own lungs, because I felt they were ingeniously inspiring, and radically eye-opening in unprecedented ways.[1]

Psychoanalysis and reading

I knew right away that Lacan was relevant to literary thinkers, not just because of his famously poetic style, but because, most crucially, he saw the whole affair of the unconscious as a phenomenon — and an affair — of reading:

> In analytic discourse [Lacan repeats in one of his later seminars], you presume the subject of the unconscious to be capable of reading. This is what this whole affair of the unconscious amounts to. Not only do you presume him to be capable of reading, *you presume him to be capable of learning how to read*.[2]

In Lacan's unique visit to Yale at my invitation in 1975, he addressed spontaneously a casual group of American psychoanalysts (possibly in his attempt to connect with them) in more familiar, more colloquial, terms, highlighting and explaining much more clearly the crucial role that the event of reading had fulfilled in Freud's foundational discovery:

> [Freud's] first interest was in hysteria (...). He spent a lot of time listening, and while he was listening, there resulted something paradoxical, a *reading*. It was while listening to hysterics that he *read* that there was an unconscious. That is, something he could only construct, and in which he himself was implicated; he was implicated in it in the sense that, to his great astonishment, he noticed that he could not avoid participating in what the hysteric was telling him, and that he felt affected by it.
>
> Naturally, everything in the resulting rules in which he established the practice of psychoanalysis is designed to counteract this consequence, to conduct things in such a way as to avoid being affected.[3]

Revolutionary readers

Freud was thus, in Lacan's eyes, a revolutionary reader. Lacan, in turn, we could say, is another extraordinarily insightful and creatively innovative, revolutionary reader of Freud's text and of Freud's reading: yet another reader whose reading is foundational, in that it constitutes (like Freud's) at once a practice and a theory.

In 1968 the French philosopher Louis Althusser (who in his turn was attending Lacan's seminar) made a historically important statement, which I have found crucially enlightening, as an interpretation of Lacan's significance to culture:

It is to the intransigent, lucid — and for many years solitary — theoretical effort of Jacques Lacan that we owe today this result [this renewed understanding of the workings of the unconscious], which has drastically transformed our way of reading Freud. At a time when what Lacan has given us that was so radically new begins to pass into the public domain and when everyone can use it, in their own way, to their profit, I would like to make a point of acknowledging our debt toward *his exemplary lesson of reading*, the effects of which (...) go well beyond its original object.[4]

Life between America and France

When Althusser wrote this, I was still working on my dissertation. I totally adhered to this historical public acknowledgement by Althusser, and wanted one day to interpret and illuminate this statement in my own way. Having pursued (as I narrated) my PhD in France, I was offered my first teaching job at Yale. My formative years, including the first years of my professional career at Yale as teacher and as literary critic, took place — pragmatically and theoretically — through a frequent physical and cultural shuttle movement between America and France. Following the publication of my dissertation (by a Parisian publisher),[5] my next two books were equally written in French and initially (in their original editions) published in Paris.[6] As a young scholar and young author, I became for some years a participant in the Parisian intellectual circles, and frequently conversed and met with writers and psychoanalysts. It was a time when almost all of Paris, intellectuals from various disciplines and trainings and virtually all artists, were customarily attending Lacan's seminars and were familiar with — and differently impacted by — the teachings of Lacan. This milieu was highly stimulating and regularly thought-provoking. Eventually, out of the seminar, I came to know Lacan in person, and had with him throughout the years several private meetings that included unforgettable exchanges.

What I had thus learned in France over the years, seemed preciously inspiring, and I wanted to bring this exciting, innovative psychoanalytic emphasis, these new possibilities for reading and this new kind of stimulating inspiration to the United States, and to the English-speaking context. This is how I conceived this *Yale French Studies* special issue.

Reading otherwise

In commenting on the significance of the issue's title and subtitle (*Literature and Psychoanalysis: The Question of Reading: Otherwise*), I tried to clarify at once the meaning of my project and the driving force of its intellectual incentive in my second 'Foreword' to the Johns Hopkins (1982) republication of the special issue of the journal as a book:[7]

> Why Otherwise? (...) The question hitherto neglected is, indeed, how to relate psychoanalysis and literature otherwise than at the (all too frequent) cost of banalizing both; how to put in contact the very genius of psychoanalysis and the (very different) genius of the thing called literature — of that which makes texts literary — without reducing their basic otherness, without compromising the differences between them which make, precisely, for the specificity of their genius.
>
> *Otherwise* suggests, then, that what is at stake in the different manner of this volume is the very question of the relation between otherness and wisdom. Psychoanalysis and literature, in attempting to derive each other's wisdom, without compromising the other's otherness, here renew the question not just of their respective meaning(s), but of their respective meaningfulness.[8]

How do we teach (lessons of) reading?

In line with Althusser's acknowledgement of the originality of the Lacanian psychoanalytic teaching as an 'exemplary lesson of reading', I wanted my edited volume of *Yale French Studies* to embody in its own way Althusser's visionary pedagogical illumination, and to become in turn nothing less, and nothing other, than 'an exemplary lesson of reading'. A reading lesson — as I understood it — was to be, however, not so much a statement, as a performance; a collective performance that was meant to illustrate an innovative kind of dialogue between psychoanalysis and literature, a dialogue embodied less in the propounding of a theory, than in a different, pioneering reading *practice*.

The issue did in fact make a collective affirmation, I believe, of the existence (and the proven efficacy) of new ways of reading, built as it was on the assembled contributions of a distinguished team of (cross-linguistic) American and French creative thinkers, including psychoanalysts, writers and literary critics. The psychoanalytic theory involved in their essays was eloquent (each time) through a concrete textual analysis, a reading practice that derived its (collective) exemplarity from its capacity — each time in unanticipated ways — both to reveal (enable a discovery), and to surprise.

Thus, Jacques Lacan's introductory, concrete analysis of 'Desire and the Interpretation of Desire' as illustrated through the glorious literary text and verbal genius of Shakespeare's *Hamlet*; Daniel Sibony's following, analytically sophisticated reading of *Hamlet* as 'a writing effect'; Gayati Spivak's philosophical and critical, pragmatic and theoretical reflections on Coleridge's *Biographia Literaria*; Roger Dragonetti's reading of Dante's *Divina Commedia*; Charles Méla's reading of *Perceval*; my own reading of the readings and the text of Henry James's literary tale *The Turn of the Screw*; Peter Brooks's analysis of Freud's *Beyond the Pleasure Principle* as an archetypal literary narrative (of ends and of beginnings); Jean-Michel Rey's reading of 'Freud's Writing on Writing', analysing the whole spectrum of Freud's references to literary writers; followed by Philippe Sollers's astonishing writerly piece on the act of writing, demonstrating how a contemporary literary writer receives, interprets and records the Lacan effect and the Freud effect, in finally envisioning and depicting, in a concrete yet imaginative tour de force, 'Freud's Hand' in the act of writing his five case histories (each finger matching in its physical description the characteristics of its own psychoanalytic case). This stunning literary piece is followed, in conclusion of the issue, by three major philosophical elucidations: Fredric Jameson's theoretical and practical reflections conjugating Marxism and Freudian psychoanalysis with Lacan's theory of 'the symbolic', 'the imaginary' and the enigmatic concept of 'the real', in so far as all these discourses mutually address the (individual and — Jameson insists — most importantly, the social) problem of the subject; John Brenkman's reading of Plato's *The Symposium* as a touchstone of the present drama of encounters (and mutual critiques) between literature, philosophy and psychoanalysis; and, finally, Barbara Johnson's ingeniously woven reading tapestry of Poe, Lacan and Derrida in so far as they mutually contest each other but in fact collectively highlight and illustrate the literary texture of Poe's tale 'The Purloined Letter'; this diverse, and today still irreplaceable, list of readings did in fact engage collectively in a new kind of creative, living dialogue between psychoanalysis and literature, the two fields speaking (teaching, learning) not from without but from within each other. This living educational dialogue must be continued and pursued today, because its teachings (as Freud said of analysis itself) are interminable: in their enticing dialogical potential and in the infinite educational wealth of their mutual implications, they can never be exhausted.

My programmatic 'Introduction' to the *Yale French Studies* issue was entitled, thus, as the dynamic point of departure it was meant to be, 'To Open the Question'.

Do I think today — forty years later — that the question (of reading, and of the dialogical relationship between psychoanalysis and literature) can be 'opened', or reopened, in the same way? I think not, or not exactly, because both the world and the university have in the meantime radically changed.

II.

Why the question of today is different

In 1977 we could take for granted the importance of the liberal arts in higher education, and thus the vital human need for literature seemed clear. The civilized world's widespread recognition, not just of the centrality of literature, but of the inherent dignity of its humanistic mission — could be taken as a given. It can no longer be so today. As we all know, the Humanities in higher academic institutions are facing an ongoing existential crisis, on a global, transcontinental scale. This global cultural, intellectual and conceptual crisis translates itself financially into repeated, major budget cuts to Humanities departments, cuts that take effect, across the board, through the amalgamation and elimination of various literature and language programmes deemed expendable or marginal. In parallel, reductions are imposed on the numbers of admitted students to these programmes. A reconfiguration of curricula responds to these administrative, corporate-style financial pressures.

The academy throughout the world materializes nowadays at once a ferocious battlefield — and an unbreachable abyss — between two competing yet incompatible and contradictory visions of academic education. On the one hand, a Humboldtian model[9] of holistic, comprehensive liberal arts education, founded on two concepts or two goals, shaped by theorists of the Enlightenment: the (classical liberal) concept of the individual's autonomy and freedom (through which the student will explore her intellectual gifts in encountering the world, and thereby unfold her subjectivity in which she will discover — and live out — her humanity), and the concept or the goal of forming world citizenship, through the so-called 'collective bond' which connects autonomous, free individuals irrespective of their different social or cultural experiences of socialization. World citizens encounter, and address, the big questions of humanity: justice, peace, care about exchange of cultures, and the rebuilding of relationships. Such comprehensive education (in what the Romans had significantly named *artes liberalis* — 'arts worthy of free men, as opposed to slaves') was to be entirely separated from job-seeking, and absolutely independent both of economic interests and of political rewards.

Facing this ideal of forming world citizenship as the goal of education, there is, on the other hand, in today's academy, a conflicting, more pragmatic vision based on economic calculations of the universities themselves (submitting to criteria that prevail in the global market), emphasizing straight away a more accelerated and more focused professional apprenticeship of specific forms of expertise and of technical career skills, seeking a more limited and targeted job-oriented academic training. This approach bypasses altogether the Humboldtian claim for a foundational, broader humanistic education. It is geared towards making the university a profit-oriented institution, and securing for the student — the professional apprentice — an accelerated economical realization as an individual, and a quicker future of individual(ist) (capitalist) economical accomplishment (measured mostly by earning capacity). In this vision, which is overpowering today and seems to be predominating in most academic high administrations, the academy is basically transformed into a financial, bureaucratic-managerial, corporate-style organization, and the university as a whole — in the very core of its educational endeavour — becomes primarily a market-driven institution, in which the truth of the market (and its sole touchstone of predictable — consumerist — market profitability) becomes an almost absolute criterion of evaluation that erases nearly all other scales of values, and overrules every other cultural or philosophical conception of the truth. Everything is measured in terms of actual or potential earning capacity, that is, profitability or non-profitability. Theories, enquiries, ideas and areas of research, are reduced to the exclusive criterion of what will sell; the scale of value is the saleability and the profitability of cultural trends. The university's constitutive academic freedom, its reputed independence from the requirements of interested parties, and in particular — currently — its independence from the private needs of world capital — have dramatically diminished, and seem to be about to disappear. This goes hand in hand with the rushed acceleration of the time of education: PhD students are pushed out of the university after four or five years of supported academic education, so as to hasten the industrial production of degrees, and to shorten the duration of the university's intellectual and financial investment in individuals.

This emphasis on market values, and more generally on the exclusive economic rationality of social goods and of the production of social values, is underwritten, motivated and increasingly reinforced by the global rise (and the triumphant political implementation) — since the third quarter of the twentieth century — of the ideology known as neoliberalism.[10] In this overbearing, domineering educational, cultural and political environment, let us now return to the relationship between literature and psychoanalysis.

The year 2017 in education: an inversion of the situation of 1977

In 1977 people knew what literature was, but very few had knowledge of French psychoanalysis, and the point of my issue was to teach how the innovations of French psychoanalysis could shed new light on literature. Today the situation is symmetrically reversed. Psychoanalysis — including French psychoanalysis — has become much better known, but we have fundamentally forgotten, and I claim that we no longer know, what literature is, in its distinctive textual specificity. We do teach literary theory in academic literature departments. But very few professors nowadays (in universities across the world) still teach literary texts in their particularity through a focus on close readings, or through detailed analysis of the uniqueness of a text's style or of its distinctive literary insight.

Education is always a relation — and a dialogue — between the known and the unknown, as well as between consciousness and the unconscious, in ways we do not always fully understand. In 1977 literature was very present in cultural and academic consciousness, whereas psychoanalysis had to be brought deeper and more fully into consciousness. Today it seems to me that psychoanalysis has found its undisputed place in our collective (educated, academic) consciousness, but literature — and what it means — has dropped out of the field of consciousness. Literature itself has become, today, our academic 'Purloined Letter' — a purloined letter, I would emphasize, both in its literary sense, ingeniously invented as a symbol by Edgar Allan Poe, and in its sophisticated, interpretive psychoanalytic sense, as highlighted later by Lacan in the wake of Poe. Because literature — submitted to the ruling economic standards and to the near-exclusive weight of market values by the accountants of the neoliberal university — has been judged summarily as 'non-profitable', and as calling for a structural re-allocation of funds and for withdrawal of financial resources, we have been witnessing for two decades a gradual, insidious and pernicious process of devaluation and depreciation of the discipline of literature, in which we (university professors of literature) are unwittingly, unconsciously participating, because we too are brainwashed by the surrounding culture and we do not want to be perceived as being left behind. Anyone familiar with the academic scene can notice how in recent years the members of the university, teachers as well as students, and literary critics in their turn, become more and more concerned with *self-marketing*, rather than with the process of creation and critical invention in itself. Thus, we all end up ourselves contributing – inadvertently – to the social and collective market process of the depreciation and *the downgrading of literature*. We all unwittingly take part in the neoliberal project of literature's agreed-upon devaluation, without noticing that this devaluation and depreciation are inculcated into us by the global interests of world capital and by its prevailing 'free market' ideology, from which literature (in its own self-definition and its history) had always radically distanced itself. Neoliberalism would be served, for its own political and economic private ends, by an erasure — and a censorship — of the power of critique inherent in the literary field. We could call this, I suggest, a project of *extermination* of literature. When Baudelaire translated Poe's short story 'The Purloined Letter', into French he called the tale 'La lettre volée' (The Stolen Letter). Can we say that the neoliberal university, in depreciating and repudiating literature, is in effect attempting (in Baudelaire's words) to *steal literature from us*? Can we resist this process and this project, by becoming conscious of it?

In this fortieth anniversary reopening or re-enacting of the dialogue between psychoanalysis and literature, the task today, I would suggest, is not so much to teach or to rethink otherwise psychoanalysis, as to recover literature from its devaluation and depreciation, to rescue it from its cultural and political eradication by the neoliberal university and by the corporate world's overwhelmingly predominant, global ultra-capitalist economic ideology. Those of us who still believe in literature must on the contrary reaffirm literature's prestige, and reassert its literary truth, as a truth which radically resists commodification, and refuses to accept — or strike a compromise with — a sound bite, materialistically shrunk and shallowly eviscerated world of 'post-truth'.

In 1977 I proposed that we had to learn how to 'read otherwise' psychoanalysis, and primarily how to 'read otherwise' *through* psychoanalysis. In 2017 I am suggesting that, in our neoliberal age, what we must 'read otherwise' — what I feel today it has become *most urgent to read otherwise* — is literature.

III.

'Between heaven and earth': the psychoanalytic homage to literature

Unlike today's predominant economists and their followers, the founders of psychoanalysis underscored the (always unexpected and surprising) relevance of literature, in highlighting their own admiration for what they saw as literature's nobility and dignity. They considered literature as a 'valued ally' in their own pioneering psychoanalytical investigation, and relied on it as a vital source of their creative inspiration. Psychoanalysis has always known, indeed, that literature encompasses at once the known and the unknown, and that — as an embodiment of the unconscious and of what exceeds the known — its teaching cannot be dispensed with in any education, and is particularly crucial to a psychoanalytic education.

Literature has always known, on the other hand, that knowledge — of whatever kind — always has its limitations, and that rationality — of whatever kind (including economic rationality) — can easily become irrational or even turn delirious by a mere 'turn of the screw', or — as Freud put it — by a mere quarter of a turn.

'There are more things between heaven and earth, Horatio,' Hamlet says, 'than are dreamt of in our philosophy.'[11] Freud — who (like Lacan) has learned a lot from Hamlet — therefore writes in his study of Jensen's *Gradiva*:

But creative writers are valuable allies and their evidence is to be prized highly, for they are apt to know a whole host of things between heaven and earth of which our philosophy has not yet let us dream. In their knowledge of the mind they are far in advance of us everyday people, for they draw upon sources which we have not yet opened up for science.[12]

Lacan, in turn, will underscore — and set up as a model for his own students — Freud's deeply deferential attitude towards art. Lacan will take this deference one step further, in talking about poetry:

And as Plato pointed out long ago [Lacan says in a seminar], it is not at all necessary that the poet know what he is doing, in fact, it is preferable that he not know.

That is what gives a primordial value to what he does. We can only bow our heads before it (...). From art we have to take seeds — take seeds for something else.[13]

The alliance between psychoanalysis and literature

In fact, Lacan's originality in highlighting and interpreting Freud's legacy and his revolutionary lesson proceeds from the important fact that Lacan perceives Freud — and is interested in exploring Freud — not merely as a theorist, but as himself in turn a literary writer (in his compelling, moving written texts), and also as an ingenious literary reader. Unique in his position among Freud's heirs and disciples, Lacan has both the courage and the genius to let himself be taught by Freud's literariness, as well as by Freud's sharp and pointed psychoanalytic insight. In Lacan's eyes, Freud's sensitivity to literature is therefore crucial: Lacan strongly recommends that literary sensitivity be acquired, cultivated and developed in the training of the future analysts, and be part of the self-education he requires and expects of psychoanalysts as such. Lacan writes:

> One has only to turn the pages of (...) [Freud's] works for it to become abundantly clear that Freud regarded a study (...) of the resonances (...) of literature and of the significations involved in works of art as necessary to an understanding of our [psychoanalytical] experience. Indeed, Freud himself is a striking instance of his own belief: he derived his inspiration, his ways of thinking and his technical weapons, from just such a study. But he also regarded it as a necessary condition in any teaching of psychoanalysis.[14]

Psychoanalysis is not what it should be without this opening, without this cultivated psychoanalytic receptivity to literature, which in practical (clinical) analysis means an analytic literary ear, a tuned-in analytic listening, attentive to the resonances and to the nuances of the patient's language. Psychoanalysis requires, therefore, something like poetic intuition.[15]

This singular literary (and psychoanalytic) lesson that Lacan derives from Freud's style and from Freud's revolutionary way of reading (his way of *listening* to the unconscious, in his patients, and in dreams), a lesson in the light of which Lacan learns *how to read Freud*, is transformed, in Lacan's own work, into a deliberately literary style of teaching. But it must be noted that what Lacan's *poetic pedagogy* is always meaningfully striving for, reaching for at its very core, both literarily and psychoanalytically, is *truth* (the truth of the unconscious): truth in its irreducible complexity; truth as an infinitely open literary question: What is (to borrow Freud's word[16]) the 'navel' of my own dream of understanding? What is the riddle I pose here under the guise of knowledge?[17]

IV.

The gadfly, or Why literature?

When Socrates (in the *Apology*) is put on trial and sentenced to death, he addresses the assembly of Athenian citizens in giving them his own literary definition of his own philosophical — and at the same time ethical and pedagogical — kind of truth:

> Men of Athens, I honor and love you; but (...) while I have life and strength I shall never cease from the practice and teaching of philosophy, exhorting every one whom I meet after my manner, and convincing him, saying: Oh my friend, why do you, who are a citizen of the great and mighty and wise city of Athens, care so much about laying the greatest amount of money and honor and reputation, and so little about wisdom and truth and the greatest improvement of the soul, which you never regard or heed at all? Are you not ashamed of this? (...) I tell you that virtue is not given by money (...). This is my teaching, and if this is the doctrine that corrupts the youth, my teaching is ruinous indeed. (...) I would have you know, that if you kill such a one as I am, you will injure yourselves more than you will injure me. (...) For (...) you will not easily find another like me, who, if I may use such a ludicrous figure of speech, am a sort of gadfly, given to the state by the God; and the state is like a great and noble steed who is tardy in his motions owing to his very size, and requires to be stirred into life. *I am that gadfly which God has given the state*, and all day and in all places, am always fastening upon you, arousing and persuading and reproaching you (...). I dare say that you may feel irritated at being suddenly awakened when you are caught napping; and you may think that if you were to strike me dead (...) you would sleep on for the remainder of your lives, unless God in his care gives you another gadfly.[18]

This role of gadfly that Socrates invented for himself, in coining it in court metaphorically and literarily, and in politically reclaiming it in his *Apology* as the quintessence of his philosophical and pedagogical vocation, and as the definition of his mission, this role that he conceptualized for the first time, and for which he was prepared to die, was transformed by the trial and the verdict into a symbolic, archetypal autobiographic destiny, whose signification was projected forward into history, beyond the individual who thereby pronounced his (unsuccessful) self-defence, and beyond the moment's punctual historic singularity.

Socrates' dramatic and traumatic execution, and Plato's publication of the *Apology* (and other dialogues) that kept Socrates alive for ever, had a tremendous impact on the history and on the shape of Western culture. Others after Socrates created (throughout history) different versions of this mission, in taking on themselves this role described in the *Apology*, and in embodying this philosophical and cultural vocation in their own life and sometimes in their own fate. In reality, all great literary writers became gadflies in one way or another, each in his or her own way. I would argue that literature itself, in its most profound lifeblood, might be considered — in its own elliptical, enigmatic ways — as a perpetual performance of the gadfly.

This is not only why our neoliberal age finds literature superfluous — and dangerous, harmful or detrimental to its various private economic interests. It is also why, in general, dictatorships would like to do away with literature, and why totalitarian regimes have always tried — and failed — not just to censor art but to persecute and to suppress the writers, to purge its artists. Albert Camus reflects that art — by virtue of what he calls its 'free essence' — works to connect people and unite them, as opposed to dictatorial regimes and tyrannies which, on the contrary, very like our neoliberal economists/philosophers, work to isolate and separate people from one another. The literary writer (by the very nature of his calling) becomes par excellence what Camus calls, in borrowing the metaphor from the Norwegian playwright Hendrik Ibsen, 'A Public Enemy'.[19] Camus writes:

Liberty alone draws people from their isolation; but slavery dominates a crowd of solitudes. And art, by virtue of [its] free essence (...) unites whereas tyranny separates. It is not surprising, therefore, that art should be the enemy marked by any form of oppression.[20]

I would suggest that among the (disguised or undisguised) oppressive forms that Camus discusses, these oppressive structures that by their very nature combat literature and attempt to censor and discredit it, striving to strangle and to stifle the potentially subversive force of literary writers, and to repress their dreaded power of expression and communication, among these structures of oppression we can count as well (although Camus could not yet target it) the current neoliberal, clandestine and covert form of oppression, that sells itself deceptively as nothing other than a promised liberty. Camus is lecturing about the mercantile society of the nineteenth century, but his wise and ironically acute critique fits our own century as well:

> There is no reason for being surprised that such a society (...) inscribes the words 'liberty' and 'equality' on its prisons *as well as on its temples of finance*. However, words cannot be prostituted with impunity. *The most misrepresented value today is the value of liberty.*[21]

Such a society, Camus argues, *must* discredit art and punish it. It delegitimizes art's compelling truth by silencing and quashing it, and (like in Ibsen's play) by reversing on the artist his own indictment of society, and by claiming that it is he, the artist, who (by spreading his 'fake news') is the real 'public enemy' who is damaging the people (in their economic welfare) and endangering the public health (the health of their prosperity).

> It is not surprising [Camus therefore writes] that artists and intellectuals should have been the first victims of modern tyrannies, whether of the Right or the Left. Tyrants know there is in the work of art an emancipatory force. (...) Every great work makes the human face (...) richer, and this is its whole secret. (...) Yes, when modern tyranny shows us that, even when confined to his calling, the artist is *a public enemy*, it is right. But in this way tyranny pays its respect, through the artist, to an image of man that nothing has ever been able to crush.[22]

This communal affirmation that Camus, in accepting the Nobel, defines symbolically as the very core, the driving force of any literary act (the generative principle of any literary work), indeed cannot avoid but be in conflict and in contradiction with the neoliberal ideological and philosophical endeavour to *bypass the collective* and to negate it, to 'free' oneself (economically, culturally, existentially) from it, and thus essentially — as Pierre Bourdieu argues — to destroy all collective structures, to *bypass and to negate* (annul) *the public realm as such*.[23]

The writer's double task

In offering contemporary literary works as testimonies to reality, literature endeavours to *take responsibility for truth*: the writer metaphorically takes the witness stand, if not before a court of law, at the very least before the court of history and of the future (as well as of his readers); the writer conjures his creative memory essentially in order to *address* another, to *appeal* to the community. To testify (through an artistic work) is thus not merely to narrate, but to *commit oneself*, and to commit the narrative, *to others*: to take responsibility, in speech, for history and for the truth of an occurrence, for something which, by definition, goes beyond the personal.²⁴ An act of literature always constitutes an affirmation of the public realm, and an implicit declaration of the existential bond of solidarity uniting individuals to one another as a collective.

In his acceptance speech of the Nobel Prize in Literature that was awarded to him in 1957, Albert Camus defined the role of the writer by two tasks: 'the service of truth' and the 'service of liberty':

> Because [the literary writer's] task is to unite the greatest number of people, his art must not compromise with lies and servitude which, wherever they rule, breed solitude. (...) The nobility of our craft will always be rooted in two commitments: (...) the refusal to lie about what one knows, and the resistance to oppression.

Literature is thus — Camus declares in his Nobel acceptance speech — 'a means of stirring the greatest number of people by offering them a privileged picture of common joys and sufferings'. Without community and without the public realm, Camus insists throughout his Nobel speech, there is no literature.

> The artist [Camus said] shapes himself as writer through a perpetual shuttle movement between his own self and the presence of the others, midway between the beauty he cannot do without, and the community he cannot tear himself away from. (...) But the silence of an unknown prisoner abandoned to humiliations at the other end of the world, is enough to draw the writer out of his exile, at least whenever, in the midst of the privileges of freedom, he manages not to forget that silence and to transmit it, in order to make it resound by means of his art.²⁵

Between beauty and pain: the unforgettable

The literary writer is thus characterized as 'vulnerable but obstinate, unjust but impassioned for justice, (...) not ceasing to be divided between sorrow and beauty'. It is interesting to note that the idea of this split — of this division and this contradictory pull inside the artist — is repeated by Camus in a lecture he gives later in the University of Uppsala: 'After all,' he tells the audience, 'perhaps the greatness of art lies in the perpetual *tension between beauty and pain*.'²⁶

Would it be correct to think, to say today that the future of civilization, of democracy, of justice, of reality, of truth, is contingent on a writer's faithfulness?

'Yes,' Camus (who did not hear my question) answered in his Notebooks of 1953, scribbled when he was just forty and could not predict, anticipate the fame he was to reach in only four years for having 'illuminated the problems of the human conscience in our times', as the Nobel citation put it.

xviii *Paragraph*

Yes, [Camus at forty promised to himself] — Yes, there is beauty and there are the humiliated. Whatever difficulties the enterprise may present, I would like never to be unfaithful either to the one or the other.²⁷

Can we in the academy live up to Camus's words and to his literary faithfulness, and become in our turn *faithful* to the two tasks he assigned to those who practice literature — 'the service of truth' ('the refusal to lie about what one knows') and 'the service of liberty' (the 'resistance to oppression', disguised or undisguised) — *by means of teaching literature*, and (like Camus) of staking both our *faith* and our *hope* in literature?

Can we — in other words — renew our teaching of both literature and psychoanalysis in unveiling once again the secret and the power of their enigmatic juncture, and in allowing both fields to put us back in touch with the sources of our own (individual and social) pain²⁸ and with our (silent or sub-textual) cultural and political unconscious, whose hidden energy alone might help us to unsettle ideologies, and to extract ourselves from the tyranny of received ideas (especially the current tyranny of those prevailing neoliberal received ideas)?

To put it differently, in summary: Can we rekindle the torch of literature and revitalize its dialogue with psychoanalysis, in rejuvenating and renewing both our search for, and our contact with, their common truth, as a perpetual reminder of what can never be forgotten, and simultaneously, as an act that is yet to come?

NOTES

1   In what follows, citations from Lacan's works refer either to the original French editions of Lacan's *Ecrits* (Paris: Seuil, 1966), or to Lacan's original published Seminars in France (Paris: Editions du Seuil, edited by Jacques-Alain Miller), S (Séminaire, followed by the Seminar number) indicating the page number in the original French edition. Unless otherwise indicated, the *Ecrits* will be cited in the English translation by Alan Sheridan: *Ecrits, A Selection* (New York: Norton, 1977). The original French edition (marked E, followed by page number) will be followed by N — for the corresponding page number in the English/American edition. When S is followed by N, the reference will also show the corresponding page number in the Norton English edition of that seminar. When citations from the Seminars give no reference to an English edition (N), there is no official English edition, and the translation from the French original is mine.
2   Lacan, S XX, 380, emphasis mine. Like Freud, Lacan acknowledged that the poets had discovered the unconscious before Freud. Yet Lacan was trying to

bring into focus something else that Freud's precursors were not in possession of, something that Lacan perceives as the unrecognized, unnoticed crux of Freud's originality, and that (in Lacan's perception) was not only insufficiently acknowledged, missed by Freud's immediate posterity, but was in effect erased or blatantly denied by the tradition of American ego psychology. The quintessential Freudian discovery that Lacan reclaims for Freud is Freud's absolutely new, unprecedented understanding that 'the unconscious is structured like a language', and consequently Freud's emphasis on language as the specific 'royal road to the unconscious', and as the methodological psychoanalytic *key* — at once clinical and theoretical — to any psychoanalytic reading of any textual, symptomatic chain of signifiers, not only in dreams but in any chain of signifiers and/or of symbolic (carnal or linguistic) signs. In Seminar XI, *The Four Fundamental Concepts of Psychoanalysis*, Lacan didactically explains his own characteristic vision of what distinguishes Freud's concept of the unconscious from all those that preceded it, and makes it incomparable to them:

> Freud's unconscious [Lacan says] is not at all the romantic unconscious of imaginative creation (...). It is not the locus of the divinities of the night (...). Freud is introducing something other (...). To all these forms of the unconscious, (...) what Freud opposes is the revelation that at the level of the unconscious there is something that at all points is homologous with what occurs at the level of the [conscious] subject — *this thing speaks* [*ça parle*] and functions in a way quite as elaborate as at the level of the conscious, which thus loses what seems to be its privilege. (S XI 26–7, N 24, translation modified).

What Lacan takes care to emphasize, in other words, is how the unconscious speaks not *from under* consciousness, but *from within* it. Although different, radically other than what is meant by consciousness, the unconscious is mixed in — 'inmixed' — with the speech of consciousness, whose meaning it displaces, and sometimes entirely subverts.

3   Transcribed from a recording of Lacan's improvised, unwritten talk in his meeting with American psychoanalysts at the Kanzer Seminar, Yale University, 24 November 1975. Translated from the original French in which Lacan delivers this talk, by Barbara Johnson; my italics.

4   Louis Althusser and Etienne Balibar, *Lire le capital* (Paris: Petite collection Maspéro, 1971), 13; my translation from the French; italics mine.

5   *La 'Folie' dans l'œuvre romanesque de Stendhal* (Paris: Jose Corti, 1970).

6   *La Folie et la chose littéraire* (Paris: Seuil, 1978) (rendered in English as *Writing and Madness: Literature/Philosophy/Psychoanalysis*, translated by Martha Noel Evans and Brian Massumi (Palo Alto: Stanford University Press, 2003)), and *Le Scandale du corps parlant* (Paris: Seuil, 1980) (in English: *The Scandal of*

the Speaking Body: Don Juan with J. L. Austin, or Seduction in Two Languages, translated by Catherine Porter (Palo Alto: Stanford University Press, 2002)).
7   *Literature and Psychoanalysis: The Question of Reading: Otherwise*, edited by Shoshana Felman (Baltimore: The Johns Hopkins University Press, 1982) (originally appeared as a double issue, Nos 55/56, of *Yale French Studies*, 1977; 1980). Citations from this volume will refer to the Johns Hopkins edition, henceforth abbreviated as JH, followed by page number.
8   JH, 2–3.
9   Named after Wilhelm von Humboldt, a Prussian philosopher, diplomat and government functionary, who founded the university of Berlin (now the Humboldt Free University of Berlin) and reformed the Prussian university system, at the beginning of the nineteenth century.
10 See, in particular, the works of the economists and the philosophers that are considered the theoretical founders — the prophets — and the advocates of the economic rationality and of the social philosophy and political ideology of neoliberalism, mainly Friedrich Hayek and Milton Friedman. The foundations of this conception are laid historically in the mid-eighteenth century by Scottish Enlightenment thinker Adam Smith (who is considered the father of modern economics) in his book *The Wealth of Nations* (1776). Smith introduces the pioneering concept of 'the invisible hand', which is a metaphoric name for the unobservable market force that helps the demand and supply of goods in a free market to balance itself and reach equilibrium automatically. By the introduction of this concept, Smith argued that society is made up of self-interested individuals, and through markets these individuals make collective life possible. 'It is not from the benevolence of the butcher, the brewer, or the baker, that we expect our dinner,' Smith said, 'but from their regard to their own interest.' In the modern neoliberal economic theory which is in essence heir to this central concept of the market, there is no ethic other than the ethic of the market. There is no need (and no justified claim) for social justice, Hayek argues. Because people's intelligence is limited (he posits), they do not know how to govern themselves and it is better to rely on the self-regulating logic of a (deregulated, privatized) free market and free trade, for the well-being of society. The individual's need for (economic, mercantile) freedom is primordial, and this *right* to private freedom must itself be liberalized, liberated from the control of the State. In the neoliberal conception, the State (and any intervention by a government in favour of social equality or protection of the weak and vulnerable) should be minimized. Margaret Thatcher and Ronald Reagan were the political implementers of this theory in government practices in the United Kingdom and in the United States, in promoting neoliberal ideals, and their political collaboration and mutual support had a great ideological and political success in spreading the neoliberal ideology (transforming it from a minority to a

majority stance and in imposing its self-interest as an accepted, prevailing 'moral' ideology) throughout the Western world.

The critics of this theory argue that what the ideology of neoliberalism (and its political, executive implementation) has in fact created is not an enhanced freedom nor a general well-being of society (which neoliberalism claimed to target, and to bring about), but rather a wild, ultra-capitalist world of fierce Darwinian competition in which all fight all, and in which the ideals of collective social goods, or of social justice and of democratic citizenship, are discredited, and almost entirely dissolved in practical reality, under the private rule of global ultra-capital and its actual, reigning global *tyranny of money*.

For a historical or political analysis of neoliberalism, as well as for a critique of its theories and practices, see, among others, David Harvey, *A Brief History of Neoliberalism* (Oxford: Oxford University Press, 2005); Wendy Brown, *Undoing the Demos: Neoliberalism's Stealth Revolution* (New York: Zone Books/near futures, 2015); Martha Nussbaum, *Not for Profit: Why Democracy Needs the Humanities* (Princeton University Press, 2010, updated 2016); Pierre Bourdieu, 'L'essence du néoliberalisme', *Le Monde*, 8 December 1998; Bill Readings, *The University in Ruins* (Harvard University Press, 1996); Frank Donoghue, *The Last Professors: The Corporate University and the Fate of the Humanities* (New York: Fordham University Press, 2008); Benjamin Ginsberg, *The Fall of the Faculty* (Oxford: Oxford University Press, 2013).

11   William Shakespeare, *Hamlet*, Act I, scene 5.
12   Sigmund Freud, 'Delusion and Dream in Jensen's Gradiva' in *The Standard Edition of the Complete Psychological Works of Sigmund Freud*, 24 vols, translated and edited by James Strachey, in collaboration with Anna Freud, assisted by Alix Strachey and Alan Tyson (London: The Hogarth Press and the Institute of Psycho-analysis, 1978), 9, 8 (this edition of Freud's writings will henceforth referred to by the abbreviation *SE*).
13   Jacques Lacan, *Les Non-dupes errent* (Séminaire XXI, 1973–4, unpublished), session of 9 April 1974. My translation from the French, from my personal notes of Lacan's seminar of this date (which I attended and transcribed).
14   E 295, N 144.
15   'Freud had, eminently [Lacan writes], this feel for meaning, which accounts for the fact that any of his works (...) gives the reader the impression that it is written by a soothsayer, that it is guided by that kind of meaning which is of the order of poetic inspiration' (S II, 353).
16   'There is', writes Freud, 'at least one spot in every dream at which it is unplumbable, — a navel, as it were, that is its point of contact with the unknown.' *The Interpretation of Dreams*, *SE* 4, 111.
17   For a more elaborate articulation of this point, see my essay 'Teaching Terminable and Interminable' in Barbara Johnson's *Yale French Studies* issue, 63

(1982), 21–45. In her characteristically paradoxical and always provocatively witty style, Johnson called her issue (and defined its topic, ironically yet profoundly, as) *The Pedagogical Imperative: Teaching as a Literary Genre*. My essay was later republished in a revised version in my book *Jacques Lacan and the Adventure of Insight: Psychoanalysis in Contemporary Culture* (Cambridge, MA: Harvard University Press, 1987).

18   Plato, *Apology*, in *The Trial and Death of Socrates*, translated by Benjamin Jowett (New York: Dover Thrift Editions, 1992), 30–2. Emphasis mine.

19   *A Public Enemy* is the title of a play by Henrik Ibsen, written in 1882. Originally (and still today) translated into English as *An Enemy of the People* (see, for instance, the text in Ibsen, *Four Major Plays*, vol. 2, translated by Rolf Fjelde, with an Afterword by Terry Otten (New York: Signet Classics, 2001). When staged and performed in theatres, however, the title is frequently abbreviated into the famous shorter title, *A Public Enemy*, which Camus (a playwright in his turn) is echoing here (citing the expression 'A Public Enemy' — as an echo to the famous Ibsen title). *A Public Enemy* is the story of a scientist — a physician, who is charged with inspecting the famous public baths (believed to be healing) which are the main tourist draw to his native town. He finds the water to be contaminated, and intends to publish these findings in a newspaper, to warn his townspeople and the tourists, and in demanding expensive and urgent repairs, be in fact a public saviour. But the town wishes to continue to financially profit from the baths and not damage the economic prosperity they had assured. When the physician refuses to be silenced despite the authorities' pressure on him to not publish what he knows to be true, he is declared 'an enemy of the people' and is ridiculed, persecuted and exiled.

Interestingly enough, Ibsen's play, and its profoundly ironic title, *An Enemy of the People*, in reality exposes and criticizes (and — like a gadfly — forcefully indicts) nothing other than the way in which the *real 'public good'* is fatally *defeated* by the overpowering economic *tyranny of money*, which in order to protect its own financial interests turns the public benefactor into 'A Public Enemy'. It is as if, from within his nineteenth-century Norway, Ibsen could foresee, anticipate and uncannily criticize before its time the coming neoliberalism, in its claim to serve the general social good, but in reality in its anti-social economic practice and its anti-democratic, (anti-social-justice) ideology.

20   Albert Camus, 'Create Dangerously', in *Resistance, Rebellion, and Death: Essays* (New York: Vintage Books, 1995; original copyright, Alfred A. Knopf, 1960), 269. This edition will be henceforth indicated by the abbreviation *RRD*.

21   Camus, *RRD*, 269–70; italics mine.

22   Camus, *RRD*, 254; italics mine.

23 'And yet the world is there,' Bourdieu writes, 'with the immediately visible effects of the implementation of the great neoliberal utopia: not only the poverty of an increasingly large segment of the most economically advanced societies, the extraordinary growth in income differences, the progressive disappearance of autonomous universes of cultural production, such as film, publishing, etc., through the intrusive imposition of commercial values, but also and above all two major trends. First is the destruction of all collective institutions capable of counteracting the effects of the infernal machine, primarily those of the state, repository of all universal values associated with the idea of the *public realm*. Second is the imposition everywhere, in the upper spheres of the economy and the state as at the heart of corporations, of that sort of moral Darwinism that, with the cult of the winner (...) institutes the struggle of all against all and *cynicism* as the norm of all action and behavior.' See Bourdieu, 'L'essence du neolibéralisme' in *Le Monde diplomatique*, 8 December 1998, English edition; Bourdieu's original italics.

24 For a more elaborate articulation of this conception, in the theoretical frame of a philosophical, psychoanalytical and literary vision I developed for the first time in 1992, see my book *Testimony: Crises of Witnessing in Literature, Psychoanalysis and History* (co-authored with Dori Laub, MD; New York: Routledge, 1992). A follow-up to this theoretical perspective, which develops it in slightly different directions, through a new inquiry into law and literature, and into the (historical and psychoanalytic) interaction between law and trauma, can be found in my later book *The Juridical Unconscious: Trials and Traumas in the Twentieth Century* (Cambridge, MA and London: Harvard University Press, 2002).

25 Albert Camus, *Banquet Speech*, City Hall in Stockholm, 10 December 1957. See http//www.nobelprize.org/nobel_prizes/literature/laureates/1957/camus-speech.html. Speech delivered in French. English translation of the speech (as transcribed officially on the website) modified by me, from the French recording (adjacent videotape) of Camus's speech.

26 'Create Dangerously' in *RRD*, pp. 267–8. Emphasis mine.

27 Camus, 'Return to Tipasa' in Camus, *Lyrical and Critical Essays*, edited by Philip Thody, translated by Ellen Conroy Kennedy (New York: Vintage Books, 1970), 169–70.

28 As Camus has put it earlier, 'perhaps what makes art great is the perpetual tension between beauty and pain'. Pain is what unites, allies, aligns and brings together literature and psychoanalysis, in their common search for — yet different explorations — of its sources and its meaning, as well as of each field's unique means (direct or indirect) for its reduction, its alleviation.

Introduction: Open Questions, Opaque Transmissions

Elissa Marder

In 1977 Shoshana Felman opened up the question of how literature and psychoanalysis speak to each other's most intimate concerns with her landmark volume of *Yale French Studies*: *Literature and Psychoanalysis: The Question of Reading: Otherwise*. That relationship, she proposed, needed to be reinvented, and what was called for was a real dialogue between two different bodies of language and two different modes of knowledge.

In the forty years that have elapsed since Felman first reopened the question, the encounter between literature and psychoanalysis has participated in the emergence of several new fields of critical inquiry, such as trauma, testimony, affect theory, neuropsychoanalysis and performance studies, and has been a privileged space for reflections on mourning, singularity, translation and translatability, the death drive, repetition, violence, cruelty, virtual reality, the clinic and sexuality.

In preparing this special issue of *Paragraph*, I approached a group of creative thinkers who have written powerfully on literature and psychoanalysis and issued an open invitation to them to think about how the relationship between literature and psychoanalysis once again needs to be reinvented. The contributors to this volume answered this call with a wide range of responses. As I read through the essays, I became increasingly aware that, despite their many differences, there was a common thread running through them. With the exception of Shoshana Felman herself (who graciously agreed to write the preface to this volume), all the authors elected to approach the question of the relation between 'literature and psychoanalysis' obliquely. Rather than providing psychoanalytically inflected readings of literary texts, for example, the contributors explore how literature and psychoanalysis share a primary concern with what one can never master or get beyond. In each essay, at stake are modes of expression and an art of reading that take up the challenge of opacity, intractability, resistance, affect and unintelligibility.

In contrast to a world that has become increasingly enamoured with modes of knowledge production that respond to demands for quantifiable verification (the science of the brain), transparent communication and programmatic applicability, literature and psychoanalysis foreground the importance of allowing what cannot be brought into the realm of conscious knowledge to become manifest through contradiction, ambiguity, over-determination, ambivalence and failure of expression. In this sense, the meaning of the term 'literature' emerges here as something like the art of cultivating the latent resources in language that make it possible to transmit feelings, affects, ideas, experiences — and even history — in ways that resist and bypass translation into known and knowable meanings. In the essays in this volume, literature meets psychoanalysis through the creation of a space for an encounter with others and the world that goes beyond the purview of consciousness and the limits of any individual self.

The essays speak to one another through a distinct set of common themes. Many of them explore texts in which the very possibility of addressing oneself to any other is put into question. Although the authors approach this question from very different angles, in each case the encounter between literature and psychoanalysis bears witness to experiences that cannot be told from within the frame of conventional structures of address. Another related theme that runs through the volume concerns occult forms of intersubjective communication. Essays addressing this theme show how Freud's writings often become most literary (and engage with literature) whenever he attempts to establish clear boundaries between psychoanalytic models of intersubjective communication (such as transference and unconscious identification) and occult operations such as telepathy, the experience of the uncanny, and communication with the dead. Exploring a third thematic thread, several of the authors show how psychoanalytic modes of interpretation (such as scansion) share significant features with formal literary analysis and poetics.

All of these essays do more than merely describe or analyse the texts they treat: they are written performances that also enact the very intractability of the literary and psychoanalytic 'thing'. The encounter with this intractability is itself a source of potential transformation: when literature and psychoanalysis meet in this way, beyond merely disciplinary concerns, the contours of the world itself are recast, and the future becomes once again unknown, even unknowable.

The Body's Testimony: Dramatic Witness in the Eichmann Trial

CATHY CARUTH

One of the enduring questions raised by Shoshana Felman and Dori Laub in their 1995 book *Testimony: Crises of Witnessing in Literature, Psychoanalysis and History* is what it means for an event to be constituted by the collapse of its witness.[1] What constitutes the specific forms of denial or not-knowing that structure such an event and what kind of testimony can proceed from that collapse? In their articulation of these questions, Felman and Laub clearly draw upon Freud's late notion of historical trauma in order to characterize the specific manner in which the Holocaust is not (culturally, socially or politically) assimilated at the time of its occurrence but is deferred as a collective, potentially recognizable event until later. By rethinking this historical trauma, however, as a 'collapse of witnessing', the authors shift the focus, I would suggest, from a purely cognitive or epistemological question — a problem of knowing and not-knowing — to a question of communicating *to others*: a problem of address.[2] It is the circumstance of having 'no one to whom one could say Thou', as Laub puts it (*T*, 82), that constitutes the Holocaust, for the victims, as what the authors call an 'event without a witness'. What kind of testimony can emerge from a historical experience that, in Felman's terms, 'annihilated any possibility of address'? (*T*, 38)

This question, I will argue, lies at the centre of Shoshana Felman's essay, 'A Ghost in the House of Justice: Death and the Language of the Law', which is the second of two chapters on the Eichmann trial in her 2002 book, *The Juridical Unconscious: Trials and Traumas in the Twentieth Century*.[3] In this chapter, Felman turns to the actual, physical collapse of a witness on the stand in the 1961 trial in Jerusalem of Adolf Eichmann, the Nazi officer accused of coordinating the annihilation of the European Jews. Yehiel Dinoor, a writer also known as

K-Zetnik and one of the few eyewitnesses to Eichmann at the trial, falls out of the stand and into a coma while attempting to provide his testimony. Framing her argument as a critique of Hannah Arendt, who, in her famous report on the trial, *Eichmann in Jerusalem: A Report on the Banality of Evil*, views K-Zetnik's fall as a moment of exorbitant testimonial failure, Felman argues that the collapse of K-Zetnik becomes central, through its traumatic disruption of the procedures of legal testimony, to the trial's larger project of witnessing the Holocaust.[4] While her focus on this collapse might appear to place an epistemological gap — a lack of knowledge or representation — at the heart of the trial, I will argue instead that her essay centres rather on a problem of address, dramatized concretely on the legal stage and between the witness and the audience in the courtroom, through which the Holocaust, as history, is effectively both enacted and passed on.

A Living Record

It is the dramatic and concrete form of communication at the trial upon which Felman focuses in her framing discussion of the event in Jerusalem. Felman emphasizes the insistence of the chief prosecutor of Eichmann, Gideon Hausner, on the fact that the Jerusalem trial (unlike that at Nuremberg) is not simply a legal tool of judgement for the criminal acts of the accused — a judicial aim supported by the marshalling of evidentiary proof–but also an act of creating a 'living record' of a history that has not yet been fully impressed upon the minds of men. Taking as her point of departure Hannah Arendt's critique of the Israeli prosecution and of its decision to use potentially fallible human witnesses (in distinction from the decision of the prosecution at Nuremberg to use documents alone as evidence), Felman cites Hausner's recognition of the prime importance of the human witness not only as a source of factual evidence but as the most effective means of communicating, to a wider audience, the nature of an unprecedented event: 'In order merely to secure a conviction', Hausner writes, 'it was obviously enough to let the archives speak (...). But I knew we needed more than a conviction; we needed a living record of a gigantic human and national disaster (...) [T]he course adopted at the Nuremberg trials was efficient (...) but (...) failed to reach the hearts of men' (*JU*, 133). It is this crucial role of the human witness not only to report but to make an impact, to 'impress' on human memory, the lived sense of a disaster that resists the imagination, that, Felman underscores in her argument with Arendt, is the function of the fragility and the very fallibility of the human witnesses' testimony:

> The Nuremberg trials had *failed to transmit*, or to impress on human memory and 'on the hearts of men,' the knowledge and the shock of what had happened. The Eichmann trial sought, in contrast, not only to establish facts but to transmit (...). The tool of law was used not only as a tool of *proof* of unimaginable facts but, above all, as a compelling *medium of transmission* — as an effective tool of national and international communication of these thought-defying facts. (133)

The task of transmission is not only a matter of telling or proving, but also of *the act of transmitting*, a specific kind of communicative act that impresses on public memory 'truth as event and as the shock of an *encounter* with events' (133).[5] The act of transmission is thus a means of passing on, through the drama of the human testimony, the impact of an unimaginable history.

K-Zetnik's role in the trial, from this perspective, is not limited to providing an eyewitness account of Eichmann's activities at Auschwitz in the service of the criminal accusation; K-Zetnik is to serve, more fundamentally, as a literary writer with a particular capacity to communicate in a language that acts upon the memory and the 'heart'. Felman points out that he is brought in by the prosecution because of the power of his literary writing, a mode of semi-autobiographical fiction in which he has become known for his Holocaust accounts. Within this context, K-Zetnik's inability to complete his testimony — a simple failure within the traditional judicial project of prosecuting the accused — is to be understood not merely as an obstacle to the trial's purpose, but also as part of the literary effect of a testimonial event: an event that itself has an impact upon memory. Indeed, Felman suggests, unlike traditional legal language, which strives to provide a form of closure that distances the Holocaust, literature — or more broadly 'art' — attempts to bring closer and to keep open, through the way it acts upon the listener, the wound of this particular event.[6] Whereas for Arendt, then, K-Zetnik's fall becomes, ironically, an 'exception that (...) did not prove the rule of simplicity or of ability to tell a story' (cited in *JU*, 145), for Felman, K-Zetnik's fall becomes part of his larger, interminable act of creating a memory in others:

> His testimony thus amounted to a legal failure, the kind of legal failure Jackson [the prosecutor at Nuremberg] had feared. And yet this legal moment of surprise,

captured on film, left an indelible mark on the trial and has impressed itself on visual and historic memory. (...) It has remained a literally unforgettable key moment of the trial, a signal or a symbol of a constantly replayed and yet ungrasped, ungraspable kernel of collective memory. (*JU*, 135)

In fainting, and thus falling mute in the middle of his legal testimony, K-Zetnik does not simply lose the power of speech; he rather, as Felman sees it, 'gave silence a transmitting power' (*JU*, 154). His fall thereby *acts*, unconsciously, to bring the Holocaust upon the legal stage. It is not the mere *absence of a story*, then, but the *enactment of its loss*, that will create history, for those who watch the trial, as a memorable *encounter with an event*.

Giving Voice to the Dead

How do we understand this encounter and the history it unexpectedly creates? It is important to recognize that its powerful effect does not derive solely, in Felman's argument, from K-Zetnik's presence as an Auschwitz victim and a literary writer. Felman argues that K-Zetnik also shares a specific aim with the trial's fundamental project. The uniqueness of this project is originally articulated by the chief prosecutor in his opening statement:

When I stand before you, Judges of Israel, in this court (...) I do not stand alone. With me (...) stand six million prosecutors. But alas, they cannot rise to level the finger of accusation in the direction of the glass dock and cry out 'J'accuse' against the man who sits there. For their ashes are piled in the hills of Auschwitz. (...) Their Blood cries to Heaven, but their voice cannot be heard. Thus it falls to me to be their mouthpiece and to deliver the awesome indictment in their name. (*JU*, 149)

The position of the prosecutor — and by extension the aim of the trial as a whole — is to give voice to the victims who have not returned. Felman juxtaposes this quotation with a passage from one of K-Zetnik's books, in which he names his own purpose in a similar manner:

All of them are now buried in me and continue to live in me, I made an oath to them to be their voice, and when I got out of Auschwitz they went with me, they and the silent blocks, and the silent crematorium, and the silent horizons, and the mountain of ashes. (*JU*, 148)

K-Zetnik aims, like the prosecutor, to 'be the voice' of the dead, to use his voice as a tool to pass on their story to a living audience. 'The writer K-Zetnik', Felman suggests, 'therefore could symbolically be viewed as the most central witness to the trial's announced project to *give voice* to *the six million dead*' (148–9).[7] When his body falls silent and as if lifeless beside the witness box, then, K-Zetnik no longer tells the story of the dead but rather takes their place (enacts their story) upon the legal stage, drawing the audience into his own role, in the camps, as the one suddenly faced with the brutal separation between life and death.

The enactment of history in K-Zetnik's fall can thus be understood as a *re-enactment* that draws the entire court into the drama of a particular moment, one that Felman suggests is part of K-Zetnik's language before he collapses, and that, I would argue, is continued, differently, in the interruption of his testimony. 'Prior to his fainting spell,' Felman writes, 'at the point where the prosecutor interrupts him, K-Zetnik tries to define Auschwitz by re-envisaging the terrifying moment of Selection, of repeated weekly separation between inmates chosen for an imminent extermination and inmates arbitrarily selected for life' (*JU*, 147). It is the moment of the division between death and life that Felman reads in K-Zetnik's words on the witness stand just before he falls: words that she cites and then interprets:

And the inhabitants of that planet had no names. They had neither parents nor children (...). They did not live, nor did they die, in accordance with the laws of this world. Their names were the numbers (...). They left me, they kept leaving me, left (...) for close to two years they left me and always left me behind (...) I see them, they are watching me, I see them. (147)

Felman then comments on this as follows:

What K-Zetnik keeps reliving of the death camp is the moment of departure, the last gaze of the departed, the exchange of looks between the dying and the living at the very moment in which life and death are separating but are still tied up together and can for the last time see each other eye to eye.

The story of the dead that K-Zetnik is unable to complete is the story of the living as they are separated from the others, the moment in which the condemned stare back at the survivors across the gap between death and life. Indeed, the moment is not told as if by a living man who sees, as he takes his departure from, the dead, but rather by the one who is 'left' by the dead who stare back at *him* as someone hardly living. Instead of testifying to the difference between death and life, then, K-Zetnik appears to switch places with the dead in his inability to tell this difference. If the breaking-off of the testimony is, in Felman's vision, an extension of his trance-like words, then K-Zetnik's fall also embodies the confusion between death and life he is re-enacting in his testimony. As Felman puts it: 'In constantly reliving through the moment of departure the repeated separation between life and death, what K-Zentik testifies to is, however, not the separation or the difference between life and death, but on the contrary (...) their interpenetration' (148). The look between the condemned and the survivors, I would add, is not a story that can be addressed to others, but a moment of division between death and life that paradoxically precludes the difference (between self and others, between the dying and the living) necessary for any form of address. This moment is, likewise, re-enacted in the courtroom as *the collapse of the address* between the witness and the audience, as K-Zetnik falls face-down to the floor and the flabbergasted audience, within the re-enacted drama, takes his place.

A Silencing Command

The moments in which K-Zetnik goes into a trance and falls out of the witness stand do not take place in isolation, or as spontaneous events, but occur by means of the intervention of the prosecutor and judge who, like the witness, wish to tell the story of the dead but do this through their own attempt to provide a legal voice to K-Zetnik. In the chapter preceding 'A Ghost in the House of Justice', Felman had focused on the way in which the framework of the Eichmann trial had permitted the surviving victims of the Holocaust to validate, and join together, their stories through the authority they acquired, on the witness stand, in narrating their experiences as legal subjects.[8] To enable K-Zetnik to carry out his mission to bear witness to the dead as part of this larger, public and collective, authoritative story, the court also addresses him as a legal subject whose testimony can then join the larger, official Holocaust narrative. The exchange between the legal language of the prosecutor and the judge and the literary language of K-Zetnik is thus central, Felman suggests, to the trial's attempt to integrate the 'ungraspable core' of the Holocaust into the larger public and collective story. And this attempt to give the literary writer his own legal voice must be understood, I would further argue, as a structure that parallels K-Zetnik's own attempt to give a voice to the dead, a project that is shared, as we have noted above, by court and witness.

Rather than reaching this goal together through their face-to-face exchange of questions and answers, however, the dialogue between the two sides (of court and witness) unwittingly becomes a series of interruptions that divide, rather than join, the two attempts to provide a witness for the dead. This takes place precisely, in Felman's account of the scene, when the judge, repeating the request of the prosecutor, interrupts K-Zetnik in his trance-like description of his fellow inmates going off to the gas chambers. The moment occurs, more specifically, when he is responding to the question of why he writes under the pen name 'K-Zetnik', a name that means 'concentration camp inmate' and which identifies him with the others. When the prosecutor and judge interrupt the trance-like testimony of the witness in their attempt to return him to his strictly legal role, they address him by his legal name, Dinoor. Felman's reading underscores the clash between the two names of the witness: the contradiction that he must experience at that moment between his literary name and his legal name:

Because he is in turn speaking for the dead, K-Zetnik must remain, like them, anonymous and nameless. He must testify, that is, under the name K-Zetnik. (...) But in a court of law, a witness cannot remain nameless and cannot testify anonymously. A witness is accountable precisely to his legal, given name.

'*Mr. Dinóor*, please, please listen to Mr. Hausner and to me,' says the presiding judge impatiently, putting an end to the account that the witness gives of his adopted name.

K-Zetnik faints because he cannot be interpellated at this moment by his legal name, Dinoor: the dead still claim him as *their* witness, as K-Zetnik who belongs to them and is still one of them. The court reclaims him as *its* witness, as Dinoor. (...) He plunges into the abyss between the different planets. On the frontier between the living and the dead, between the present and the past, he falls as though he were himself a corpse. (*JU*, 149)

At the moment that the judge interrupts K-Zetnik in order to return him to his position as a legal witness, K-Zetnik essentially interrupts the legal questioning by falling into a faint. The attempt *to address K-Zetnik as a legal subject* is answered by a physical breakdown that deprives both the prosecutor, and the witness, of a mutual address. It is this collapse of address between court and witness, I would suggest,[9] that is then transferred, at the moment of K-Zetnik's fall, to the relation between K-Zetnik and his audience, as he becomes mute and the moved audience begins to speak and vocalize, as though drawn into the drama in his place. At this moment, then, the prosecutor and the judge step inadvertently into a third role that belongs to neither side.[10]

If the fall occurs 'between' court and witness, as Felman reads it, it is because — I would suggest — the interruption of their mutual address re-enacts the incursion of another, radically different language that unexpectedly ruptures the relation between court and witness – even as it confuses the relation between the witness and the audience — before any party in the courtroom drama can grasp what has taken place.

The incursion of this other language must be understood in terms of a concrete and specific moment of traumatic re-enactment that occurs when K-Zetnik responds to the judge's insistence that he pay attention to the prosecutor's questions. Felman's recounting of the scene emphasizes the unexpectedness of the drama that gathers around the sudden fall:

'What is your full name?' asked the presiding judge.
'Yehiel Dinoor,' answered the witness. The prosecutor then proceeded.
'What is the reason that you took the pen name K-Zetnik, Mr. Dinoor?'
'It is not a pen name,' the witness (now seated) began answering. 'I do not regard myself as a writer who writes literature.' [And he proceeds:]

'This is a chronicle from the planet of Auschwitz. I was there for about two years. Time there was different from what it is here on earth. Every split second ran on a different cycle of time. And the inhabitants of that planet had no names. (. . .) Their names were the numbers 'K-Zetnik so and so' (. . .). They left me, they kept leaving me, left (. . .) for close to two years they left me and always left me behind. (. . .) I see them, they are watching me, I see them –'

At this point, the prosecutor gently interrupted: 'Mr. Dinoor, could I perhaps put a few questions to you if you will consent?'

But Dinoor continued speaking in a hollow and tense voice, oblivious to the courtroom setting, as a man plunged in hallucination or in a hypnotic trance. 'I see them . . . I saw them standing in the line. . . '

Thereupon the presiding judge matter-of-factly intervened: 'Mr. Dinoor, please, please listen to Mr. Hausner; wait a minute, now you listen to me!'

The haggard witness vacantly got up and without a warning collapsed into a faint, slumping to the floor beside the witness stand.

Policemen ran toward Dinoor to lift his collapsed body, to support him and to carry him out of the courtroom. The flabbergasted audience remained motionless, staring in disbelief. 'Quiet, quiet, quiet!' ordered the presiding judge: 'I am asking for silence.' (*JU*, 136–7)

The disproportion between the judge's final entreaty to K-Zetnik and the radical response of the physical collapse into a fall that occurs 'without warning' reveals this moment as a traumatic repetition, the reliving of a violent command that had taken place in the concentration camp, Felman suggests, before it could be grasped:

> K-Zetnik undergoes severe traumatic shock in re-experiencing the same terror and panic that dumbfounded him each time when, as an inmate, he was suddenly confronted by the inexorable Nazi authorities of Auschwitz. (...) The call to order by the judge urging the witness to obey (...) impacts the witness *physically* as an invasive call to order by an SS officer. Once more, the imposition of a heartless and unbending rule of order violently robs him of his words and, in reducing him to silence, once more threatens to annihilate him, to erase his essence as a *human* witness. (146)

The judge's command to listen to the questions of the court is experienced by K-Zetnik as the command of a Nazi officer, whose 'call to order' annihilates him 'as a human witness'. The fall of K-Zetnik in the courtroom, therefore, repeats this traumatizing moment by dramatizing this annihilation of the human: an event that does not simply eliminate K-Zetnik's humanity but more specifically eliminates his humanity *as a witness*. It is indeed, one might point out, each time that he begins to say 'I see them' that K-Zetnik is interrupted, first by the prosecutor, and then by the presiding judge: at the moment that he wishes to fulfil his function as a witness to those who are going off to die. The 'call to order' of the Nazi, which K-Zetnik relives in the judge's words, must be nothing other, then, than 'the terrifying moment of Selection' itself, the ultimate Nazi command that divides the ones who will die from the ones who will remain and that, at that moment, obliterates K-Zetnik's capacity to bear witness to this very command.

What does it mean to say that K-Zetnik is obliterated as a witness at this moment? It would appear that he is precisely, as survivor, the only one who can bear witness to the dead and who indeed, as he had written in his later books, felt he must spend his entire life carrying out this task. Yet the brutality of the Nazi utterance, K-Zetnik seems to be showing in his collapse, lies not only in its arbitrary condemnation of the others to a dehumanizing death but also in its equally arbitrary selection of the ones who will survive, and who also lose their humanity at this very moment. The judge's order to K-Zetnik when he interrupts him and addresses him by his legal name is thus relived by K-Zetnik as a command that precisely *eliminates him as an addressee*: as one who could respond, as a human being, to the question of another and who likewise, in his turn, could find an addressee for his own story. It is, thereby, a command that eliminates the very possibility of witnessing — of addressing to another — the arbitrariness of the division between death and life, an event that K-Zetnik passes on, without intending to, through the re-enactment, by the entire courtroom, of the story that he cannot tell.

The Body on the Stage

From the perspective of this re-enactment, the historical reality of the Holocaust can be said to emerge, in the courtroom, as the annihilation of its own witness. This is a specific history, bound up with the re-enactment of what the Nazi's called 'Selection' and that, as I have suggested, Felman implicitly analyses as what is returning in K-Zetnik's fall. The court does not embody knowledge of the past, framed by the process of the trial; this history, as we have seen, rather draws the court into its framework:

> I have argued [Felman writes] (. . .) that the law is, so to speak, professionally blind to its constitutive and structural relation to (both private and collective, cultural) trauma, and that its 'forms of judicial blindness' take shape wherever the structure of the trauma unwittingly takes over the structure of a trial and wherever the legal institution, unawares, triggers a legal repetition of the trauma that it puts on trial or attempts to cure. (JU, 146)

I wish to propose my own elaboration of Felman's insight, which might take it one step further. In taking over all positions in the courtroom, the drama re-enacts a process that involved all segments of society, including, markedly, the legal structures that should have prevented the dehumanization of the Jews.[11] It is thus, in my eyes, particularly important that Felman reads K-Zetnik's collapse not as a private experience that overcomes him simply as an individual, but as a response to the legal language of the judge (and prosecutor), whose words, relived by K-Zetnik as an echo of the order of a Nazi, erase precisely for the witness the legal and humanizing address that they are in fact meant to provide. Indeed, I wish to underscore the understanding that the fall of K-Zetnik must not be read as an emotional response to the brutality of the command he is reliving but as a dramatization of the annihilation of address that has *already taken place* within the Nazi's words.[12] In other words, the temporality of the deferred event re-enacted in the courtroom is the temporality that makes the fall of K-Zetnik not an ordinary 'response' to an address but a reaction that appears to come *too late* to be able to prevent, or to resist, the annihilation of address — of the victim's humanity and capability of witnessing — that has *already happened* in the command. What cannot be told at this moment of collapse of the witness is the institutional, political and societal participation borne by the language of the Nazi as it annihilates, in those at whom it is aimed, the very possibility to receive, or pass on, a human story.[13]

Yet Felman also points to a certain shifting, within this re-enactment, of the nature of the drama that is here played out: a double role, we might say, that is enacted, at the moment of the fall, specifically by the witness's body. As we have noted above, K-Zetnik's fall must be seen, according to the logic of Felman's argument, as part of the testimony he is giving just before it, an attempt to speak of the moment when the living are separated from the dying. The fall, however, communicates this moment in a different manner:

> K-Zetnik's testimony does not simply tell *about* the impossibility of telling: it dramatizes it — *enacts it* — through its own lapse into coma and its own collapse into a silence. 'It was the most *dramatic* moment of the trial,' writes Tom Segev, 'one of the most dramatic moments in the country's history'. (...) For Arendt as a critical legal observer and as a conscious representative of the traditional conception of the law, however, *the dramatic* as such is by definition *immaterial* and extraneous to the trial. (...) I would argue here, in contrast, that the dramatic *can* be legally significant. I submit that in the Eichmann trial (as the passing comment of the judges has in fact conceded) the dramatic *was* indeed endowed with *legal meaning*, meaning that the classical jurisprudential, legalistic view was programmed to miss. (JU, 161)

If K-Zetnik's fall *dramatizes* the 'impossibility of telling' through 'its own lapse into coma and its own collapse into a silence', then this fall is not only the repetition of the 'physical' response of K-Zetnik to the Nazi's order in the concentration camp, but also — in the present of the courtroom — a *making visible* of something *not visible* in the event. In Felman's words, what is thus dramatized is 'the impossibility of telling'. In my turn, I have argued here that it is precisely the annihilation of address that is dramatized in the body's fall and in its reduction into sudden silence, an annihilation that is now made visible to the trial audience and to the court itself upon the legal stage. It is indeed this *sight of the falling body* that draws the audience and the court into K-Zetnik's drama. The body not only *repeats an earlier physical event*, we would have to say, but also *plays a role in a present drama enacted upon a public stage*, an unprecedented public stage that is itself, moreover, suddenly made visible — as we can see in the film of this scene in the trial — when K-Zetnik falls outside the witness box.[14] In the manner in which I read it, Felman's argument reveals the body as a pivot between the trauma of re-enactment that continues to envelop the courtroom in unconsciousness[15] and a different kind of action that, while drawing the audience into the scene, also, potentially, breaks the trance of the reenactment by focusing the audience on the collapsed body and on the events taking place outside of the witness stand. When the body falls, Felman suggests, the testimony 'is invaded by the body':

> The speaking body has become a dying body (...) The body's testimony (...) creates a new dimension of the trial, a *physical legal dimension* that dramatically expands what can be grasped as legal meaning. (163)

If K-Zetnik's body thus not only re-enacts, but testifies, in its fall, then the new, expanded 'legal meaning' to which Felman draws attention must include — I would propose — this new position of the trial's audience in its own participation in the events as it responds to the collapse. The audience is both placed in K-Zetnik's position (as seeing a falling body) and reverses this position at the same time: as K-Zetnik suddenly falls into unconsciousness and silence, the audience stands up and mutters, trying to see what it cannot yet grasp. If the body thereby becomes 'a site of memory' (162), as Felman states, it is not only a memory of what has already occurred in the past (for K-Zetnik) but also an attempt to discover (for the audience) what is not yet known.[16] The new legal meaning introduced by the collapse of the witness, I would argue, thus passes, through the body, between a re-enacted past and the call for a future: between an unconscious re-enactment and a wider imperative of witness. This imperative extends the trial beyond its own strictly legal boundaries and links its encounter with trauma to a call for a new and broader form of cultural and historical address.

This broader imperative of witness must be distinguished, slightly, from the project of the chief prosecutor Gideon Hausner, a difference that ironically brings Felman's insertion of K-Zetnik at the centre of the trial's 'project' closer to Hannah Arendt's hopes for the trial in one particular way. By making K-Zetnik's fall a fundamental aspect of the trial's ultimate effect in national and world memory, Felman reinterprets the trial's meaning differently than Hausner, whom she had brought close to K-Zetnik through their shared project of giving voice to the dead. In a footnote, Felman remarks, in passing, that '[K-Zetnik's] terrified collapse is at the same time an improbable act of resistance, a gesture of defiance of the court and of its ruling' (*JU*, 233). K-Zetnik's fall is in fact, as noted above, an interruption of the trial and a non-response to the prosecutor's pleas, a failure of response that shifts the action from the legal to the traumatic spheres. It could be argued that in enabling this shift, K-Zetnik unconsciously denies the court its larger goal of integrating him into a narrative that could be used in the political service of the Israeli state, as the prime minister of Israel had hoped, a hope Arendt had criticized and rejected (as is discussed by Felman in her previous chapter in *The Juridical Unconscious*, 'Theaters of Justice: Arendt in Jerusalem and the Redefinition of Legal Meaning in the Wake of the Holocaust').[17] K-Zetnik's fall cannot be easily integrated into a heroic narrative of Jewish survival, and it is this very vulnerability that, in Felman's reading, makes K-Zetnik's story of exemplary and urgent (global) interest as a site of memory and a site of testimony, an imperative that can be passed on to others. It is not a site of testimony as knowledge, but rather — as we see enacted in the attempts by the concerned audience at the trial (as we notice in the film) to stand up and see what is happening to K-Zetnik's body — a testimony in the form of a collective cognitive, emotional, and bodily response to an event that has not yet been told.

A Promise

This unique relationship between K-Zetnik and his audience — a not fully conscious, partly bodily, *passing on of the imperative to tell* — is what Felman tries to capture, I believe, in her explanation of 'the dramatic', a term whose significance she develops through its use and definition by Walter Benjamin.[18] Felman cites Benjamin's emphasis on the dramatic, in his well-known essay on Goethe's *Elective Affinities*, as a gesture in a text that goes beyond words: 'Therefore, this moment cannot be expressed in words (...) it is the "dramatic" in the strictest sense' (*JU*, 162). Felman associates this with the gesture of K-Zetnik's fall:

Law in principle *rules out* what cannot be disclosed in words. In contrast, the dramatic, Benjamin says, is a beyond of words. It is a physical gesture by which language points to a meaning it cannot articulate.
    Such is K-Zetnik's fall outside the witness stand. It makes a corpse out of the living witness who has sworn to remain anonymous and undifferentiated from the dead. (162)

Felman interestingly associates Benjamin's analysis of the dramatic as a 'gesture by which language points to a meaning it cannot articulate' to the actual, physical fall of K-Zetnik, thereby emphasizing, once more, the dramatic element of K-Zetnik's fall that I have suggested makes visible the violent performative gesture of the Nazi's speech.

In making visible, through K-Zetnik's body, what has happened in the Nazi's command, the fall dramatizes a relation between the Nazi and K-Zetnik, even as it also dramatizes, at this moment, a relation between K-Zetnik and the condemned, those whom the Nazi Selection condemned to death.

We see how the dramatic can also be understood to signify the relation between K-Zetnik and the courtroom audience witnessing his fall when we turn to the text by Walter Benjamin that Felman uses to illustrate the dramatic. Benjamin uses two literary examples to describe a relation between the characters and those who observe them — the ones narrating the scenes — in which the observer's response dramatizes something that the characters cannot grasp of their own situation.[19] In the second of these examples, from Dante's *Inferno*, the narrator, Dante, watches the condemned lovers Paolo and Francesca, in the second circle of Hell, as they remain poised, for ever, at a moment before they are discovered and killed. Dante — like K-Zetnik with the condemned he watches, like the audience watching K-Zetnik — is so moved that he falls into a faint. For Benjamin, Dante's faint illustrates the response of an observer who takes up, in his body, the not-yet-fulfilled fate of the others:

> It is he alone who, in the feeling of hope, can fulfill the meaning of the event — quite as Dante assumes in himself the hopelessness of the lovers, when, after the words of Francesca da Rimini, he falls 'as if a corpse fell.'[20]

The fate of the hopeless lovers, Benjamin suggests, is taken up by their observer and narrator Dante, who falls 'as if a corpse fell', a physical (re-)enactment of the hopeless fate of the condemned. Felman apparently echoes this line unconsciously in one of her own descriptions of K-Zetnik's fall when she writes 'On the frontier between the living and the dead, between the present and the past, he falls as though he were himself a corpse' (*JU*, 149), thus underlining the unconscious passing-on, in K-Zetnik's fall, of his own position *as a witness to the condemned*, and more specifically as a witness *who cannot simply tell, but passes on through a bodily gesture*, the moment of their deaths.[21] In passing on this moment to the audience, I would suggest, K-Zetnik's bodily act also partakes of the 'dramatic' because it does not simply belong to, or is not simply locatable in, the actual body of K-Zetnik, since it only becomes visible (in the film recorded of the trial, and perhaps for the audience in the trial as well) when the audience effectively (dramatically) takes his place by standing up and seeking to see his fallen body. In Felman's text, too, the passage between the *figure of falling* and the bodily gesture, the bodily gesture and her own critical text, can only be called 'dramatic', a moment of writing that refuses the confines of either legal or literary language and, in its own way, 'fulfils the meaning of the event': it binds the hopelessness of the event to the hope of a new mode of witness.

This new mode is figured in Felman's own text, in part, through another term that she borrows from Benjamin, the notion of *das Ausdruckslose*, 'the expressionless'. Thus, she writes, citing Benjamin's text:

Only the expressionless completes the work [completes the trial], by shattering it into a thing of shards, into a fragment of the true world, into the torso of a symbol. To borrow Benjamin's inspired terms to describe the trial, I would argue that K-Zetnik's fainting and his petrified body stand for the 'expressionless' — *das Ausdruckslose* — that suddenly erupts into the language of the law and *interrupts* the trial. (JU, 163)

In her interruption of her own language with Benjamin's *das Ausdruckslose*, naming the disfigured figure, the faceless face, of the 'expressionless', Felman identifies K-Zetnik's fall with a mode of communication that evokes, and evades, a straightforward face-to-face encounter.[22] We also find a trace of this figure, I believe, in K-Zetnik's full testimony, at the trial, at the moment he ascribes his own source of commitment and strength to the final looks of the condemned:

If I am able to stand here in this court before you, and retell the tale of this planet, if I, out of this planet of Auschwitz, am able to be here with you today, then I believe with all my being that this is thanks to the oath I made to them there. They gave me the strength. This oath was my armor and this was the unnatural part above nature which sustained me, as a Muselmann, to withstand Auschwitz. They always left me. They always took leave of me. And the look in their eyes had the promise of my oath in them.[23]

If K-Zetnik's commitment to testify for the condemned can be passed on, it is because the 'promise of [his] oath' comes not from him alone, but from 'their eyes'. When K-Zetnik falls to the ground in a coma and draws us into his drama, he also passes on this oath that he can no longer see reflected back to him but that he hands over, at this moment, to the audiences who watch him. If K-Zetnik breaks his promise as he falls, he also passes it on, in this collapse, to another audience and to the possibility, at least, of a future addressee.

NOTES

1. Shoshana Felman and Dori Laub, *Testimony: Crises of Witnessing in Literature, Psychoanalysis and History* (New York: Routledge, 1991). Henceforward abbreviated as *T*.
2. See, for example, *T*, xviii and 80 for explicit articulations of the 'collapse of witnessing'.
3. Shoshana Felman, *The Juridical Unconcious: Trials and Traumas in the Twentieth Century* (Cambridge, MA: Harvard University Press, 2002). Henceforward abbreviated as *JU*.
4. See Hannah Arendt, *Eichmann in Jerusalem: A Report on the Banality of Evil* (New York: Penguin, 1994 [1963]). I have discussed Felman's relation to Arendt in 'A Ghost of the House of Justice' in a previous essay; see Cathy Caruth, 'Trauma, Justice, and the Political Unconscious: Arendt's and Felman's Journey to Jerusalem', in *The Claims of Literature: A Shoshana Felman Reader*, edited by Emily Sun, Eyal Peretz and Ulrich Baer (New York: Fordham, 2007). Felman writes two, connected chapters on the trial that engage with Arendt, the first of which — 'Theaters of Justice: Arendt in Jerusalem, the Eichmann Trial, and the Redefinition of Legal Meaning in the Wake of the Holocaust' — concerns the witnesses whose speaking creates a collective Holocaust history and the second about K-Zetnik's fall into silence.
5. See Felman's use of the notion of transmission in *Testimony*. This is bound up, I believe, with Clause Lanzmann's use of this term in 'Hier ist kein Warum' in *Au sujet de Shoah: Le film de Claude Lanzmann*, edited by Bernard Cuau et al. (Paris: Belin, 1990), discussed by Felman in her introduction to 'The Obscenity of Understanding: An Evening with Claude Lanzmann' in *Trauma: Explorations in Memory*, edited by Cathy Caruth (Baltimore: Johns Hopkins University Press, 1995).
6. See, in particular, 'Theaters of Justice', 106–7 and 'A Ghost in the House of Justice', 153–4.
7. The prosecutor and the writer both engage, from this perspective, in the use of the literary figure of prosopopoeia, the giving of a mask or face to the dead so that the dead may speak. But they do it differently and for different purposes, and, interestingly, through their own, mutually constituting, face-to-face encounter. The final part of this essay returns to this implicit figure as it emerges in the courtroom through a disfigured face.
8. See 'Theaters of Justice' and note 5, above.
9. Felman refers to the exchange, at one point, as a 'missed encounter', drawing thus upon a Lacanian psychoanalytic language in which the 'missed encounter' is also the encounter with the Real. I am, in part, using the problem of address to reread the 'missed encounter' as she articulates it in this context.

10   While Felman does not discuss this exchange of positions among the parties in the courtroom, this exchange recalls an analysis she does provide in a completely different context: her reading of Lacan's analysis of Poe's 'The Purloined Letter' in her essay 'On Reading Poetry: Reflections on the Limits and Possibilities of Psychoanalytic Approaches', in *The Purloined Poe: Lacan, Derrida, and Psychoanalytic Reading*, edited by John P. Muller and William J. Richardson (Baltimore: Johns Hopkins University Press, 1987). In that essay she discusses Lacan's reading of Poe in terms of the repetition of scenes, another instance of repetition compulsion and also his own reading of Freud's *Beyond the Pleasure Principle* though in a non-catastrophic context.

11   I am thinking here, for example, of the Nuremberg Laws. Hannah Arendt had argued that the final movement toward absolute totalitarian control by the Nazis involved the 'annihilation of the juridical person', followed by the 'murder of the moral person', followed by 'the destruction of individuality'. See Hannah Arendt, *The Origins of Totalitarianism* (New York: Harcourt, Brace, Jovanovich, 1973 [1951]). Felman touches on the history of law in relation to persecution of the Jews in 'Theaters of Justice', specifically in relation to the Dreyfus affair, alluded to in Hausner's citation of Zola's 'J'accuse'.

12   I would argue that Felman is implicitly taking a new step, here, in the speech act analysis that she famously articulated in her book *The Scandal of the Speaking Body: Don Juan with J. L. Austin, or Seduction in Two Languages* (Stanford: Stanford, 2002 [1983]). Felman argued, there, for the bodily dimension of the speech act, whose effects are produced not simply through its success (or 'felicity') but also and more fundamentally through its lack of success, or displaced effects ('infelicity'), the central example being there the promise (and specifically the promise to marry). (This infelicity is exemplified in Austin's own theoretical text, interestingly, by the figure of slips and falls of the theoretician.) In that text, she is concerned with the realm of desire and the unconscious, in which the performative works within a social register in which the address is not in question. In 'A Ghost in the House of Justice', however — I am arguing in my essay — she is concerned with catastrophic death and the radical denial, or 'collapse of witnessing', of a society, in which the undoing of the social bond — what Françoise Davoine and Jean-Max Gaudillière have called the 'social link' in their book *History beyond Trauma* (New York: Other Press, 2004) — is broken by means of a performative that includes the annihilation of its own presumed address. The fall is no longer on the stage, we might say, but off of it.

This is not a psychological theory but a linguistic, social and political one, even though Felman uses language that at points appears psychological (like 'terrified' when referring to why K-Zetnik falls in response to what he perceives as a Nazi command). To clarify this from the point of view of speech act theory: what would ordinarily be called the 'perlocutionary' dimension of the speech act — the effect of the speech act upon its addressee — is in the case of the Nazi command already contained within the illocutionary act (the speech act itself). This is because, unlike an ordinary speech act, which assumes an addressee, the Nazi utterance (in the Felman essay, as I have argued, the utterance that separates life from death) does not address the person it is aimed at but eliminates its addressee, hence containing its effect already in its utterance. Thus K-Zetnik's fall is already, in a sense, contained in the utterance.

The implications of this analysis are, I think, profound. In the essay 'The Resistance to Theory', in his book *The Resistance to Theory* (Minneapolis: Minnesota, 1986), Paul de Man notes that the perlocutionary act is usually banished from 'true' speech act theory to the emotional and psychological realm (it would be understood, thereby, as merely a psychological effect). He suggests that this must be rethought. I would argue that Felman's essay allows us to imagine what that means by thinking through the problem of the 'collapse of address' within the Nazi utterance. (Claude Lanzmann's discussion of an anecdote by Primo Levi in 'Hier ist kein Warum' — see above, note 5 — could also be seen as bringing out the non-address in the Nazi who, when the inmate asks him 'Why?' responds with 'Here there is no why' — something I would read as saying 'there is no address and response between you and me'.) We might ask what it would mean to go back and reconsider the earlier work from the perspective of the non-psychological interpretation of the perlocutionary act as well. But what is important for my essay is to note that trauma theory, as it emerges in Felman's analysis, is not simply a psychological phenomenon but carries with it the reality of a radical social act.

The movement from desire to death, in the history of Felman's speech act theory, could also bear some analysis, if one were to take into account this illocutionary–perlocutionary rethinking in both texts and the role of trauma theory as it enters the later work (as trauma theory would return in Freud's later work). In both cases, for Felman, the speech act — bound up with desire, or with annihilation — is inextricably linked to the body, and specifically a falling body (notably, in 'The Resistance to the Theory', de Man also provides a story, an example, of falling to speak about the effects of rhetoric).

13 I would thus argue that the temporality of trauma, at least in this context, must be thought in terms of the temporality of a particular, annihilating utterance. What does it mean when one is by definition 'too late' to respond to a violent utterance aimed precisely at eliminating one's humanity? The notion of 'helplessness' in victimization could be thought usefully from this perspective, I believe, with regard to 'relational' trauma — the trauma that has to do with relationships between people — and/or 'betrayal' trauma — the trauma experienced as the betrayal of another. (It has been argued that it

is difficult to find any trauma that is not on some level relational or betrayal-related, since even in so-called natural disasters human elements are often at play.) This also means that trauma would be engaged with an inherently political issue of disempowering; in this case, that is also an ethical issue of dehumanization. The temporality of trauma, in other words, seen from this perspective, is not simply a cognitive or individual phenomenon, and the theory that emphasizes this temporality — specifically the psychoanalytic theory of trauma — has to be seen as a meditation on social, political and institutional phenomena, as is clearly the case in Felman's essay. This emphasis also suggests — along with the problem of address in general — that the problem of 'representation' is not the best way to talk about what is at stake in the experience or theory of trauma as it emerged in the late nineteenth and early twentieth centuries and has been developed through the early twenty-first century.

14 It is interesting to note that K-Zetnik twice goes out of the box, when he is mentioning seeing the others; first he goes out and comes back in, and then falls out of it. We actually don't see the moment of the fall in the film, which contributes to the sense, in watching it as audiences of that recording, of a missed, traumatic moment.

15 Felman writes, 'it is the law itself that for a moment loses consciousness' (164): another way of emphasizing that the analysis of K-Zetnik is the analysis of a 'traumatic kernel' not reducible to the individual experience.

16 It is interesting that the phrase 'the speaking body becomes a falling body' is also a kind of site of memory in Felman's own text, as 'the speaking body' echoes the title of her book *The Scandal of the Speaking Body* (see note 12). The sentence thus traces a trajectory within, or tells a story about, her own theoretical work. Another analysis of her text might look at the relation between the historical trajectories of law (articulated briefly by Felman when she mentions the historical relation between the law and trauma), psychoanalysis (which had a very complicated relation to Nazi Germany) and Felman's literary theoretical itinerary.

17 See 'Theaters of Justice', pp. 109–10. Arendt's view is not only legal but political, then; while Felman does not address the political directly in her argument, I would argue that there is a potential thinking of it here through the rethinking of the nature of the 'act' constituted by K-Zetnik's fall. I suggested, in 'Trauma, Justice, and the Political Unconscious', that Felman's and Arendt's two projects could be seen communicating with each other; I believe, now, that we might try to think this communication through the nature of the vulnerable — yet in some sense resistant — witness.

18 Felman turns to Benjamin after a section in which she reinterprets Arendt's to K-Zetnik in terms of Arendt's own, unarticulated, grief for her friend Benjamin after his suicide at the border between France and Spain in his own flight from fascism. In her reading of Arendt's claim that K-Zetnik's testimony

and fall do not 'prove the rule of simplicity or of ability to tell a story', Felman suggests that Arendt unconsciously alludes, here, to Benjamin's 'The Storyteller', and that her writing on K-Zetnik, and more largely on the trial, unconsciously transmits this unspoken grief. Felman's own use of Benjamin, after her analysis of Arendt, could be said to link Felman herself to Arendt. Indeed, an extended analysis of her essay might explore the way in which the passage from trauma to testimony in Felman's analysis of K-Zetnik's fall passes unconsciously through a kind of address between Felman and Arendt.

19 Benjamin's essay is in fact very complex and enigmatic; I am summarizing, here, for the parallels I see between it and Felman's analysis of K-Zetnik. Benjamin describes what he calls 'the narrator's stance' in Goethe and in Dante, where the narrator (as objective observer in *Elective Affinities* or inscribed in the text, as Dante in the *Inferno*) produces a figure (in Goethe's case) or an action (in Dante's case) that dramatizes something that the characters cannot grasp of their own situation.

20 Walter Benjamin, 'Goethe's *Elective Affinities*', in *Walter Benjamin: Selected Writings*, vol. 1, edited by Marcus Bullock and Michael W. Jennings (Cambridge: Belknap Press–Harvard University Press, 1996), 355.

21 The precise meaning of Dante's fall at the end of Canto 2 of the *Inferno* is debated; it is linked to Dante's 'pity' as well and, in its specific context, has been seen by some to have erotic meaning ('the little death'), as Paolo and Francesca are reading a romantic story in the scene in Hell. I am summarizing the Dante in terms of what I see as its significance in the passage from Goethe to Benjamin to Felman. Felman's own use of it might itself be considered 'dramatic' in so far as K-Zetnik's fall is also, in her text, arguably making visible the notion of 'the collapse of witnessing'.

22 Felman also, it should be noted, suddenly introduces into her own text here Benjamin's German when she cites his term *das Ausdruckslose*. It is interesting that this term can also allude to the face, which brings us back to the problem of prosopopoeia that centrally underlies the project of the trial for Hausner and K-Zetnik, in Felman's argument (in so far as she emphasizes the wish by both to give voice to the dead). What returns here might be called a de-facement of sorts, which is nonetheless the site of a transmission. Behind this I believe we might also trace de Man's face, through the dynamics of figure and disfigurement operating in Felman's own text. See Paul de Man, 'Autobiography as De-Facement' in his *The Rhetoric of Romanticism* (New York: Columbia, 1984).

23 For a clip of K-Zetnik's testimony at the trial, see: https://www.youtube.com/watch?v=o0T9tZiKYl4&t=349s.

The Transfer of Complaint: A Narcissistic Time-Share

AVITAL RONELL

I can't complain. I belong to a generation that was fired up by the provocations of Lacan, Derrida, Lyotard, Kofman and the rest of that irretrievable world. We were succoured by outstanding texts and motivated to discipline ourselves around their relentless demands. The great transmitters and innovators were nearby, unstoppably broadcasting their breakthrough arbitrations. The books piled on, making us giddy, feeding an unknown addiction. When bound and released, the new arrivals called us to huddle around them, becoming instantaneous hits and fabulous hermeneutic puzzles. It was a time to which my students refer with grudging acknowledgement, a slightly toxic mix of envy and gratitude. Still, it was not always easy to be on the receiving end of such abundance.

Despite the good fortune and copious portions — the prod is still coming from remembered times of fevered productivity, a 'dangerous proximity', as Hölderlin would say, to greatness of thought and determination — despite the generosity and generativity we witnessed, it wasn't all parousia. One stood before hard choices, some of which were admittedly no-brainers; nonetheless, these choices met with serious institutional dilemmas, a series of low-blow persecutions, pulling up a desert of jobless waiting periods. Nothing, henceforth, was to be taken for granted. We had to choose or lose our mentors, trade off sides and historical lineage, file down reading lists, form agonistic gangs, go up against establishment scholars — most of whom were not ready to tap out as quickly as we had anticipated. Our nerves were chronically on edge. Not all the time, and not everyone, I suppose, was meant to reach her limits and launch into successive *Untergänge*, the experience of Nietzschean cracks and breakups. But if you had your finger on the pulse of the *Weltgeist*, you'd have found that many things in those days were moving hard and fast. Perhaps we were, for the most part, overstimulated, too swiftly headed for burnout and unsecured reboot. Still, as an archipelago of disciple-formations and quasi-schools we kept it together, for a spell at least — managing to hold steady with a stash of blockbuster works that quickly became events, not mere containers of knowledge or academically sanctioned discourse. One of these events was Shoshana Felman's volume, putting out the colon-call ': *Otherwise*'. Nietzsche and Heidegger had trained us to stalk the significance of a diacritical mark, and Felman had it settle in the subtitle as *Reading: Otherwise*. A generation of scholars became hooked on the call put out to a type of 'otherwise than reading', though reading, split by the colon-call, was henceforth always about stocking up on imponderables, internal fissurings, ironically pitched, and otherwise driven. A whole grove of new unintelligibilities opened up to us and drove our universities crazy.

To the degree that influence can at all be measured and appropriately rendered, anxiously tabulated, I knew right away that my debt to Felman's work would be sizable. Not only did she create the volume's impressive sequencing and inflection, but she contributed her own work, a riveting article entitled 'Turning the Screw of Interpretation', where she discusses, among other things, 'the desire for ignorance' — an articulation, in terms of my subsequent itinerary, an early springboard for the work on stupidity and the fading empire of cognition. Knowing what you unconsciously know and what you don't know you know yet are propelled by the knowing repressed and secretly activated — such stealth displacements of stances in knowing are part of the textual repertory that Felman had us seek out. To this day, I feel as though her work keeps fanning out in subtle ways in my own/dispossessed relation to writing and, most recently, I parleyed the title of her essay by reflecting on 'The Turn of the Screwed', offering another consideration of aporia and non-relation in literature and psychoanalysis, themes that she had initiated in strong and lasting terms of engagement. In my capacity as Miss Prison (the codename I used as a graduate student), I ran them unrecognizably, in relentlessly aberrant directions. Many of my cohort's themes are trackable to Felman's archival predilections and critical elaborations. The fate of the screwed, for instance, and epic fails has recently shown up for me in the drama of adolescence, what Freud called 'a strong alteration' when designating puberty.

My academic puberty, traumatic and ongoing, entailed a passage through that book, the way it contoured the jolting unsaid and italicized its insight. In some specific ways the volume cast Hamlet in the lead role, giving ground to the great adolescent that haunts our desperate search for justice. Trained by this work, its many facets and directives, and the new essays recruited by Felman, I soon saw Hamlet as the cipher for the modern engine of *complaint*. The complaint doubles down on the riot of injustice strapped to the very fact of being — announcing psychic despair over the fact or facticity that our days are borrowed, that language lashes out arbitrarily, grievously misfires intention, dowses meaning, outsources feeling to remote and approximate fields of saying, sideswiping the aims of lament, downsizing the house of praise — hinging the advent of evil on the demand for justice.

Still adolescent, but slightly matured, I run with the lessons delivered to my custody. Let me now turn to the way *Hamlet* turns back on the way language says its piece, tossing complaint into the abyss of the unanswerable, inching towards the unsendable envoi for which Rilke and Celan would later vouch. What can it mean to soliloquize and turn the steady howl of disjointure upon oneself?

★ ★ ★

In the article headlining Felman's volume, Jacques Lacan analyses how Hamlet's father appears as the Other barred.[1] Hamlet's father 'must complain for all eternity that he was interrupted, taken by surprise, cut off in midstream — that to him the possibility of response, of retribution, is forever sealed off' (44). Lacan does not dwell on the mode of address and disturbed pose that he identifies as those of the father: the complaint. Though eternally appointed, complaint as part of the constraint of barred being does not catch Lacan here, but it is where I would like to linger, particularly in consideration of the way the complaint is transferred to the son who must carry the burden of a language at once binding and dismissible.

Prince Hamlet, attached to language — 'It speaks!'[2] — swung by its over-the-top lapse into the madness of saying and reciting and recycling phantomal horror, toppled by the Opheliac demise, drives his complaint home to the essence of man, to the way the *anthropos* works, is worked and chronically disjuncts: 'What a piece of work is man!' The enigma of man, whether or not it is worked out, riveted by destructive impulse, continually readjusted by considerations of warlike tactical forces, theoretical adherences and the clutch of reason, focuses the complaint. What is man? How does this thing, human all too inhuman, *work*? Often latched on to the work of mourning the functioning of man, like the work of mourning, according to Derrida, does not work. Nowadays we continue to say, when downscaling, 'She's a piece of work!' indicating trouble and a coded history of difficult behaviours.

Shuttling between father and son in *Hamlet*, how does the tragic adherence to the complaint implicate man, what does it tell us about the stalls and neutralizing tendencies of acts (or passivities) of complaining? How does the complaint struggle for legitimacy in the rhetorical bid for power? Or are the thrusts of complaining just the necessary accompaniment to powerlessness, capable only of showcasing the illegitimate lunges made at referential authority and what it means consistently to fall flat on the face of linguistic positing feints? The complaint bickers constantly with its stated insufficiencies, the limits it hits with regard to reach and intention. Proffering only the spectacle of a failed bid for its own authority, the complaint incorporates its flailing dumb show as it tries to latch on to its recalcitrant auditor.

It's touch and go in *Hamlet*, for the plaint that triggers the dumb show hits home, suffices to 'catch the conscience of the King', sending Uncle Claudius reeling and kneeling like no other language form of attack. To the extent that charging with language can be at all gendered — a contestable but inescapable temptation of comprehension and argument — thus failing the test of maintaining even a hint of manliness in the making of claims and executing turnarounds, the plaintive bout is not only the destitute cousin to all language, coming from the wrong side of the referential tracks, but says something about the plight of those beings that take recourse to language and lose ground, fight it out time and again with only paltry results and downpowered amplifiers.

Hamlet sets into gear a drama of flouted sovereignty, for the throne of Denmark has been seized illegitimately, by intimate usurpation. That the power grab extends inextricably to Gertrude tightens the knot of sovereign assumption and desire. Dethroned, the ghost can only rattle his son, who in turn can only rattle his chains, locked into a signifying chain that allows for little latitude. Fogged in and frozen in place, Hamlet constructs the precarious edifice of his complaints. There are moments when he breaks loose from his peculiar confinement, when he lunges at Polonius and arranges for the execution of his friends as part of a demonstration of rage misfiring, going after a secondary tangent.

The complaint as premier attribute — as zero stage of linguistic feint — offers up a sense of man in relation to the decline of sovereignty. No sovereign, no pose of subjective mastery, would be caught dead complaining! Or, more to the ghostly point, the sovereign must be dead in order to complain. The supreme complainer, Hamlet's ghost attracts doubt to the veracity of his claims, inspires his interlocutor to pull in, to suspend action if not belief. Both Hamlets strain the terms of their suspension, in air and as heir. All possibility for dramatically conceived action famously hangs fire. He cannot target a first responder, someone who would be roused to vengeance by a readably convincing war cry. What gets transmitted is not so much an order, a perlocutionary speech act, but the suspensive stance, occupied by the phantomal utterance, of the supreme complainer — the dead paternal trope. Fathers are not supposed to complain; mothers, well, this is another story, currently under investigation, for mothers can go at it: they do not commonly risk in terms of language games the threat of castration and no one really cares about their gripe, the on-switch of an inconsequential cannonade of nagging. Sometimes, however, they are pushed to murderous extremes in order to lodge a complaint, make it take hold in view of an entire, horror-stricken community of onlookers, the so-called 'innocent' bystanders who have, to some degree or another, let it come to this.

★ ★ ★

It is in the nature of the complaint to hammer a point home, without establishing residency in the House of Being. It insists and harps; it increases its velocities, becomes a shrill sonic signature travelling behind its possible meaning-fields. It goes to work on nothing but spares no one. An abrasive counter-example to philosophical demonstration, and responsible for the disruption of normative types of rhetorical and political dispute, the complaint pulls down the aspiration of the language-bearer to change the world and become, despite it all, an enduring host for the occasional outburst of meaningfulness, even purposiveness, if without purpose — a structure that Kant has taught us to welcome and integrate. The complaint brings every transcendental signified down to earth.

A problem that undergirds any serious study of the complaint involves its tendency to prolong the span of an injurious misdeed. Lining up as a species of mourning disorder, it just won't let go but repeals any petition for reprieve. Tenacious and often enough exhausting, drearily unrelenting, the complaint can bring movement — one of Hannah Arendt's definitions of freedom: freedom of movement — to a standstill, shuttering a world closing in on itself, drained of vitality. At the same time, it makes an unceasing production of annoyance stand out with a kind of whistle-blowing poise, as emblem of strength, almost as if complaining emanated from a position of pure and laudable conviction.

In a way, the complaint's rumble through the neighbourhood of being represents one way of saying, 'No justice, no peace', influencing a shakedown of that which should not be tolerated. Whether in *Hamlet* or on the streets, the complaint, in its clumsy, diminished yet partially befitting manner, takes aim at the unbearable. It almost makes the unbearable bearable to the extent that it arranges a reduced rate, a place for its charge within the bargained spectrum of mere annoyance — the bickering firing range that makes life's hardships manageable, maybe containable, if hopped up on repetition compulsion. Under favourable conditions the complaint eventually can bring a defective structure down, though mostly, let's face it, disturbed minds are left impervious to the nattering insect-like bites of language. The target often enough stays intact. Regardless of its effective range of motion, it can never be cleared of suspicion when it comes to determining what side of the complaint lands with justice or promotes further evildoing. For the complaint looks like it is in collusion with the very iniquity it criticizes, if only to the extent that the picked-off problem extends its shelf-life when becoming the object of the reviler's fixation.

In the German language, one form of complaint or lament, the *Klage*, flips easily into *Anklage*, accusation. The undecidable limit between complaint and accusatory claim — a rollover prompted by Walter Benjamin's study of Karl Kraus — will provide a basis for some of the analyses I present here. Pursuing the underworld of 'phrase', one can consider, in the shuttle between philosophical and literary points of urgency, the unsystematizable contingency, an environment of failed performatives that motor micro-events unleashed by complaints and their lethal counterparts — for instance, one can explore what it means to throw a curse at someone, to nag the target towards and to death.

At certain points the effort to understand the nature of the complaint may seem like menial labour in the fields of language theory and political advocacy. Yet, caught in the crosswinds of vanishing protest and the newly visible stoppage of social movement, it seemed relevant to return to the drawing boards of language that slogans, pleads, accuses, demands and despairs, calling out with no assured address or hope for a beseeched rejoinder. Besides, I am a partisan of non-canonized tropes of moaning and bitching, a language stash of which I fear I haven't produced enough myself, even though, as born troublemaker, I tend to veer towards mined zones and difficult access routes to marginalized objects or themes of thought with noisy trespass. Few would want to claim the degraded realm of language's castoffs and get into the down and dirty grit of language usage, the gutter of *Gerede* or gossip, with me and my girl squad of alpha bitches.

In some ways, the complaint serves up the antidote to the *parole du maître*, staving off, in terms of tonality and rhythm, any master discourse. Yet, running a low profile, unmanly and coarse, angling, in terms of cultural codifications, with the intent mostly to target women and children, it is also behind and ahead of the scenes of its deployment, serving as the ground of language, the place from which any act of phrasing takes off. Language begins and expires in protest of its own dispossession and broken ability to ensure the solidity of world.

(Then there are those who can't complain. They squeak by with the rejoinder of meek desistence, 'I can't complain.' A blockbuster, nearly congenial utterance, a staple of amiable denial that I examine closely, it runs like a street translation of a Celan poem: they know that there is no address in the era of the becoming anonymous of God. Who would pick up your call? Those who live in stubborn destitution cannot complain. Nor do sovereigns, those who rule in Shakespeare or in scattered world posts. All the same, by stating that they 'can't complain', the abstainers, those who resolutely desist, raise the issue of the complaint, its necessity and futility, insinuating a store of complaints at the ready, but withheld: I could complain, but I renounce the temptation to do so. Anyway, who, in a Rilkean syntax of being, would hear me?) On some level of ethical responsiveness, I am mandated to refrain from unloading the complaint. But, maybe, as in the surprise ending of *Portnoy's Complaint*, an analyst would hear me? I turn the screw now on psychoanalysis and the ends of complaint.

★ ★ ★

Deserving their own dossier and inventory, medical and legal complaints call for a considerably concise treatment of body, institution and language. Psychoanalysis deals routinely with complaints. In most cases the delivery of a complaint functions as the 'open sesame' of a psychoanalytic encounter. According to psychoanalyst Anne Dufourmantelle, the complaint made during the analytic work initiates a wager, poses a dilemma and defies analytic arbitration. The complaint, she warns, should not be confounded with the *demande* (demand), and actually dismantles the scene and coordinates of analysis, throwing the analyst into crisis. Neither fully developed as *demande* nor as description, the complaint throws a wrench into the system, no matter how non-systematic and pliant it proves to be. The complaint serves to show the impotence of the other. In conversation, Anne says that she feels diminished by the subversive function of the complaint in analysis, shining a harsh light on the bareness of our being-there, together, in the language that subjects us.

Another analyst, François Roustang, tries in his work, *La Fin de la plainte*, to mark an end to the complaint, a way out of the debilitating and repetitive stances of the complaining subject.[3] According to the analyst, the complaint must be brought to an end; it must complete its rounds, even if this means re-describing the analytic experience. Analysis should not be used as pretext for extending the life cycle of the complaint and its strategic epistemological underpinnings.

Roustang offers interpretations of Narcissus and Psyche in light of the 'illusion of healing by means of self-knowledge'. What Narcissus teaches us is that self-knowledge can be fatal. Locked in embrace with himself, 'Narcisse 1er', Narcissus the first, proves to be a paranoid dictator, having lost all distance, blinded to any possible sense of alterity and differentiation (27). There are other ascensions of Narcissus, including 'Narcisse II', second or secondary, who is essentially inexistent (27–8). The Narcisses rallied by Roustang are 'champions de la plainte' (29) (champions of complaint), and the analyst goes after them ferociously. I admit that the encounter with such severity, his uncompromising pushback on the complaining subject, have taken me by surprise. At first, I was startled by the severe beating, or at least bad rap sheet that Dr Roustang gives the complaint, the subject that ticks off a mechanism of grievance as well as ticking off the analyst. This guy would decimate me if I went to him, vulnerable and raw. OK, maybe he's not talking to or about me, and my customized stock of problems. I'm not so sure that I'm all that narcissistically wrought to the point of needing paring down (I'm not kidding — if anything, I need periodically to *renarcissize*, but that's another story). From the start, he seemed harsh to me. I was developing from page 1 a negative transference. But he's not my analyst, so I dial it down, bracket the misgivings. I can always get at him critically, detached and cold, I tell myself. But the 'rights of nerves' rarely prompt me to be detached and cold. Should his relentless pursuit really be taken at face value, though?

Then I remember the legions of narcissistic snivellers that have come my way, always hankering after more, rarely in touch with or jolted by the spark of alterity, except for what has existentially bamboozled them en route to my phone number or office or table. I have had entire conversations with those who not once asked how I was doing, what I was doing, if I was even capable of doing, my face practically dropped on the desk, fists pounding, I was in so many ways crawling. But now I am complaining. Pardon me.

★ ★ ★

Still, Roustang really sticks it to 'les plaintes qui se prolongent au-delà de la décence d'un chagrin ou d'un deuil [et] se développent comme un cancer qui va tout dévorer' (29) since, instead of proliferating like cellular life in the service of growth, 'elles prolifèrent sur le vide de l'intérêt pour soi' (29) (the complaints that go on and on, exceeding the decency of the time of distress or grief, developing like a cancer that devours everything, proliferating in the void of self-interest). In some respects, this guy tops Claudius, counting down the right and restricted period of proper mourning. He has no patience with what he sees as a senseless emptying born of self-involvement — a precarious position for an analyst to occupy. He must know the risks he is taking, because he is smart as a whip, and, I'm told, worthy. I've heard from a friend who used to go to him to air her complaint that he is an excellent analyst. Another friend found him to be on the harsh side of rigorous. I suppose that only an analyst would authorize and specify the sense of decency and measure when it comes to timing one's period of grief or pain, but, really, what a smack down. I'm smarting! That part of my superego permanently occupied by Derrida wonders: He's a little off, no? — Who dares to hold a stopwatch over suffering, the time of catastrophic wounding? Of course, it would be nice to stop the pain, call it a day, but to call it a cancerous growth owing to self-indulgence? Yes, and no. No — and yes. He really has it in for *les Narcisses*.

I'm not that far behind on this assessment, I must admit. They have become unbearable to me: I would love to unstick them from my skin — grand reception area. Champions of the complaint, 'les Narcisses ferment les yeux à ce parcours fatal et tentent de justifier par une répétition inlassable la direction erronée qu'ils ont prise. Ils pensent soulager la souffrance qui s'exhale de leur recherché folle, alors qu'ils s'enferment dans ce dont ils prétendent sortir. Il n'y a plus d'issue pour eux que l'appel à la pitié ou à la compassion' (29) (The Narcissi close their eyes to the fatal course on which they embark, attempting to justify by unrelieved repetition the wrong path taken. They think they can subdue the suffering that emanates from their mad search, but in fact they lock themselves into what they claim to overcome. There is no exit for them other than an appeal to pity or compassion).

★ ★ ★

For Roustang, the complaint issues from one who wants to keep intact her *chagrin* or suffering, if only to avoid confronting it head on. In a way, he rebukes the complaint for not becoming a lamentation, a rite of passage — in fact, for not *becoming*. The complaint, he argues, ought to have given way to an aesthetic *mise en forme* of pain, a reorganization of the beauty of expression trying to catch up with a disorder perceived in its first stages as irreparable, an elegy meant to begin the work of closing a mourning period. But to the extent that the complaint persists, it remains instead a repetitive fixation that feeds chagrin rather than exhausting its course. The complaint that does not finish itself off or move up the ladder of formal transformation increases pain, opening only on a condition of depression that, with each day, is more irremediable. In this way, the complaint complies only with the refusal of an imposed reality — something that may have overwhelmed my existence and relational systems, a terrible event, disruptive and inassimilable.

Faced with the unmovable event, I become tired, depleted, unable to effect the existential and material modifications required of me if I am to change things: I remain in the rote of the complaint, over and over again, preferring to deny that something has happened to me, to my world of structured accommodations, specific grammars of avoidance. The event 'insists', however, for it won't go away. When the complaint runs out the clock, stabilizing only its concourse, it has become a way to evade facing the event. Instead, Roustang argues, one can regret its occurrence and encroachment, one can deplore attendant facts; one wants, wishes for, demands a time and place when things were different. Continual complaining means that I have been unable to appropriate the overwhelming event and assume responsibility in some way for its onslaught and implications. This is when fault is assigned to another, be it destiny, society, heredity, the genitors: my messed-up parents. 'La plainte en vient à porter plainte et à se répandre en accusations' (10) (The complaint shows up to register a complaint and to spread out in the form of accusations).

In a way that proves critical, judgement is suspended by the complaint and condemnation staved off as the event continues to develop consequences. One develops a pervasive sense of encroachment: one feels shaken down, squeezed and surrounded by enemies, and begins permanently adopting the figure of one persecuted. As much as the complaint resembles a rebuttal to injustice, evoking recrimination, maybe indulging a subtle Nietzschean dose of vengeance — Nietzsche claims to detect a subtle dose of vengeance in every complaint in the *Untimely Meditations* — nothing of the sort will rise up or amount to much, for the subject of complaint remains obstinate, stuck in process with the faulty understanding that the order of things must change, and not 'mes propres sentiments' (11) (my own feelings). What happens is that a state of division reigns where no reconciliation becomes viable. Complaint has existential takeover plans, attaching to everything and nothing, crowding out life's capacity to endow and enrich.

One of the sticking points of complaint, according to Roustang, is found in the way it blocks out forms of consolation or overcoming. The complaint issues from the stunted lifeline of childhood wounding. Something happened — and has not ceased to happen, continues to hurt — that cannot be ignored by an analyst or therapist who needs to consider how the complaint 'était le fruit de l'impossibilité de vivre' (12) (was the fruit of the impossibility of living), arising as it does as the impossibility of living life at an early age: the wounding struck so deeply that it prohibited any new growth. In this area of being, obstinacy holds intact an infantile part of the self. The complaint is an effect of the refusal to grow up, or it expresses, at least, regret over having grown up. Staying in place, dissatisfied and stunted — this still shot keeps one hooked on the cherished self of childhood that remains frozen in a pout. The complaining subject is thus protected from plunging into the pain of growth spurts, which limits the astonishing abundance of life's donations, so readily available, according to the therapist, as part of the very risky prompts of overflowing generosity, free-floating gratuity, and the adventurous frontiers of friendship and love. Resentment, reproaches, requiring that others give us what, in principle, we cannot receive — these stymied uprisings are held in place by the complainant closed in on himself.

Roustang profiles two relations to the stall of being on which he appears to hang the complaint. They prove contradictory and rich. On the one hand, the therapist is enjoined to induce mobility, pull the complainer out of the ditch. This pull-out and push cannot be accomplished by turning away from the emptiness to which the complaint attests. The narcissistically retrograde patient, running at top speed on empty, needs to learn how to *wait*. Maybe in French this directive becomes more eloquent, for the patient need to *patienter*, to assume her patience-ness. (I add this disclaimer: Roustang would be unlikely to approve this Freudo-Heidegger inflection of being that waits; moreover, he has long ago booked out of psychoanalysis, a practice that he believes feeds the complaint. I resume.) The patient needs to assume his patience-ness the way one assumes one's castration (ditto on the unlikeliness of obtaining Roustang's approval on the concern with castration as moment of truth). The patient needs to show patience, to assume 'une attente dépouillée' (16) (a bare sense of waiting) that resembles despair. Emptiness itself, the voided space of our existence, is what goads the breath and breeze to enable movement in existence. Roustang admittedly goes far here, to the Far East, in order to stir up some movement, seeking to locate a syntax of light but firm prompting, a tug that would let things and beings touch, get in touch with one another, giving them over to 'l'unité d'une caresse' (16) (a caress's unity), an existential tap both French and Asian. A force that comes from yonder yet stays with us, a pulse from elsewhere that prompts and gently prods; this is what the Chinese call Tao.

However, remodelling existence so that it releases from the tether of complaint is not a given. The complaint does not let up of itself, often tantalizing the complainer into complacent standstill. Nothing moves or budges, nothing unsticks from the standpoint of narcissistic tenacity. Towards the end of the work, Roustang therefore offers another approach. Pushing off from the 'plainte meurtrière' (39), a kind of lethal complaint, condemned to stasis ('il se condamne à ne plus se mouvoir') (39), repeating incessantly the same grievances, the therapist Roustang chooses to follow a path not taken (39).

How does one break into the closed circuit of the narcissistic economy? One way is to deploy *disrespect* — 'l'irrespect inclus dans l'impératif' (170) (the disrespect inherent to the imperative). There is no way to avoid a rhetoric or pose of disrespect in the address to an apprentice, student or patient. This nettling structure becomes apparent in hypnosis, to which Roustang returns, which induces the subject to heteronomize, to learn to situate 'la dépendance comme source de l'indépendance' (170) (dependence as springboard for independence). At the same time, the narcissist must learn to make the leap that is freeing on her own, outside herself, for no one else can fend for the event of self-freeing that comes out of relatedness.

The therapist's radical incapacity to free up the analysand in place of the other comes to the fore, and in the aporetic retreat the chronic complainer becomes unbound, prompted by the 'suprême irrespect' (171) ('supreme lack of respect') of the imperative. The very set-up of the encounter and its impotent inflections serve the purpose of shaking up the hold of narcissistic stagnancy. The asymmetrical relatedness presupposed by the scene and sentence, 'You will now close your eyes', means that the subject has sought and yielded to a commanding other, one who has broken the narcissistic seal by giving an order, delivering an instruction to the now suggestible subject. The staging of heteronomy cracks the sealing fantasy of independence, breaking open the myth of some individualistic autonomy by instituting the diverting fields of heteronomy. Such a mutation in relation, and towards relation, is effected by a disrespecting move on the self-enclosed sufferer that comes about as a kind of slap of 'snap out of it', bringing the sufferer abruptly to relationality and world. In Freud, differently set and otherwise marked up, the movement from narcissism to identification introduces the possibility of a just politics.[4] For Freud the narcissi must be able to get over themselves, identify with others, if the political were ever to hold sway. But group psychology and the sorry state of mankind left Freud pessimistic about the prospects for such a leap.

Roustang, who has distanced himself from Freud, but still remains in some disrespects on course, looks for a detox remedy for unbridled narcissism, cipher of our era. What can serve as 'cure de désintoxication narcissique' (175) (rehab for toxic narcissism)? How can one desituate narcissism, the suicidal inclination of self-internment? Roustang seeks 'un autre type de sensorialité' (183) (another type of sensoriality), a spacing of being that would make room for replunging into the field of the unconscious, if only to find some relation to it, simply by being there and getting one's bearings, without fulfilling the prophecy to which Liriope, mother of Narcissus, was privy. When Liriope, in Ovid's *Metamorphoses*, asks the oracle if her son's life will span to old age, the response is distinct: '*Si se non nouerit*,' if he does not know himself. Roustang interprets the oracle as saying that the condition for longevity rests on the injunction *not to know oneself*, not to know who one is, for such knowledge signs off on a death sentence: 'L'autoconnaissance est fatale' (19) (self-knowledge is fatal).

Under such constraints and prohibitive conditions, how can the plaint of the narcissist, the worried comprehension of Liriope be stilled? Sometimes, the way to disrupt narcissistic burrowing, archaeological and specular in nature, is to thread the narcissist through an experience of stupidity, or by the sheer idiocy of non-experience, to instigate a reduction or mineralization of being condensed into inanimate thereness. In other words, the narcissist needs to be cupped in a place already sketched out in such phrases as 'I feel heavy, like a stone', 'I cannot move; I feel as dense as a slab of concrete, as thick as wood' (173). A lot depends on *placing* the narcissistic body, letting it take its place in world — something that is not assured or easy to attain. In order to achieve movement, the narcissist may need to go through a phase of stupefying thereness, allowing for nothing but the stupefaction and stupidity of hunkering down in existence. The sheerness of being-there that the analyst seeks to encourage may be the opposite of nomadic transversals or schizoid mobility, no matter how stationary their itineraries remain. Becoming-thing in other words, *unbecoming*, petrified, emptied and still, the complainer neutralizes, drops heavy into life, a recovering complainer fettered neither by the pause of stupor nor by the myth of ecstatic emancipation.

Ach!

★ ★ ★

About this contribution: It should have been an elegy, a way of 'Reading: Otherwise'. It should have closed a mourning period or quietly marked the end of an era of critical abundance, shuttling the stubborn schedules of unsepulchred pain. Instead, it grabbed on to a scrap of language, an instance of dismissible speech, letting the **COMPLAINT**, obdurate by nature, turn over its hoarse engine.

NOTES

1 Jacques Lacan, 'Desire and the Interpretation of Desire in *Hamlet*' in *Literature and Psychoanalysis: The Question of Reading: Otherwise* (Baltimore and London: The Johns Hopkins University Press, 1982).
2 I have decided to leave intact a possible trip-up — something that may or may not amount to a lapsus. The last time I jammed on the quote 'It speaks!' was in seminar. In 'The Poets Take Philosophy' class at New York University in 2015, we took a time out to consider Celan's 'Meridian' and the exclamation 'It speaks!' Derrida gave serious thought to the exclamation mark, which I realize now resembles a ghostly figure, perhaps Hamlet's father hovering over the globe, or *Shakespere's* (a spelling that accrues to this name) Globe Theatre. Perhaps I should have left the more recognizable quote on the page, namely, 'Speak to it, Horatio!' The way that poetic language speaks or communicates infrastructurally, without the anchor of strict chronicity or

historical build-up, should open new dossiers. I am not the only one to note that Hamlet mysteriously calls out for the 'doctor in Vienna' when he plunges a sword into the membrane hiding Polonius, one of his victims. Who would be so small-minded as to deny the evidence showing that Hamlet was already telepathizing with Freud? 'It speaks!' (*Ça parle!*)

3 François Roustang, *La Fin de la plainte* (Paris: Editions Odile Jacob, 2000), 19, 29. Henceforth, all references to this work will be to this edition.

4 I have addressed the movement from narcissism to identification, reading Nancy and Lacoue-Labarthe's work on political panic in *Loser Sons: Politics and Authority* (Champaign: University of Illinois Press, 2012).

Nothing to Say: The Negative Phrase of Affect

Claire Nouvet

'I have nothing to say.' I will not recount the cases reported by therapists from which I extract this phrase. It will stand alone, cut off from its histories — for its irruption marks the refusal of all storytelling as well as the rejection of the transferential address that therapy presupposes. For those who encountered a certain silence and the annihilation to which it reduced everything that could be said, there is no longer any possible interlocutor. Silence is irremediable. What, then, is the task of the talking cure? And what position should the therapist adopt once s/he has been summarily dismissed from the position of addressee?

Confronted with such a challenge, the therapist may want to turn to literature, and specifically to the poem about nothing, 'Farai un vers de dreit nïen' (I'll do a song about nothing at all),[1] that Guillaume IX, 'the first known troubadour', wrote.[2] In this poem, lyric poetry puts itself in relation to the muteness of what Jean-François Lyotard, after Lacan, calls the Thing. It sets for itself the task of both presenting and transmitting its affect, an affect that Lyotard theorizes as a negative phrase since it negates the four coordinates used to orient and respond to any phrase: addressor, addressee, meaning, referent. 'The phrase of affect "says" it is something, as *Da*, here and now, inasmuch as this something is *nothing*, not meaning, not referent, not address.'[3] Literature, I will argue, transmits the intractable resistance of this inarticulate 'nothing'. It in fact defines literary 'tradition' as a transference of affect, which is also the transference of a peculiar kind of address from which the address of psychoanalytic transference has much to learn, especially when 'nothing' has to be said.

I Have Nothing to Say

'I have nothing to say': someone apparently says that s/he is empty, a blank that has nothing to give. Thrown between patient and therapist as a challenge, it is the verbal equivalent of the silence that threatens to interrupt the exchange once and for all. The therapist will be all too eager to treat this phrase as a mere resistance. The patient does not have 'nothing' to say as s/he claims. On the contrary, s/he has plenty to say, but not to 'you', the therapist, who will point out that the very elision of 'you' from the sentence proves that it does not mean that 'I' am void of ideas or feelings, but only that 'I have nothing to say *to you*'. Whatever 'I' am thinking/feeling will not be said to the disappointing 'you' that 'you' are, a 'you' so disappointing that it deserves to be erased from the sentence, reduced to nothing, to radical irrelevance.

The therapist has a point when s/he translates the sentence 'I have nothing to say' as 'I dismiss you as my interlocutor on the basis of some unvoiced complaint'. S/he is also probably right in assuming that, whatever might be his or her deficiencies, s/he only provided the occasion for the patient to rediscover a childhood lesson of sorts, the basic lesson of abandonment and of betrayal: that there is no 'you' to hear what one has to say. The active erasure of 'you' in the 'here and now' of the session repeats and, in so doing, bears witness to a previous erasure over which 'I' had no control. 'You' has been vacated long ago, in a past that remains forever present, ready to irrupt in the 'here and now' if only given the chance by some occasional deficiency. The present tense of the sentence 'I have nothing to say' is the extension of an infantile present that engulfs chronological time in all of its dimensions: there was no 'you' then; there is no 'you' now; there can never be any 'you'.

But — and here is my resistance to the therapeutic treatment of this sentence as a mere resistance — if there is no 'you', then whatever 'I' may have to say is 'nothing', that is, devalued by not being heard. 'I have plenty to say' and 'I have nothing to say' are not mutually exclusive sentences. Whatever 'I' may have to say is reduced to nothing by the absence of a 'you' capable of hearing it. When not heard, words are emptied out, unbearably light. One speaks in vain. And this is precisely what the sentence 'I have nothing to say' enacts. In the marked absence of any possible 'you', anything 'I' may have to say is reduced to the 'nothing' that is thrown in-between 'I' and the vacated spot that is 'you'. There, where there should be someone, there is no one. Or: 'I may indeed have something to say as you suspect, but the void that you have become has voided anything that I may have to say at this very moment.' As for the 'I' who is apparently still speaking, it too is reduced to nothing. If there is no 'you' to hear what 'I' must say, then 'I' is annihilated, reduced to muteness in the very gesture of speaking. 'I' is speaking, words are uttered, but words which are muted by not being heard.

'I have nothing to say' enacts a linguistic annihilation that explodes the four coordinates of a phrase. This explosion starts with the annihilation of the addressee pole, which launches a chain reaction: if there is no 'you', no addressee to speak to, then there is no 'I', no addressor, and nothing to say (meaning) about anything (referent). All referents and meanings are pre-emptively dismissed by the voiding of the axis of destination. Whoever is saying this negative phrase is re-enacting the annihilation of the universe where s/he should be able to dwell, the explosion of all of the coordinates that should articulate it. S/he floats in the void. As she re-enacts this traumatic annihilation, she unknowingly phrases the negative phrase of its affect, an affect that passes undetected in this most unsentimental of sentences: 'I have nothing to say.'

Is this explosion punctual? The therapist may want to believe that it is the case. After some tuning of the transferential axis, that is, the axis of destination, the patient who claimed to have nothing to say starts speaking again about something to 'you'. The therapist, no doubt, will be reassured. We are speaking to each other about something, constructing meanings, moving along the path of language. And, indeed, very interesting things can be said following the apparent roadblock of 'I have nothing to say'. But does the fact that 'you' and 'I' start speaking again prove that we have left the roadblock behind us? Did we progress from 'nothing' to 'something'? To believe in a therapeutic progress that simply moves out of nothing into something is, in my opinion, to be deaf to the war that is being waged. 'I' may have plenty to say, but this apparent plenitude can always be — and will always be — reduced to nothing. 'Nothing' is not opposed to 'something': it underlines, undermines and infiltrates 'something' at all times. This is a *guerre sourde,* a French expression that I use for its double meaning. A *guerre sourde* means a war that is latent, undeclared. But *sourde* also connotes deafness and the stifling of sounds. The constant voiding that a patient can perform on everything that s/he says constitutes a *guerre sourde* in both meanings: it is both a latent warfare, below the surface, undeclared and unnoticeable, and a war that is *sourde* because it remains unheard by both therapist and patient.

What I am trying to describe is a concealed annihilation, all the more devastating for being concealed. An explosion has devastated language. It is empty, exploded from within, while still apparently standing, as if nothing had happened, a beautiful façade behind which there is nothing. Where 'I' apparently stand and speak, a 'no one' reduced to muteness. Where 'something' is apparently said, 'nothing', since something can always count for nothing. Where a 'you' should stand as an interlocutor, this other 'you' who has been there all the time: the unresponsive one who does not receive and return the gift of language, thereby turning the gift into nothing, and the giver into no one. And it is no use to try to treat this unresponsiveness by tracing it back to a singular face or proper name. There was, of course, one face through which silence came for the first time, one name through which it was learned that language makes no difference, and that its gift is futile. But, in the aftermath of this discovery, there can no longer be any 'first' time. The 'first' time will be annihilated by being reduced to nothing more than the occasion to discover that there is an empty spot in the world from which no response will ever come, a deaf spot that annihilates language and turns it into an unbearably futile exercise. This deafness draws the line of an intractable resistance; it will refuse all treatment. All other deafness, therapeutic or otherwise, will be treated as mere occasions to re-find that empty spot.

This deaf and deadening spot is what 'I' have when 'I' say: 'I have nothing to say.' It is a guarded treasure: 'Nothing is what I keep for myself in everything I say.' I suspect that whoever says 'I have nothing to say' contemplates in silence everything that s/he says reduced to meaninglessness and muteness by 'you' who cannot hear it. In front of that deaf spot, better to give up speaking: aborted words fall in silence on the floor. And s/he who lets them drop silently is the only witness of this linguistic abortion. This secretly guarded annihilation is a weapon in the latent warfare, the *guerre sourde*, being waged: everything that we say can always count for nothing. The words that we weave between us and that constitute our relationship unravel in their very utterance. Therapy aborts as it progresses, and the more it progresses.

Faced with such warfare, the therapist may be tempted to step in as the responsive addressee who repairs the addressee pole. Someone steps in at the precise spot where there was no one. Analytic listening substitutes for a non-listening that it claims to eradicate in that very gesture. Such eradication is the final negation. It negates deafness, and, in so doing, exposes its own deafness. The patients who say nothing know better. They know that the deaf spot, once opened, cannot be negated. No amount of responsive listening can ever eradicate the fact that language has been put, once and for all, in relation to that which annihilates it: deafness and, through it, indifference, non-relation itself. The deaf and mute spot is intractable. It cannot be eliminated. It will stubbornly resist all treatment that claims to do away with it. It permanently stamps speech with utter futility.

Why indeed speak? One does not deal with this question by eradicating it. What, then, is one to do? This is a question of analytic technique that I could address to therapists, leaving it up to them to answer. This would be a slightly disingenuous move. For what I hear in the phrase 'I have nothing to say' is not just an intractable resistance, but also an opening, a challenge that the patient, at that very moment, addresses to her/himself and to the therapist: this annihilation of 'you', and 'me', of what we talk about, and of the meanings that we construct about it, this is what 'I' must say. 'I' must present, that is, describe and not just enact, the negation that attacks all the coordinates (addressor, addressee, referent, meaning) that articulate a phrase. 'I have nothing to say' is a double-edged sentence, simultaneously a refusal ('Nothing is what I'll keep for myself in everything that I say') and an injunction that the speaker unknowingly phrases: 'This nothing, do not just enact it. Find a way to say it.' A clenched fist over nothing and the precarious outline of an open hand that might open some kind of future.

But what can it possibly mean to 'say nothing', to say this annihilation around which the sentence wraps itself like a clenched fist protecting an empty core? And can this presentation of nothing fit the transferential model that presupposes that all phrases are addressed to the analyst? I do not think so. And here, the talking cure may have something to learn from poetry, and from the strange address that Guillaume IX stages in his poem about nothing. This poem exposes the negation that undoes everything that is said as it is being said, and, in so doing, gives a 'sense' of an affect — the sorrow intimated at the very core of the poem — that the futility of words such as 'sorrow' can only betray.

I Have to Say Nothing

'I'll do a song about nothing at all'[4] proclaims defiantly the lyric 'I' in the opening line before doing so by negating all the available topics of lyric poetry:

> It won't be about me or about others,
> It won't be about love nor about happiness
> Nor about anything else,
> For it was composed earlier while (I was) sleeping
> On a horse. (vv. 2–6)

Once everything that could be said has been discarded, the poem seems completed. In the blank between 'I will not speak about anything' and 'I have composed a poem', in the jump from the future tense to the past tense, here is 'nothing'. The poem wraps itself around a blank that is not allowed to stand in the present tense of chronological time.

And still a voice continues to negate by taking as its target the 'I' who spoke about nothing:

> I don't know what time I was born,
> I am not happy or sad,
> I am not a stranger or an intimate friend,
> Nor can I do anything about it;
> For so I was enchanted at night
> Upon a high hill.
> I don't know when I am asleep,
> Nor when I am awake, if someone doesn't tell me. (vv. 7–14)

Out of chronological time, since he does not know 'what time [he] was born' (v. 7), neither conscious nor unconscious, since he does not know when he is awake or asleep, neither 'a stranger or an intimate friend', neither 'happy' nor 'sad', the anonymous 'I' who took on the strange task of saying nothing is floating in limbo, straddling a deadly in-between as he straddles his horse, emptied out of any positive qualification. Without qualities, 'I' is no one, indeterminacy itself.

This 'no one' nevertheless claims to feel a pain that he immediately negates by depriving it of any value:

> My heart is almost split apart
> By a heartfelt pain;
> But that is not worth an ant to me,
> By Saint Martial! (vv. 15–18)

However devastating, pain counts for nothing. An 'I' reduced to 'no one' thus feels nothing. Feeling nothing does not mean not to feel anything. It means depriving one's feelings of any value and significance. One feels intensely and at the same time feels the emptiness and meaninglessness of feeling anything. One feels in vain. Such voiding of meaning explains the opening stanza: it leaves nothing to talk about.

Feelings are worthless, as insignificant as 'an ant', for they cannot match the pain that sickens the heart:

> I am sick and I am afraid of dying,
> Yet I know nothing about it except what I hear;
> I'll search for a doctor to my liking,
> Yet I don't know any;
> He will be a good doctor if he can heal me,
> But not if I worsen. (vv. 19–24)

The lyric topos of the 'love sickness' is evoked through its negation, since 'I' knows nothing of this sickness 'except what I hear about it', for instance from a poetic tradition that calls it 'love'. By naming 'love' the unknowable pain from which 'I' suffers, this tradition turns an indeterminate affect that exceeds cognition into a knowable and qualified 'feeling'. But this unknown affect resists qualification, and drives writing to the precise extent that it resists ever being qualified into a determinate feeling. As the very persistence of the lyric tradition testifies, no amount of 'love' and sentimental meaning will manage to write once and for all the affect that afflicts the lyric 'I'.

As he searches for a 'doctor' who might heal him, a Lady emerges as both the cause and the remedy of the indeterminate affect that threatens to kill him. But the cause is itself indeterminate and unknown:

> I have a woman-friend, I don't know who she is
> For I never saw her, so help me;
> She never did anything which I like or dislike,
> And I don't care;
> (...)
> I never saw her and I love her greatly;
> She has never yet done right by me, or wrong.[5] (vv. 25–31)

'She' who can presumably heal him by returning his love is precisely the one who cannot return anything. He does not know who she is; he has never met or seen her. As Jacques Roubaud notes, Guillaume's poem is 'an anticipated parody of one of the most famous cansos of the trobar',[6] the song where Jaufré Rudel invokes the figure of a Far Away

Lady whom the lyric 'I' loves although he has never seen her. Before Jaufré Rudel composed this seemingly ideal figure, Guillaume both sketches her outline and 'parodies' — that is, de-idealizes — her in advance by exposing her negativity. What passes for the object of love is no object at all, but something else entirely, something so maddening in fact that one might prefer breaking all relation to it. 'She' whom the lyric 'I' does not know and has never seen is indeed deprived of all the characteristics of an object. Thus voided, the 'object' of love emerges as a non-object. 'She' is but the contour of a void, of no-thing.

This nothing is, paradoxically enough, the mark of the 'Thing', a notion that Lacan foregrounds in the Freudian text and considerably extends in an argumentation that reads the Lady of courtly love as its indexical sign. Lacan highlights a passage of the *Project* where Freud 'dissects' two components in the perception of the 'fellow human being', the *Nebenmensch*, the neighbour.[7] While some features of this 'fellow' who 'resembles the subject' can be 'understood by the activity of memory — that is, can be traced back to information from the subject's own body', another part falls from this process of (re)-cognition through 'association' or comparison, and 'stays together as a *thing*' (*SE* I, 331). Freud calls *das Ding*, the thing, this uncognizable component for which no predicates are available, these 'residues which evade being judged' (*SE* I, 334). Following Freud, who noted that the subject is interested in cognizing the 'fellow human being' in so far as it resembles the 'first satisfying object and further his first hostile object, as well as his sole helping power' (*SE* I, 331), Lacan extends the encounter with the Thing to the relation with the other as 'mother' — that is, the caretaker whose proximity and good neighbouring guarantees survival. The libidinal encounter with this primordial other carves out an unknowable, unassimilable and radically alien 'Thing' at the very core of the 'neighbour'.

Lyotard will inflect some of the traits of the Lacanian account when he too invokes the 'Thing', albeit within a different philosophical elaboration, which contests the extent to which the unconscious can be said to be 'structured like a language', and which expands on the notion of affect, mentioned but left undeveloped by Lacan. Of relevance for the Lyotardian notion of affect will be the characterization of the Thing as that which exceeds both the imaginary and the symbolic, since it is 'the beyond-of-the-signified' in relation to which, as Lacan notes, the subject constitutes itself 'in a kind of relationship characterized by primary affect, prior to any repression'.[8]

The Thing is 'at the heart' of the 'subjective world' (*SL* VII, 71), but as 'an excluded interior' (*SL* VII, 101) since it is the presence 'within' the psyche of an unknowable 'something' for which it has no representation, and which can therefore only 'appear' negatively within representation as the void signalling that which cannot ever be signified. The Lady of courtly love indexes, for Lacan, such a 'Thing'. Courtly love is 'an exemplary form, a paradigm of sublimation' (*SL* VII, 128) that, in his definition, 'raises an object (. . .) to the dignity of the Thing' (*SL* VII, 112). Deprived of the attributes that would constitute her as an object of any substance, the courtly Lady becomes the index of the Thing that exceeds the representation necessary for the constitution of a determinate object.

In a gesture that pre-empts idealization, Guillaume's poem exposes the complete voiding of the love-object: 'she' is, from the start, crudely defined as the pronominal index that points to the 'thing', that is, the non-object that escapes representation.[9] But she, this Thing, is also identified as that which affects the lyric 'I', an identification that Lyotard stresses in his own elaboration of the Thing as the unconscious affect for which no representation is available and which, as such, does not belong to the unconscious constituted by secondary repression. This affect is not a qualified feeling, but an inarticulate nothing which has no meaning, no referent and no address. Guillaume places at the very heart of the lyric subject this inarticulate affect. The indeterminate 'sickness' of which he knows nothing, it strips him of his identity,[10] and performs the 'depropriation' that affect, according to Lyotard, inflicts: 'Affect necessarily inscribes itself in the order of the proper as the event of a depropriation.'[11] The affected subject of lyric poetry cannot indeed be localized on a map or in a chronology. 'Enchanted at night/Upon a high hill' (vv. 11–12), he steps into the atopic space of 'enchantment' that love names and out of chronological time — he does not know 'what time I was born' — since affect, for which no representation is available, cannot be inscribed in a chronology that requires such representation. Outside chronology and hence biographical history, he enters the 'now' of the lyric poem, the achronological 'now' of affect, and the enchanted space of affectivity where one loses all 'sense' of oneself. Deprived of his history, he becomes as nameless and indeterminate as the affect that nearly splits his heart. In its grip, he is 'neither happy nor sad' since it exceeds what he knows how to feel, not 'a stranger or an intimate friend' since it is the incomprehensible 'alien within' that maintains him at an irreducible distance even in the closest proximity. Having no meaning since no qualified feelings can ever capture it, this affect has also no referent and no addressee since it cannot ever provide a determinate object (a 'cause' or reason for its affliction) about which and to which anything could be said. As Guillaume's poem rudely insists, 'she', the affecting 'thing' within, cannot be a 'you', an interlocutor, since she is not a determinate object. 'She' to whom lyric poetry addresses its love is thus revealed to be the exact opposite of what an addressee should mean. 'She' marks the vacant spot where there is no one to address, no 'you', no interlocutor to hear, receive or return speech.

Why go on speaking to that? Shouldn't 'I' find an object worthy of the name? This is the therapeutic solution that Guillaume apparently proposes when he dismisses the vacant Lady and replaces her with a better one, more 'noble' and 'beautiful', 'who is worth more' because she presumably gives at last an 'object' to love:

> When I don't see her, I'm happy about it,
> It's not worth a rooster to me!
> For I know one more gentle and beautiful,
> Who is worth more. (vv. 33–6)

From this better Lady, whom Guillaume calls the 'Good Neighbour' in other poems,[12] one can expect to receive a response. A close and responsive neighbour, she obliterates the silence and distance of the Thing. But her proximity is undermined by the distance that the following stanza reinstates:

> I don't know the place where she stays,
> Whether it's in the hills or on the plains;
> I don't dare speak of the wrong she has done to me,
> I'll just drop it. (vv. 37–40)

To whom does 'she' refer? To the better Lady or the vacant one? The very indeterminacy of the reference suggests that the Thing returns at the very core of the responsive neighbour who was supposed to negate it. As Leupin notes, the nobler Lady provides the fantasmatic veil that represses the absence of the first 'unnamable and unrepresentable' Lady, a veil that is denounced as an imaginary construction when she turns out to be, as he puts it, 'sans lieu', without any assignable place (*Mélanges*, 302): 'I don't know the place where she stays' (v. 37).

Far from obliterating the Thing, the better Lady becomes the empty vista through which it returns to absent the 'Good Neighbour' on the spot: she who seemed so close and responsive is suddenly nowhere to be found.[13] Even worse, she is now accused of having caused a 'wrong': 'I don't dare speak of the wrong she has done to me' (v. 39). The lyric 'I' (and his speech) has indeed been wronged, that is, damaged by an affect that cannot be qualified within the register of pleasure or morality since she never did anything that he could either 'like' or 'dislike', or even call 'right' or 'wrong', an indeterminate affect that he dares not speak because he *cannot* speak it. This affect is both a wrong and ongoing grief: 'E peza.m be quar sai rema' (v. 41), a line that Bond translates as 'And it grieves me to stay here' while noting an alternative translation: 'And it grieves me that she stays here'. I will suggest that the lyric 'I' cannot 'stay here' precisely because 'she stays here'. At the end of the poem, the Lady is both nowhere to be found, and right here. She is both absent and present, or rather she is the very presence of an absence that grieves the lyric 'I' who is forced to take his leave under the insistent pressure of the affect that she inflicts: 'And it grieves me to stay here/So I am going' (vv. 41–2). The affected 'I' is gone on the spot, a disappearance that the beginning of the poem enacted when it deprived him of all personal characteristics and history.

In a final negation, Guillaume negates the therapeutic solution that he offered. No responsive interlocutor, no Good Neighbour, will ever manage to cancel the Thing. Through the empty vista that the better Lady becomes, it hovers and insists. In the end, it is to 'her' (the Thing as affect) that the lyric 'I' sends his song, to 'her' who marks the spot where there is precisely no one, no 'you', no interlocutor. It is to this empty spot that the troubadours sing. They address 'no one'. To address no one does not mean that one gives up addressing. It means addressing the vacant spot where there is no interlocutor to address, the deaf and mute spot that neither hears nor responds, the inhuman silence that threatens language with utter futility. And it is to that, to this affecting 'thing' at their very core, that the troubadours address the song that phrases the inarticulate nothing that is its affect. They sing nothing, out of nothing, and to nothing. With this address, they set their song in relation to that which refuses all relation since, as Guillaume puts it, 'she' who affects me never did anything to intentionally please or displease me. 'She' is indifference, non-relation itself.

An Address to No One

Therapy has much to learn from Guillaume's negation of a certain kind of therapeutic solution. The patients who faced, in their own distinct way, a traumatic unresponsiveness also know that the deaf spot cannot ever be eradicated. For them to move from 'I have nothing to say' to 'I have to say nothing', from the enactment of annihilation to its presentation, the analyst will therefore need to shift position. At one crucial point, s/he will need to vacate the position of the responsive addressee (the better Lady) in order to become the witness of phrases that are, strictly speaking, addressed to no one. Patients who say nothing know indeed that they must find the strength to address no one, to speak to the deaf spot instead of being simply suffocated by it. To find this strength, they need the analyst to become a witness.

To become a witness means first, not to confuse oneself with the deaf spot, either by responding for it, or by not responding in its place. Responding for it would be playing the role of the 'better', because responsive, Lady who covers up the unresponsive one and, in so doing, redoubles the annihilation by negating it. 'Playing dead' will not do either, since it would only repeat the annihilation on a mediocre scale. No amount of analytic silence and dead-like neutrality can ever match the annihilating silence that those patients have faced. From their point of view, the analyst who plays 'dead' is simply laughable.

To be a witness also means that the therapist is there to hear that which the deaf spot cannot by definition hear: the pain of annihilation and its inarticulate affect. And, by hearing it, this witness allows the patient to hear it. Even more, s/he confirms that something has been said, that 'I' has managed to say nothing to no one — and that this nothing was hers to say. Does this presentation of nothing mean renouncing it once and for all? Not quite. Far from being given up in the act of phrasing, nothing becomes what I 'have' at last, and have to say, over and over again, an inexhaustible secret that no phrasing will ever open once and for all. The clenched and open fist are now one and the same gesture.

While therapy stops here, literature requires a bit more work. Guillaume's poem culminates indeed in an *envoi*, an enigmatic sending:

> I've done the song, about whom I don't know;
> And I'll send it over to the one
> Who will send it for me through another
> Toward Anjou,
> So that (she/he) might send me a copy of the key
> To his/her coffer. (vv. 43–6)[14]

Literary reception is defined as the transmission of Guillaume's poem, that is, of the affective nothing that disarticulates his lyric phrasing. It clearly takes a 'poet' to receive a poem in such a way, one who can hear the affective nothing that silently unravels the 'something' that lyric poetry seems doomed to say, and who can send it, that is, transmit it again in another poem. In the wake of Guillaume's poem, literary tradition becomes the transmission of the negative affect-phrase that infiltrates and disarticulates all the lyric phrases that Guillaume has composed, will keep composing, and that others, after him, will go on composing.

As he sends nothing again, the troubadour will send to Guillaume the 'contraclau' (the 'counterkey') of his 'estui', his 'case' or 'little box', which, as Stanesco suggests, refers to the poem itself that is here 'sealed'.[15] And it is not just the poem of the other troubadour that is locked, but Guillaume's poem as well when it wraps itself, in this last stanza, around the riddle of this line: 'I've done the song, about whom I do not know' (v. 43). The lyric subject does not know about whom/what he sang when he sang about nothing. The 'key' to what he said, it is not he who has it, but the anonymous recipient to whom he sends it.

Is Guillaume asking this recipient to send him the key that will belatedly open his own sealed poem? It would be relatively easy — and it has been done — to read this 'key' as the hermeneutic key that will solve the riddle of his text. By transmitting and rephrasing the nothing that Guillaume sang, troubadours would be expected to make this nothing more legible and intelligible, to explain the enigma that his own song is for Guillaume. I do not believe that this is the kind of key that troubadours are invited to send back. A key, after all, can lock as well as open. And the 'contra' of *contraclau* connotes opposition, resistance. To ask for a *contraclau* is not to ask for the key that will unlock the riddle of the poem and of the enigmatic 'she' around which it gravitates, but for a redoubling of the lock. As they transmit and rephrase the nothing that Guillaume sent, troubadours will duplicate the key that sealed his poem. They will, in turn, compose a poem about the one whom they do not know, from whom no knowledge can ever be expected, the intractable spot that does not hear, speak or care. In so doing, they will lock the song again around the enigmatic spot that resists all intelligibility. What is asked, in other words, is not to make the intractable spot more intelligible, but to maintain it in its intractable resistance, and to address it as such. A transference of affect, literary tradition is the transference of this address to no one. This is the gesture that is expected from those who wish to practise the 'trobar'. Only those who have the strength to perform such an address will be the 'companions' of the 'trobar' whom Guillaume calls as witnesses at the very beginning of his first poem: 'Companho, faray un vers', 'My companions, I am going to make a *vers* that is refined.'[16]

Troubadours are 'companions'. The companion is not an addressee. When he sings, 'I' addresses nothing to no one. He addresses the mute, deaf and indifferent spot where language makes no difference. The companion is the one who can be the witness of this address. To be its witness means listening to what its addressee will never hear, the affective nothing, foreign to articulation, that disarticulates the lyric phrasing. And to hear it means sending it, transmitting it again, in a new gesture, a new poem.[17] For such a sending to take place, one must already be there where there is nothing to say. One must also find the strength to say this nothing, to stamp everything one says with its foreign accent, and, in a last gesture that defies all reason, to address it to absolutely no one.

NOTES

1 *The Poetry of William VII, Count of Poitiers, IX Duke of Aquitaine*, translated and edited by Gerald A. Bond (New York: Garland Publishing Co., 1982), 14–17. Hereafter referenced as *PW*.

2 As Jean-Charles Huchet notes, the formula, 'the first known troubadour', does not place Guillaume IX 'at the origin of a tradition': it suggests that others 'whose works and names have not been preserved came before him' (*L'Amour discourtois. La 'Fin'Amors' chez les premiers troubadours* (Toulouse: Privat, 1987), 60); my translation. Alexandre Leupin insists that this poem is nevertheless inaugural of a poetic tradition. Coming out of 'nothing', it 'proffers' Love in a way 'that had not been profferred before' and that delineates the very structure of 'fin'amor' ('Dieu, le poète et la Dame' in *Le Moyen Age dans la modernité: Mélanges offerts à Roger Dragonetti; études recueillies et présentées par Jean R. Scheidegger; avec la collaboration de Sabine Girardet et Eric Hicks* (Paris: Champion, 1996), 300, my translation; hereafter abbreviated as *Mélanges*.

3 Jean-François Lyotard, 'Emma: Between Philosophy and Psychoanalysis' in *Lyotard. Philosophy, Politics, and the Sublime*, edited by Hugh J. Silverman (New York and London: Routledge, 2002), 33. I have addressed Lyotard's conception of affect in 'The Inarticulate Affect: Lyotard and Psychoanalytic Testimony' in *Minima Memoria: In the Wake of Jean-François Lyotard*, edited by Claire Nouvet, Zrinka Stahuljak and Kent Still (Stanford: Stanford

4 *PW*, 15.
5 I am substituting here Frederick Goldin's translation for the one Bond proposes: 'I was never right and she did me no wrong' (in *Lyrics of the Troubadours and Trouvères: An Anthology and a History* (New York: Anchor Press/Doubleday, 1973), 27). Hereafter referenced as *LT*.
6 Jacques Roubaud, *La Fleur inverse: Essai sur l'art formel des troubadours* (Paris: Editions Ramsay, 1986), 38; my translation.
7 Sigmund Freud, *Project for a Scientific Psychology* in *The Standard Edition of the Complete Psychological Works of Sigmund Freud*, vol. I, translated and edited by James Strachey, in collaboration with Anna Freud, assisted by Alix Strachey and Alan Tyson (London: The Hogarth Press and the Institute of Psycho-analysis, 1957), 331. Hereafter abbreviated as *SE*.
8 Jacques Lacan, *The Seminars of Jacques Lacan: The Ethics of Psychoanalysis*, vol. VII (New York and London: W. W. Norton & Company, 1997), 54. Hereafter abbreviated as *SL*.
9 Both Huchet and Leupin have identified the problematic of the Thing in Guillaume's poem and pursued a Lacanian interpretation that opens onto the question of sexuality. Huchet reads the Lady as the 'nien' that indexes the surplus of *jouissance*. Leupin, as we shall later see, proposes an intricate reading of the Lady as the 'nothing' outside the symbolic and imaginary registers that the *fin'amor* both marks and covers, and addresses the question of sexuation in the last stanza of the poem (see note 14). For Sarah Kay, who explicitly engages the Lacanian account of the Thing, the poem stages artistic creativity as the creation of 'something' out of the nothing (the void within and beyond representation) that is the Thing; it 'exposes' the 'mechanisms' of sublimation by showing 'the contradictions inherent in creativity in which the valueless and the nonexistent are transformed into the meaningful and the esteemed', while still maintaining the author as 'origin', a godlike creator *ex nihilo*. See *Courtly Contradictions: The Emergence of the Literary Object in the Twelfth Century* (Stanford: Stanford University Press, 2001), 158.
10 Huchet notes the loss of 'biographical or psychological anchorage' (*L'amour discourtois. La 'Fin'Amors'*, 109), while Leupin notes his loss of 'identity, place and time', which he links to the absence of the Lady as cause of desire (*Mélanges*, 301–2).
11 Lyotard, *Misère de la philosophie* (Paris: Galilée, 2000), 87; my translation.
12 Lacan relates Guillaume's use of 'Bon Vezi', that is, 'Good Neighbour', to the expression that 'Freud uses in connection with the first establishment of the Thing, with its psychological genesis, namely, the *Nebenmensch*' (*SL* VII, 151–2).

13 As Leupin argues, the enigmatic 'solution' that Guillaume's poem gives to 'the question of sexuation' forever marks the 'fin'amor' that it inaugurates: the 'fin'amor' will go on 'proffering' and 'covering' the nothingness of the first Lady with the imaginary construct of the better Lady, whom it defines as 'unreachable' (*Mélanges*, 303).

14 I have modified the translation of the last two verses to reflect an ambivalence that Bond notes. Although he chooses the following translation 'So that (she) might send me a copy of the key/To her coffer', he points out that these verses could also be translated as 'So that (he) might send me a copy of the key to his coffer.' Bond translates 'sui estui' as 'her coffer' (and therefore supplies 'she' and 'her', which, as he notes, 'are not specified in the text') because, he argues, 'his' is 'less likely' given the sexual connotations attached to the 'counterkey', which is used as an 'erotic symbol' in some troubadours' poems (*PW*, 64). Leupin shows how this poem complicates the apparent 'transparency' of the sexual metaphors of the masculine 'key' and feminine 'box'. As he points out, the key metaphor does not solve the question of the very possibility of a sexual relationship with the Other sex: it neither gives the key to the enigma that the Lady is nor clarifies the meaning of desire (*Mélanges*, 303).

15 Michel Stanesco, 'L'expérience poétique du "pur" néant chez Guillaume IX d'Aquitaine', *Médiévales* 6 (1984), 66; my translation.

16 *LT*, 21. As he notes, *vers* means here 'song'.

17 Amelia E. Van Vleck suggests this reading: 'The possibility that the addressee in Poitou (MS E, Anjou MS C) in sending *la contraclau* [the counterkey] would be sending another poem is supported by the fact that many of the *senhals* poems' recipients have been shown to designate other poets. A skilled poet, in fact, would be a likely choice for a retransmitter in the process of relay. Poems sent via a first jongleur to a recipient named *Joglar* (performer) or *Messager* (messenger) or *Drogoman* (interpreter) are almost certainly expected to be sung again, until the song is publicly known' (*Memory and Re-creation in Troubadour Lyric* (Berkeley: University of California Press, 1991), 54.

What Are the Chances? Psychoanalysis, Telepathy, and the Accident

Elizabeth Rottenberg

Telepathy or the Communist Manifesto

To set us on our way, I would like to begin with two lines by George Eliot that describe to a T Freud's attitude towards occultism (so T is for Telepathy; T is for Thought Transference):

In such states of mind the most incredulous person has a private leaning towards miracle.[1]

Who supposes that it is an impossible contradiction to be superstitious and rationalizing at the same time?[2]

The first quotation is from *Middlemarch*, and I quote it not only because it resonates with what, in the 'Occultism' chapter of his three-volume biography, Ernest Jones calls Freud's 'exquisite oscillation between skepticism and credulity',[3] his 'ambivalent attitude' (J3, 390) towards the world of mysticism, his being 'in two minds' (J3, 392) about whether to make public his views on telepathy. I also quote it because it foreshadows, uncannily, almost to the letter, Freud's own statement, in 'Dreams and Occultism', about 'the secret inclination towards the miraculous'[4] of someone who regards himself 'as a sceptic' (*SE* 22, 53). The second quotation comes from *Daniel Deronda*, and it is posed as a rhetorical question, a question asked in order to make a statement rather than to elicit a response.

Now if you read the 'Occultism' chapter in *The Life and Work of Sigmund Freud*, you will see that what was simply a rhetorical question for the great English novelist becomes, for Freud's biographer, a remarkable but also a lamentable fact. For analysts who, like Jones, 'have undergone a biological, and particularly a neurological, training' (J3, 376), the fact that 'highly developed critical powers may coexist in the same person with an unexpected fund of credulity' (J3, 375) is a hard fact to swallow. And Jones makes no bones about it. In anecdote after anecdote, letter after letter, Jones will bellyache about Freud's primitive thinking and pre-scientific attitude:

> In the years before the Great War, I had several talks with Freud on occultism and kindred topics. He was fond, especially after midnight, of regaling me with strange or uncanny experiences with patients (...). When I would protest at some of the taller stories Freud was wont to reply with his favorite quotation: 'There are more things in heaven and earth than are dreamed of in your philosophy.' Some of the incidents sounded like mere coincidences, others like the obscure workings of unconscious motives. When they were concerned with clairvoyant visions of episodes at a distance, or visitations from departed spirits, I ventured to reprove him for his inclination to accept occult beliefs on flimsy evidence. His reply was: 'I don't like it at all myself, but there is some truth in it', both sides of his nature coming to expression in a short sentence. I then asked him where such beliefs could halt: if one could believe in mental processes floating in the air, one could hold on to a belief in angels. He closed the discussion at this point (about three in the morning!) with the remark: 'Quite so, even *der liebe Gott*.' This was said in a jocular tone as if agreeing with my *reductio ad absurdum* and with a quizzical look as if he were pleased at shocking me. But there was something searching also in the glance, and I went away not entirely happy lest there be some more serious undertone as well. (J3, 381)

Jones is not amused. He is not amused by Freud's 'jocular tone' or 'quizzical look'. Making light of occult topics is no joke for Jones. It's no joke because he suspects that behind Freud's levity lies a more serious, and therefore a more dangerous, undertone. Were the father of psychoanalysis truly to believe in ghosts, were he to take seriously the existence of telepathy and thought transference, it would be a terrible setback for psychoanalysis. An association with 'hocus-pocus and palmistry' (J3, 395), as Jones puts it, 'could only add to the odium that already invest[s] the "unscientific" subject of psychoanalysis' (J3, 386). Not only does telepathy call attention to the already shaky marriage between science and psychoanalysis, but it also risks exposing psychoanalysis to further condemnation. Indeed, it is clear from Jones's letters and the tone of his 'Occultism' chapter that the censorious spirit conjured up by Freud at the end of 'Dreams and Occultism' is none other than that of Jones: '"Here's another case," laments the spirit, "of a man who has done honest work as a scientist all through his life and has grown feeble-minded, pious and credulous in his old age"' (*SE* 22, 54).

For Jones, then, psychoanalysis must be defended. The prejudice against telepathy is so strong that any association with it could only have the effect 'of delaying the assimilation of psychoanalysis' (J3, 393) and giving strength to its opponents. Thus, when Freud publishes the short text entitled 'The Occult Significance of Dreams', a text in which, Jones tells us, Freud 'pretty plainly indicated his acceptance of telepathy' (J3, 394) and then, only a few months later, sends out his circular letter of 18 February 1926, in which he not only avows his 'conversion to telepathy' but also declares that he is no longer interested in shielding the body of psychoanalysis from the 'scandal' of its association with occultism, Jones goes ballistic. It is as if Freud has thrown a 'bomb into the psychoanalytic house' (J3, 394). Indeed, this breach of homeland security seems to have provoked in Jones something like an 'anticathexis' on a grand scale. Jones must scramble to master and bind the large amounts of stimulus that have broken in and threaten psychoanalysis at the very core of its rationality. In his letter of 25 February 1926, Jones tells Freud to cut it out, to keep his seditious speech to himself: 'In your private political opinions you might be a Bolshevist, but you would not help the spread of psychoanalysis by announcing it. So when "considerations of external policy" kept you silent before I do not know how the situation should have changed in this respect' (J3, 395). Because the personal is political — because, as Jones insists, '"psychoanalysis is Freud"' (J3, 395) — Freud must keep his commie pinko telepathic leanings to himself.

Now if I mention this exchange of letters it is because Freud's response to Jones exemplifies something rather remarkable about his treatment of telepathy and thought transference more generally. As he later writes in 'Dreams and Occultism': 'We are once again left with a *non liquet*; but I must confess that I have a feeling that here too the scales weigh in favor of thought-transference' (*SE* 22: 54). I declare the area of thought transference unclear, unproven, undecidable *but* at the same time I decide. In his response to Jones, this *ambitendency* is even more pronounced: Freud accepts *and* simultaneously rejects telepathy.[5] On the one hand, he assimilates telepathy to his person, that is, to his bodily person (to the Jewish smoker that he is). On the other hand, he eliminates telepathy from the body or being of psychoanalysis. That is, he eats his cake and he vomits it too:

I am extremely sorry that my utterance about telepathy should have plunged you into fresh difficulties. But it is really hard not to offend English sensibilities (...). When anyone brings up my Fall into Sin, just answer calmly that my conversion to telepathy is my own private affair, like my Jewishness, my passion for smoking (...) and that the theme of telepathy is in essence alien to psychoanalysis. (J3, 395, modified)

That is, Freud responds to Jones by splitting his (Jewish) body from the body of psychoanalysis. It's true, says Freud, that I believe in telepathy, but long live (the science of) psychoanalysis.

Freud splits the ticket: 'yes' to telepathy when it comes to himself, 'no' to telepathy when it comes to psychoanalysis. But isn't this dissociation between the body natural and the body politic a rather abrupt way of gathering things up and marking limits? When we know that Freud took a public position on the topic of telepathy, when we know that he struggled for years with its theorization, can we be satisfied with a distinction or opposition of this kind? And then, of course, there are the testimonies. We know from Anna Freud that telepathy 'fascinated as well as repelled' her father;[6] we know from Max Eitingon that it '"perplexed [Freud] to the point of making him lose his head"' ('Tel', 258). And, finally, we know from Freud himself that the subject of telepathy was a never-ending source of resistance for him: 'Nothing can be done', he tells us in 'Psychoanalysis and Telepathy', 'against such (...) clear resistance' (*SE* 18, 190). All of which would suggest that there is something about Freud's resistance that makes it more cryptic — and more interesting — than Jones's.

Certainly, there is resistance, one might say, 'but resistance to what? To whom? Dictated by whom, to whom, how, according to what routes?' ('Tel', 423 n. 1). We begin with this paradox: if Freud returns again and again to telepathy, if he struggles with its theorization, it is not, as Jones would have it, in order to thwart 'the relentlessness and monotony of the laws of thought (...) and the demands of reality-testing' (*SE* 22, 33). On the contrary, as we see in all of Freud's telepathy texts, it is in order to drive science beyond the state or system of contemporary science. Psychoanalysis, Freud writes as early as 'Psychoanalysis and Telepathy', is driven 'by a sense of shame that science has (...) refused to take cognizance of what are indisputable problems' (*SE* 18, 178). Psychoanalysis does not renounce its 'descent from exact science' (*SE* 18, 178). On the contrary, it is 'ready to believe what is shown (...) to deserve belief' (*SE* 22, 31). Thus, in all of his essays on occultism, Freud appeals to telepathy because it 'seems actually to favor the extension of the scientific' (*SE* 22, 55). What is more, Freud will remind his audience quite pointedly that the history of science abounds with examples in which new hypotheses were prematurely (and erroneously) condemned. The best example, of course, is that of psychoanalysis itself, which was met with nothing but contemptuous rejection when it argued for the existence of an unconscious.

So, in a way, Jones is too *earnest*. And too *literal*. He misses the *spirit* of Freud's engagement with telepathy. By fearing that Freud may have abandoned or betrayed psychoanalysis by turning to telepathy, it is — ironically — he, Jones, who ends up being not scientific enough. For Freud's interest in telepathy reflects an understanding of science and scientific revolution according to which the challenge to orthodoxy may actually advance the cause of science. Freud's intention in his telepathy texts is to extend the scientific through the psychoanalytic.

And there's method to his madness. If Freud wants to extend the scientific, if he wants to argue for the existence of telepathy, it is for a very particular reason: in order to incorporate into psychoanalysis, to bring into the deterministic fold, those psychical events that appear to defy analytic interpretation. As we will see, Freud introduces the question of occultism (whether he is *for* thought transference in 'Dreams and Occultism' or *against* superstition in *The Psychopathology of Everyday Life*) precisely in order to exclude the accident from the internal, psychical domain. When psychoanalysis finally decides to swallow or stomach so-called occult phenomena, when Freud proposes occultism as a solution, it is as a means of expelling something else — the accident. Hence psychoanalysis takes in the strange (and seemingly unscientific) — telepathy — in order to rid itself of what is stranger still: the accident. The accident must be evacuated. For it is only by isolating a domain 'into which external randomness no longer penetrates' that psychoanalysis gives itself a 'chance as a science'.[7] To put it more bluntly: Freud uses telepathy as a purgative.

But how, then, are we to read Freud's resistance? If telepathy does not represent a 'threat against [his] scientific *Weltanschauung*' (*SE* 22, 54), if it has a cleansing effect, why this ongoing resistance? Could it be that the telepathic tonic is unpalatable in some other way? Could it be that T (telepathy, thought transference) is the X that brings psychoanalytic theory to a halt precisely because it marks the spot of some indigestible idea? In which case, of course, we have our work *cut out* for us. We must *follow the resistance*.

Freud's Resistance to Telepathy

I would like therefore to point to the many parapraxes that plague Freud's texts on telepathy, beginning with 'Psychoanalysis and

Telepathy'. In this text, Freud tells us that he had intended to give reports of three cases of telepathy but that when he sat down to write his presentation, the material for the third case was missing. Here is Freud's account of his parapraxis:

I had also intended to bring you [a third] example (...). But I can now give you visible proof of the fact that I discuss the subject of occultism under the pressure of the greatest resistance. When (...) I looked over the notes which I had put together and brought with me for the purpose of this paper, the sheet on which I had noted down this last observation was not there, but in its place I found another sheet of indifferent memoranda on quite another topic, which I had brought with me by mistake. Nothing can be done against such a clear resistance. I must ask you to excuse me for omitting this case, for I cannot make the loss good from memory. (*SE* 18, 190, modified)

One can only imagine that Freud was saving the best for last, and now the last goes missing — for twelve years. The original third case, Strachey tells us, did survive as a separate manuscript to which Freud later appended the following: '*Postscript*. Here is the report, omitted owing to resistance, on a case of thought transference during analytic practice' (*SE* 18, 175). Nowhere in the *Standard Edition*, however, does this original manuscript ever appear. This is because, as Strachey writes in another note, this time to the 1932 essay 'Dreams and Occultism', where the third case does finally appear, the original draft was never published: 'It resembled the version given here [in 'Dreams and Occultism'] so closely that it was doubtful whether it was necessary to print it separately' (*SE* 22, 48). At which point Strachey adds the following detail: 'It should be added, however, that since that volume of the *Standard Edition* was published, in 1955, the manuscript has once again unaccountably disappeared' (*SE* 22, 48). So we might say that what the editorial history makes 'visible' is a *surprising* resistance to this case, which might well be called 'The-Case-of-the-Disappearing-Case'.

Moreover, this vanishing act seems to have been passed on to the text itself. The manuscript of 'Psychoanalysis and Telepathy' is the next thing to disappear:

Toward the end of [1925] Freud asked Eitingon for the manuscript of the (...) essay, perhaps with an idea of publishing it at last. Eitingon assured him he had brought it back personally, but apparently it got mislaid. It was found among Freud's papers after his death. (J3, 396)

Similarly, there seems to have been great difficulty in getting 'Some Additional Notes on Dream-Interpretation as a Whole' (the chapter of which 'The Occult Significance of Dreams' is the *third* part) to see the light of day. As Strachey explains in a complicated editorial note, Freud had intended to include 'Some Additional Notes on Dream-Interpretation as a Whole' (otherwise known as Supplementary Chapter C) to all editions of *The Interpretation of Dreams* starting in 1925. But this 'Supplementary Chapter C' (and, even more so, the third section, section C, of this Supplementary Chapter C) 'seemed dogged by misfortunes' (*SE* 19, 126). Not only was it completely left out of the eighth edition of *Die Traumdeutung* and thus omitted from the revised translation of 1932 and the double volume of Freud's *Gesammelte Werke* in 1942, not only was it 'accidentally overlooked' and not included 'at the correct chronological point in *G.W.*, 14' (*SE* 19, 126), but even when the chapter ('Some Additional Notes on Dream-Interpretation as a Whole') was included in a collective volume of Freud's shorter writings on dreams, it was not reprinted *as a whole*. What was cut out of Supplementary Chapter C was ... yes ... its C-section, 'The Occult Significance of Dreams'. What are the chances, you may ask?

What are the chances that these occurrences are accidents without any further meaning? What are the chances that Freud's resistance to telepathy should raise the question of chance in a way that is so literal ... and literally cut out for us?

The 'Accident' in Psychoanalysis

As we know from *The Psychopathology of Everyday Life* and the *Introductory Lectures*, 'nothing in the mind is arbitrary or undetermined' (*SE* 6, 242). As Freud demonstrates again and again in hundreds of examples of parapraxes, the accident is no accident for the analyst who is able to recognize and interpret an unconscious purpose behind an apparently random event. Unlike the layperson, the analyst understands the random event to be the result of an '*unconscious yet operative*' intention (*SE* 6, 272 n. 1). As Derrida puts it both succinctly and provocatively: 'There is no random chance in the unconscious' (MC, 369). There is no random chance in the unconscious because psychoanalysis symptomatizes contingency; it puts the apparent facts of randomness 'in the service of an ineluctable necessity' (MC, 369).

So how does chance operate in an economy of psychical determinism? If Freud leaves no room for the accident, if, on the contrary, he argues for 'the strict determination of apparently arbitrary psychical acts' (*SE* 6, 254 n. 1), how are we to understand chance occurrences in psychoanalysis? How are we to think chance together with analysis's hermeneutic drive, that is, with its compulsion to make the accident unhappen? In the final chapter of *The Psychopathology of Everyday Life*, Freud tries to do both things at once. On the one hand, he claims that 'determination in the psychical sphere is (...) carried out without a gap' (*SE* 6, 254) assuming one takes into account unconscious as well as conscious motivations. On the other hand, and in the wake of this claim, Freud suddenly finds room for chance. Suddenly, the difference that makes all the difference when it comes to distinguishing science from superstition, a *scientific* belief from a *superstitious* belief, hinges on, is determined by, *chance*. In the (C)-section of the final chapter of *The Psychopathology of Everyday Life*, Freud turns his attention to chance in order to prove that he is not a superstitious person.

Freud believes in chance, but a chance that lies safely outside of his mental life; chance is in essence alien to psychical life. With the superstitious person, it is the other way around: psychical life is full of accidents and external reality is full of unknown, secret (and futural) meaning:

I am therefore different from a superstitious person in the following way:

I do not believe that an event in whose occurrence my mental life plays no part can teach me any hidden thing about the future shape of reality; but I believe that an unintentional manifestation of my own mental activity *does* on the other hand disclose something hidden, though again it is something that belongs only to my mental life. I believe in external (real) chance, it is true, but not in internal accidental events. (*SE* 6, 257)

For Freud accidents are limited to those events that take place outside of psychical life. For the superstitious person, it is the other way around: not only does the superstitious person believe that there are psychical accidents but s/he also has a tendency to attribute to what are merely random external events a meaning that will become manifest in real — that is, future — events. Unlike Freud, the superstitious person interprets and gives meaning to 'external chance happenings' (*SE* 6, 257) by projecting outwards what are really repressed thoughts, fears, and wishes: the superstitious person 'projects outwards a motivation which I look for within' (*SE* 6, 257). By appealing to an opposition between inside and outside, science and projection, truth and fiction, Freud maintains a distinction between the hermeneutic drive of psychoanalysis, on the one hand, and the hermeneutic drive of superstition, on the other. What the analyst believes and what the superstitious person believes are not the same even if 'the compulsion not to let chance count as chance but to interpret it' (*SE* 6, 258) is common to both of them. There is belief and there is belief, one might say. Indeed, one might say of belief exactly what Freud says of knowledge in his *Introductory Lectures*: 'Belief is not always the same as belief: there are different sorts of belief, which are far from equivalent psychologically' (*SE* 16, 281, modified). In the field of a scientific psychoanalysis, there is belief and there is credulity.

And just to prove the difference, in *The Psychopathology of Everyday Life* Freud suddenly, for the first time, produces a chance event, a non-interpretable accident. Having just returned from holiday, Freud is thinking of the many patients he has to visit. One of them is an elderly, ninety-year-old woman. On this particular day, however, Freud is running late so he hails a cab to take him to this patient's house. The cabman knows the old woman's address perfectly well, yet on this particular day makes a mistake and draws up in front of the wrong house. '[I]s it of any significance', Freud asks, 'that I was driven to a house where the old lady was not to be found?' (*SE* 6, 257). Does the error reveal some kind of truth? 'Certainly not to me', says Freud, 'but if I were *superstitious* I should see an omen in the incident, the finger of fate announcing that this year would be the old lady's last (...) *I* of course explain the occurrence as an accident without any further meaning' (*SE* 6, 257).

The accident is an accident, end of story. Though it would have been a different story if Freud had been the source of the error. In that case, the occurrence would not have been an accident but an action with an unconscious aim requiring interpretation. In that case, the interpretation would have been that Freud did not expect to see the old lady for much longer. In that case, 'there would have been *Vergehen* — misconduct and mistaken path' (MC, 366). But that is not the case, and the accident can teach Freud nothing: neither about 'the future shape of reality' (*SE* 6, 257) nor about his own mental activity. The accident is an accident, pure and simple.

'Not so fast', I hear the voice of my analyst saying, 'reality is always the best excuse'. Indeed, how not to be reminded, in this analytic context, of Lacan who opens 'Tuché and Automaton' by recalling that, as analysts, on principle, we never allow ourselves to be taken in by what occurs '*as if by chance*'.[8] As good analysts, that is, we must wonder whether what has occurred *as if by chance* were not precisely the *occurrence of chance* itself. Here it would seem that Freud had simply repressed — from within the very text of *The Psychopathology of Everyday Life* — his chapter on 'Bungled Actions' where we find not one but two 'prequels' to this story. On (at least) two other occasions, as it turns out, this old woman was implicated in a very similar — and all-too-interpretable — bungled action.

The first prequel takes us back to Freud's discussion of bungled actions of a medical nature and to one of his own medical blunders. Freud tells us he had been in the habit of visiting the old woman twice a day for some years and that his routine consisted in putting eye-lotion into her eye and giving her a morphine injection. On this particular day, he puts the morphine into her eye instead of the eye-lotion. He is much alarmed by his mistake, but his fright seems exaggerated given the harmlessness of his action: 'a few drops of a two per cent solution of morphine could not do any harm even in the conjunctival sac' (*SE* 6, 177). Concluding that his fright must have come from another source, he analyses his mistake and discovers that his first association is to the phrase 'sich an der Alten vergreifen' (to do violence to the old woman). As Strachey explains in a footnote: 'The German word "*vergreifen*" means both "to make a blunder" and "to commit an assault"' (*SE* 6, 178 n. 1). This phrase — 'sich an der Alten vergreifen' — Freud tells us, provides him with 'a short cut to the solution' (*SE* 6, 178). It gets straight to the point: no mistaken path, no misstep here; 'it puts [Freud] on the trail of Œdipus and Jocasta' (MC, 368). That is, Freud's association to *vergreifen* leads directly to *begreifen*, to understanding; his *Vergeifen* exemplifies the *Begreifen* or the *Begriff* that will be so central to psychoanalysis, namely the Oedipus complex:

> I was under the influence of a dream which had been told me by a young man the previous evening and the content of which could only point to sexual intercourse with his own mother (...). While absorbed in thoughts of this kind I came to my patient, who is over ninety, and I must have been on the way to grasping the universal human application of the Œdipus myth as correlated with the Fate which is revealed in the oracles; for at that point I did violence to or committed a blunder on 'the old woman'. (*SE* 6, 177–8)

A funny thing happens on the way to the old woman's house: Freud and the future of psychoanalysis come together in a parapraxis. Freud is 'on the way to grasping the universal human application of the Œdipus myth' when he arrives at the old woman's house and wrongly puts morphine into her eye: 'at that point I did violence to or committed a blunder on "the old woman"'. At that point, a harmless parapraxis, a bungled action of no consequence, turns into an Oedipal scene. Freud's bungled action tells us not only about Freud's unconscious psychology. It also tells us about the *'psychology of the unconscious'* (*SE* 6, 259), about the transformation of *'metaphysics* into *metapsychology'* (*SE* 6, 259), about the transition from Oedipus myth to Oedipus complex. So it's not just any old parapraxis.

Which brings me to the second prequel. Again, Freud is on his way to visit the old woman, and again there's a hitch:

There is a house where twice every day for six years (...) I used to wait to be let in outside a door on the second floor. During this long period it has happened to me on two occasions (...) I have gone a floor too high — i.e., I have *'climbed too high [verstiegen]'*. On the first occasion I was enjoying an ambitious day-dream in which I was 'climbing ever higher and higher'. On this occasion I even failed to hear that the door in question had opened as I put my foot on the first step of the third flight. On another occasion, I again went too far while I was deep in thought; when I realized it, I turned back and tried to catch hold of the phantasy in which I had been absorbed. I found that I was irritated by a (phantasied) criticism of my writings in which I was reproached with always 'going too far'. This I had now replaced by the not very respectful expression 'climbing too high [*verstiegen*]'. (*SE* 6, 164–5)

Twice more, then, something happens to Freud on his way to the old woman's house. Twice more, there is a bungled action because Freud is thinking and dreaming about his future/the future of psychoanalysis. This gives us no fewer than three parapraxes, all involving the same patient. Together these parapraxes epitomize what Freud calls 'combined parapraxes'. 'Accumulated and combined parapraxes', Freud writes, are the essence of the parapraxes. They are 'the finest flower of their kind' (*SE* 15, 56) because they contradict 'in a far more energetic way' (*SE* 6, 238) the notion that a parapraxis is a matter of chance and needs no interpretation. With no other patient is Freud as *parapraxis-prone* as he is with this old woman. And yet... it is precisely with this patient, on his way to her house, that Freud claims to find *an accident without any further meaning*. What are the chances? Is this not an extravagant (*verstiegen*) claim?

To ask this in a more analytic vein: what does Freud mean by singling out a particular 'accident' and insisting that it is in itself full confirmation of the difference between psychoanalytic belief and superstitious belief, science and fiction? How should we *read* this 'accident'? Is one not led to suspect that Freud's unconscious intention here is to throw a 'bomb into the psychoanalytic house' (J3, 394)? What if the *reality* of this 'accident' lay precisely in its resistance to a certain (scientific) psychoanalysis? For if the accident fails to be an accident, if it succeeds in being a symptom, then it precisely fails to secure the boundaries between psychoanalysis and superstition. In this way, Freud's 'accident without any further meaning' leads to a questioning that is both psychoanalytic and eccentric, ex-centering in relation to psychoanalysis.

Freud's Conversion to Telepathy

Psy-fi
And this brings us back to telepathy and thought transference, which is where we started out from. That is, it brings us back to the theoretical fiction according to which the unconscious mental processes in one person are transferred to another person 'through empty space without employing the familiar methods of communication by means of words and signs' (*SE* 22, 39). One might say that Freud's debt to *fiction* — to a kind of *psy-fi* — brings with it a strange *theoretical* foresight. For when Freud *calls up* the analogy between the tele- of tele-pathy and the tele- of the tele-phone, when he *makes the connection* between an 'original, archaic method of communication' and other forms of tele-communication, he is, very literally, *ringing in* the future, that is to say, a certain thinking of originary technicity:

> The telepathic process is supposed to consist in a mental act in one person instigating the same mental act in another person (...). The analogy with other transformations, such as occur in speaking and hearing by the telephone, would then be unmistakable (...). It would seem to me that psychoanalysis, by inserting the unconscious between what is physical and what was previously called 'psychical', has paved the way for the assumption of such processes as telepathy (...). One is [also] led to a suspicion that this is the original, archaic method of communication between individuals and that in the course of phylogenetic evolution it has been replaced by the better method of giving information with the help of signals which are picked up by the sense organs. (*SE* 22, 55)

Thus, the telepathic process begins to resemble nothing so much as a wire-less, router-less, network-less communication. As 'the original, archaic method of communication between individuals', telepathy is the *Ur-Wi-Fi*, the *prototype* of all (future) tele-communication devices including but not limited to the telephone. Freud's first analogy is in fact to the tele-graph; telepathy, he says, would be 'a kind of psychical counterpart to wireless telegraphy' (*SE* 22, 36).

But how not to recall another instance of tele-communication, one that grounds the very practice of psychoanalysis? For Freud's most elaborate description of psychoanalytic technique — in the *third* of his six papers that make up 'The Papers on Technique' — begins with an extended simile involving once again the telephone. Right from the start, at the heart of the analytic situation, there is, and always was, a 'technical interposition':[9]

> To put it in a formula: he [the analyst] must turn his own unconscious like a receptive organ towards the transmitting unconscious of the patient. He must adjust himself to the patient as a telephone receiver is adjusted to the transmitting microphone. Just as the receiver converts back into soundwaves the electric oscillations in the telephone line which were set up by sounds waves, so the [analyst's] unconscious is able, from the derivatives of the unconscious which are communicated to him, to reconstruct the unconscious, which has determined the patient's free associations. (*SE* 12, 115–16)

'Can you hear me?' says the patient's transmitting unconscious to the analyst's converting receiver. Though we may find Freud's telephonic simile rather amusing, it is precisely the quality of the analyst's 'reception' that allows her/him to bring forth the patient's repressed raw material. Still, perhaps this game of tele-phone, prefiguring as it does the mechanism of transmission of tele-pathy, tells us something about the tele-system (of which tele-pathy would be both the first and final chapter in Freud's work). Does it not tell us that tele-pathy can never guarantee the destination of a communication? that a transmitting unconscious, much like an outgoing call, can always be tapped, bugged, interfered with, recorded? Does it not suggest that, through the transference, the analyst — like an *écouteur* — taps into a difference within the patient's own unconscious? Such that one may wonder whether it is not the unconscious that telephones itself to itself? Would this not be the most accurate description of what Freud is calling 'telepathy' or 'thought-transference': is thought transference not a call (on) which the other happens to pick up?

A rendezvous with literature
This is where the missing third case, the 'Case-of-the-Disappearing-Case', comes in. Not only does it pick up where Freud left off in 1921, but it also exemplifies a case in which the other (here a

patient) miraculously picks up on the thoughts of his analyst. Among all the cases of telepathy or thought transference, Freud tells us, this one leaves the 'strongest impression' (*SE* 22, 47) on him; it is also the only case in which the question of thought transference merges with the transference/counter-transference relation between analyst and analysand. In every other example, the telepathic communication takes place outside of analysis. This is the only case — or call — in which we have (at least) two transferences on the line.

The case is that of Herr P., an 'intelligent and agreeable' man (*SE* 22, 48), whom Freud has continued to see, for free, even though the case offers no chance of therapeutic success. One day Herr P. comes to his session just minutes after the London analyst Dr Forsyth has left Freud's office and brings up a startling series of jealous thoughts and associations beginning with the revelation that the young woman he is dating and with whom he is afraid to have sex calls him 'Herr von Vorsicht [Mr. Foresight]' (*SE* 22, 48).

What is so astonishing about P.'s associations is that P. seems to know things he couldn't know: 'Could P. have known that Dr. Forsyth had just paid me his first visit? Could he have known the name of the person [Dr Freund] I had visited in his house? Did he know that Dr. Jones had written a monograph on the nightmare? Or was it only *my* knowledge about these things that was revealed in his associations?' (*SE* 22, 52). What did P. know and when did he know it?

Though the evidence for the occult nature of P.'s associations to Dr Freund and Dr Jones remains inconclusive, Freud notes that the miraculous emergence of the name 'Herr von Vorsicht' would be enough to support 'the apparent fact of thought-transference' (*SE* 22, 53). What allows the scales to 'weigh in favor of thought-transference' (*SE* 22, 54) is an event that both *says Vorsicht* (foresight) and *brings* foresight.

Concretely, what Herr von Vorsicht foresees is the end of his own analysis: 'He had been warned that his analysis (...) would come to an end as soon as foreign pupils and patients returned to Vienna; and that was in fact what happened shortly afterwards' (*SE* 22, 51). So if P. brings the name *Vorsicht* into his analysis unheralded right after it has become significant to Freud as a result of Dr Forsyth's arrival, it is because P.'s unconscious sees the writing on the wall. Watch out! — *Vorsicht!* — says his unconscious, the end is near. But because he also wishes to continue his analysis, this name out of nowhere is also an unconscious attempt to keep Freud on the line: '"I'm a Forsyth too:

that's what the girl calls me (...). Do come back to me; after all I'm a Forsyth too"' (*SE* 22, 51). Forsyth, here ... hello, hello.

But there is also another (English) name that Freud's converting receiver is able to reconstruct from the name 'Vorsicht': not 'Forsyth' but 'Forsyte'. Indeed, he reminds us that, for a German speaker, the two names 'can scarcely be distinguished' (*SE* 22, 49). What is more, the name 'Forsyte' has become a kind of cipher between analyst and patient:

[P.] possessed a rich English library and used to bring me books from it. I owe to him an acquaintance with such authors as Bennett and Galsworthy (...). One day he lent me a novel of Galsworthy's with the title *The Man of Property*, whose scene is laid in the bosom of a family (...) bearing the name of 'Forsyte' (...). Only a few days before the occurrence I am speaking of, he had brought me a fresh volume from this series. The name 'Forsyte', and everything typical that the author had sought to embody in it, had played a part, too, in my conversations with P. and it had become part of the secret language which so easily grows up between people who see a lot of each other. (*SE* 22, 49)

'Forsyte' thus means the same to P. as it does to Freud. And it is to this name 'Forsyte' that Freud first calls our attention when he considers P.'s association. What Freud deems so remarkable is not only the name itself ('Herr von Vorsicht') but also the manner in which this name has managed to weave itself into P.'s own experiences. P. does not say, for example, "'The name 'Forsyte', out of the novels you are familiar with, has just occurred to me."' No — and here Freud shifts names — 'what he *did* say now was: "I'm a Forsyth too: that's what the girl calls me"' (*SE* 22, 51).

In other words, P.'s message is clear. Unlike the linguistic accident that creates static on the line in the case of P.'s association to Dr Freund — 'the evidential value of this case is totally destroyed by a chance circumstance. The man whom I had visited (...) was not only called "Freund"; he was a true friend [*Freund*] to us all' (*SE* 22, 52) — in the case of P.'s association to Dr Forsyth, there is no such indetermination:

[H]ow is it to be explained that [Herr P.] became receptive to [Dr Forsyth's] presence on the very day of his arrival and immediately after his first visit? One might say it was chance — that is, leave it unexplained. But it was precisely in order to exclude chance that I discussed P.'s (...) associations [to Dr Freund and Dr Jones], in order to show you that he was really occupied with jealous thoughts about people who visited me. (*SE* 22, 53)

Three associations all occupied with jealous thoughts about foreign doctors visiting one's analyst: this can be no accident, *as we all know*. For Freud the meaning is clear: 'come back to me [Doctor] (...) I'm a Forsyth too' (*SE* 22, 51). But, for this to be the case, something else must also be true: 'P. had in fact selected from his personal concerns the very name with which I was occupied at the same time as a result of an occurrence of which he was unaware' (*SE* 22, 49). No chance occurrence has come, in this case, to destroy the possibility of a telepathic communication. Freud has found it necessary to deny chance in order to make room for telepathy. And this, one may conclude, was the whole point of telepathy in the first place.

Yet, *on the way there*, on the way to his confession of faith, there is that other name, that other name which is really the same, since, as Freud says, one can speak interchangeably of the 'name "Forsyte" or "Forsyth"' (*SE* 22, 50). '"Forsyte" or "Forsyth"', says Freud, same difference. Yet the name 'Forsyte' and 'everything typical that [Galsworthy] had sought to embody in it' has also become part of the 'secret language' between Freud and P. So what if P. were saying 'I'm a Forsyte too'? After all, as we are reminded by this endlessly proliferating chain — *Vorsicht*-Forsyte-Forsyth-foresight-*Voraussicht* — 'psychical acts and structures are invariably overdetermined' (*SE* 13, 100) ... that is, *every call* is a conference call (and we didn't need the NSA to tell us this).

As it happens, *The Forsyte Saga* gives us a very precise definition of a 'Forsyte' in the volume to which Freud refers. As one Forsyte explains it: 'a "Forsyte" is a man who is decidedly more than less a slave of property. He knows a good thing, he knows a safe thing, and his grip on property — it doesn't matter whether it be wives, houses, money, or reputation — is his hall-mark'.[10] He is, as the title of the first volume makes clear, 'a man of property', his most distinctive feature his 'possessive instinct' (*FS*, 349). To be a 'Forsyte', as the 850-page saga makes abundantly clear, is to act in accordance with the 'possessive principle' (*FS*, 807), a principle that consists in 'avoiding the unexpected' (*FS*, 237).

Yet *The Forsyte Saga* is nothing if not the disturbing encounter of this 'possessive instinct' with 'something strange and foreign' (*FS*, 80), the unfathomable 'enigma' (*FS*, 111) that exceeds calculation, 'a sort of visitation' that impinges on, and 'brings destruction' to (*FS*, 549), a possessive world. In the course of the saga, the 'possessive principle' is unsettled by what the 'man of property' calls 'infernal mischance' (*FS*, 823). 'Chance', as the narrator declares ironically at the end of the trilogy, 'visits the lives of even the best invested Forsytes' (*FS*, 723). Though this visitation may take the rather predictable form of Beauty and Passion in Galsworthy's novels, by the end of the saga one thing is clear: the name 'Forsyte' will never again be separated from the disruptive possibilities of chance.

Perhaps one might say that what returns with Freud's remarkable third case is not only the resistance to chance but also a very Forsytean impasse. For something rather remarkable happens in the wake of telepathy's *Vorsicht*-Forsyte-Forsyth saga. It is a little as if the psychoanalytic saga of 'telepathy' had encountered its own dispossessive principle at the very end of 'Dreams and Occultism'. On the very last page of this text, psychoanalysis runs into something it can neither assimilate nor eliminate in the form of a gold coin.

A mother speaks during her analytic session of a gold coin from her childhood and then — 'immediately afterwards' (*SE* 22, 56) — her ten-year-old son (also in analysis) brings her a gold coin for her to put aside for him. At which point Freud confesses that psychoanalysis can make neither heads nor tails of the occurrence:

> The mother reported the occurrence to the child's analyst and asked her to find out from the child the reason for his action. *But the child's analysis threw no light on the matter;* the action had forced its way that day into the child's life like a foreign body [*wie ein Fremdkörper*]. A few weeks later the mother was sitting at her writing desk to write down, as she had been told to do, an account of the experience, when in came the boy and asked for the gold coin back, as he had wanted to take it with him to show in his analytic session. *Once again the child's analysis could discover no explanation of his wish*. (*SE* 22, 56, my emphasis)

'Failure, then', writes Derrida, 'in the face of the foreign body' ('Tel', 257). But we must also read this failure as a kind of chance, for psychoanalysis's failure to discover an explanation for what forces itself into the psychical life of the child is also a chance (to) return to the *Fremdkörper*, to a figure that, from the earliest days of psychoanalysis, testified to what was both inside and outside the psyche — as a result of 'accidental factors' (*SE* 2, 4).

In the final analysis, the name 'Forsyte' and the child's gold coin return us to what was 'alien to psychoanalysis'. Yet they do so with a twist. Not only do they suggest that 'telepathy' marks the necessity of suspending our naive confidence in distinctions or oppositions such as inside/outside, science/superstition, self/other. They also recall to us the importance of the 'foreign body' for psychoanalysis. And they do so through telepathy, through Freud's discussion of telepathy. What connects the 'foreign body' of *Studies on Hysteria* to the 'foreign body' of 'Dreams and Occultism' is *telepathy*. Now what is miraculous, if I can put it this way, is that this 'telepathic' *connection* occurs in or as a *break* in analytic understanding: 'analysis threw no light on the matter', 'again (...) analysis could discover no explanation'. As a result, the 'foreign body' has a curious *ring* to it. For it has, in fact, *cut in* on the line between patient and analyst; it cuts in and in so doing establishes a *chance connection*, a connection made possible by disconnection, by a failure or breakdown in the communication system. That is, the 'foreign body' disturbs the very systematicity of the telecommunication system by *dialing up*, as it were, both the reserves of chance and the powers of overdetermination. In other words, Freud's 'foreign body' strikes gold: it allows for determinism but only by reintroducing the chance that telepathy set out exclude.

But how are we to read the end of 'Dreams and Occultism', and in particular its final line: 'And this brings us back to psychoanalysis, which was what we started out from' (*SE* 22, 56)? Was telepathy a departure from psychoanalysis? Was it a mistaken path? Or has the 'foreign body' returned us to the kind of 'chance observation' (*SE* 2, 3) with which psychoanalysis began? And what if this *Vergehen* were, in the end, a close encounter not with scientific insight but with literary foresight, with what George Eliot calls 'air-blown chances, incalculable as the descent of thistle-down'?[11]

NOTES

1. George Eliot, *Middlemarch*, edited by Bert Hornback (New York: Norton, 1977), 417.
2. George Eliot, *Daniel Deronda*, edited by Terence Cave (New York: Penguin, 1995), 19.
3. Ernest Jones, *The Life and Work of Sigmund Freud*, 3 vols (New York: Basic Books, 1957), 3, 375. Hereafter J3.
4. Sigmund Freud, *New Introductory Lectures on Psychoanalysis*, *The Standard Edition of the Complete Psychological Works of Sigmund Freud* (hereafter *SE*), 24 vols, translated and edited by James Strachey, in collaboration with Anna Freud, assisted by Alix Strachey and Alan Tyson (London: The Hogarth Press and the Institute of Psychoanalysis, 1953–74), 22, 53, modified.
5. See Jacques Derrida, 'Telepathy', translated by Nicholas Royle, *Psyche 1: Inventions of the Other*, 2 vols, edited by Peggy Kamuf and Elizabeth Rottenberg (Stanford: Stanford University Press, 2007), 261. Hereafter 'Tel'.
6. Peter Gay, *Freud: A Life of Our Time* (London: Papermac, 1989), 443.

7 Jacques Derrida, 'My Chances / *Mes chances*', translated by Irene Harvey and Avital Ronell, in *Psyche 1*, 375. Hereafter MC.
8 Jacques Lacan, *The Seminar of Jacques Lacan Book XI: The Four Fundamental Concepts of Psychoanalysis*, edited by Jacques-Alain Miller, translated by Alan Sheridan (New York: Norton, 1998), 54.
9 Jacques Derrida, *Resistances of Psychoanalysis*, translated by Peggy Kamuf, Pascale-Anne Brault and Michael Naas (Stanford: Stanford University Press, 1996), 58.
10 John Galsworthy, *The Forsyte Saga* (Oxford: Oxford University Press, 1995), 194. Hereafter *FS*.
11 George Eliot, *Romola* (New York: Penguin, 1996), 407.

SF*

Forbes Morlock

> *For Shoshana (as we never dared address her),*
> *who taught a dozen of us in a 'Freud and Lacan' seminar*
> *what transference is — and what the classroom can be.*

Sigmund Freud, Sándor Ferenczi, Shoshana Felman.
SF. Es F.
What follows will not be science fiction. Nor will it be a psychoanalytic novel. It wants still to take stories seriously. And to insist that the story of psychoanalysis — the stories of psychoanalysis — be told psychoanalytically.

Imagining Freud and his intimates — among them Ferenczi — gathered around a fire in a mountain hotel, he reading aloud a treasured manuscript about the supernatural, they following its unfolding with rapt attention, it is easy to see this story haunted by Henry James's *The Turn of the Screw*. It does follow from Felman's 'Turning the Screw of Interpretation', but rather differently.

With an eye to James's governess' drive to prove her mastery, Shoshana Felman's extraordinary essay locates interpretations of James's story in terms of their authors' own desire for mastery — over it and each other.[1] Famously, she reads the readings of Henry James's text as texts towards the theoretical undoing of just such mastery, and such a drive for mastery, in the name of the unconscious. Reading or analysis may enact the desire for mastery, but the reader or analyst after Freud is never master of him- or herself. However he or she turns the text, he or she is turned by it.

---

* With thanks to Bryony Davies of the Freud Museum, Michael Molnar, Pascal Griener, Andrew Bolger, John Walshe, Clare Connors, Sarah Wood, Deborah Luepnitz, Gabrielle Brown and Elissa Marder, many of whose insightful thoughts are transferred here.

Felman's own turn extends to her organization of the 1977 double issue of *Yale French Studies*. As its editor, she opens *Literature and Psychoanalysis* with the words of the master Lacan on the master Shakespeare — and follows them with those of another Parisian analyst on *Hamlet*. Daniel Sibony opens with a question: 'To be or to produce a writing-effect: that was the question. But what is a writing-effect?'[2] She politely lets him answer, before in her own essay, placed next, displacing the question.

Her first words are the short heading 'An Uncanny Reading Effect' (TSI 94). In what she casts as the scandal 'not simply *in* the text', but 'in *our relation to the text*, in the text's *effect on us*, its readers', Felman formulates the idea of the reading effect (97). '[W]hile the governess as a reader *strives to get hold of the story*, the reading-effect is such that it is rather the story itself which *takes hold of its readers*' (184). We who read texts are also read by them... in ways we feel and recognize but cannot entirely control. In the forty years following *Literature and Psychoanalysis* literary studies has learned to work in what psychoanalysis might call the counter-transference.

Starting from the premise that the reading effect is a translation,[3] a literary rewriting, of the psychoanalytic notion of the counter-transference, what follows is an account of that counter-transference. And of what reading may be after SF — and psychoanalysis. It is a narrative of translation, transference, and the uncanny doubling of thought-transference and counter-transference. It is a tale about Ferenczi and Freud — and the latter's posthumously published paper 'Psychoanalysis and Telepathy'.[4] It is the story of a lost manuscript, a secret essay and a road trip. It is also, after 'The "Uncanny"', a ghost story.[5]

The story itself begins a little further back.

The Telephone

We ought not to think of a cerebral path of conduction as resembling a telephone wire which is only excited electrically at the moment at which it has to function (that is, in the present context, when it has to transmit [*übertragen*] a signal). We ought to liken it to a telephone line through which there is a constant flow of galvanic current and which can no longer be excited if that current ceases.[6]

In 1899 Freud published *The Interpretation of Dreams* and was given a new telephone number. 'It is easy to find a factor common to these two events.'[7] At this point it was not the technology of the telephone that transfixed Freud — as a metaphor for transmission, transference or indeed for metaphor itself. It was his phone number: 14362. In the year of Wilhelm Fliess's attack on Freud, his secret [*geheimer*] influence was still at work (*F/Jun* 219).

Ten years later Freud would explain to Carl Jung: 'In 1899 when I wrote *The Interpretation of Dreams* I was 43 years old. Thus it was plausible to suppose that the other figures signified the end of my life, hence 61 or 62. Suddenly method entered into my madness. The superstitious notion that I would die between the ages of 61 and 62 proves to coincide with the conviction that with *The Interpretation of Dreams* I had completed my life's work, that there was nothing more for me to do and that I might as well just lie down and die' (*F/Jun* 219). The superstition that will give rise publicly to an autobiographical passage in the 'The "Uncanny"' in 1919 is already in force privately in 1909.

1909: A Coincidence

To put it in a formula: [the doctor] must turn his own unconscious like a receptive organ towards the transmitting [*gebenden*] unconscious of the patient. He must adjust himself to the patient as a telephone receiver is adjusted to the transmitting microphone [*wie der Receiver des Telephons zum Teller eingestellt ist*]. Just as the receiver converts back into sound-waves the electric oscillations in the telephone line which were set up by sound waves, so the doctor's unconscious is able, from the derivatives of the unconscious which are communicated to him, to reconstruct that unconscious, which has determined the patient's free associations [*Einfälle*]. (*SE* 12, 115–16)[8]

No longer in splendid isolation in 1909, Freud was about with Jung and Ferenczi to embark on a journey to America. His first ocean voyage. Psychoanalysis's first road trip. 'They don't realize we're bringing them the plague', Felman remembers Lacan remembering Jung remembering Freud's words as the Statue of Liberty came into view (TSI, 189).[9] Freud, Jung and Ferenczi return from America as more than three doctors. They come back as one body. For the first time, it may be possible to affirm: there is psychoanalysis. Something more than a clinical technique, something more than the ideas or practice of one individual.

Within a year the Vienna Psychoanalytic Society and the International Psycho-Analytical Association (the IPA) are formally constituted and legally established. Psychoanalysis comes to life as a corporate body — with two literary organs and a border, an inside and an outside. Freud is sensitive to threats to it from both directions. He addresses the external threats under the title of a public essay, '"Wild" Psycho-Analysis'. The internal threats — those that individual analysts' (most strikingly Ferenczi's and Jung's) interests and behaviour pose to the reputation of psychoanalysis — he speaks to more privately. *Gedankenübertragung. Gegenübertragung.* In an uncanny correspondence — and one strangely unremarked except perhaps by Helene Deutsch[10] — Freud names both within four months of each other, either side of the voyage to America. Thought-transference. Counter-transference. They take their names and express their dangers — and opportunities — in odd parallel.

Thought-Transference — Sándor Ferenczi

Ferenczi's first letter to Freud on their return from America reads as one long 'postscript to my story [*Erzählung*]'.[11] Everything we read in their correspondence today follows from an original narrative of telepathy spoken and lost. Evidently the story involved a visit to a Frau Seidler and what Ferenczi variously calls '"mind reading"', 'reading *my* thoughts', '"psychic induction"', 'real clairvoyance, telepathy, etc.' (F/Fer 1, 75, 77). He proposes seeing other 'soothsayers'. His visit engaged him and the tale of it shared in the intimacy of travel engages Freud: 'the transference of *your* thoughts in incomprehensible ways is the strange thing and possibly something new' (1, 79). Ferenczi writes in German of *Gedankenlesen, das Lesen meiner Gedanken, psychische Induktion, wirkliche Clairvoyance, Telepathie* and *Wahrsagerinnen* — for all those possibilities Freud substitutes *die Übertragung* Ihrer *Gedanken*. In a casual reference to thought-transference [*Gedankenübertragung*] Freud sets the terms of their shared interest in telepathy for the next quarter of a century.[12] Ferenczi will often abbreviate 'thought-transference' as 'transference'; Freud never will.

All this comes as Ferenczi is reviewing proofs of a paper on hypnosis — the investigation of extraordinary and not-fully-understood powers of the mind occupies both men as scientists. At stake in both hypnosis and thought-transference is what lies inside and what outside the mind, where the intrapsychic ends and the interpsychic begins. Ferenczi sets one limit to their common research in his first letter: 'In conclusion, I want to assure you (…) that I am not in danger of lapsing into occultism' (*F/Fer* 1, 77). Freud in his reply draws another: 'Keep quiet about it for the time being' (1, 79). The questions of whether thought-transference exists, what it is, when to speak publicly of their research into it, and what happens to psychoanalysis if they do, will divide and bind them until Ferenczi's death.

At the moment, all this — the initial story, the correspondence and their research project — is a secret even from their shipmate Jung. A year after their initial exchange, Freud writes on 15 November 1910: 'Quickly, a piece of news for you to fix [*fixieren*] (in your possession), which brings strong evidence for thought-transference. That will certainly be *your* great discovery. So listen' (*F/Fer* 1, 232). It is news from the couch — about predictions from a court astrologer in Munich of someone's death by mid-November, which have come true that very day... in the acknowledgement of a patient's *expectations* of his brother-in-law's death, that is, of the patient's murderous wishes towards him. Six weeks later Freud provides another clinical example: 'As a New Year's present, the following prophecy for your collection, perhaps the nicest piece that you have to date' (1, 249).

Between the two letters, Freud sends Ferenczi the astrologer Frau Arnold's address, and himself goes to Munich to meet Jung. Freud travels to the very city where the soothsayer whose prophecies he has found compelling practises — and finds he has forgotten to bring her address. Resistance is manifest. At last initiated into Ferenczi and Freud's joint research, 'your findings, my confirmation through that prophecy, and my proposal of a latency period until 1913[, Jung] laughed and admitted he had been convinced for a long time' (*F/Fer* 1, 246). As if he could see it coming — indeed, as Freud can see thought-transference taking its place in psychoanalytic theory... in the future. Prophecy is the image of mastery — and mastery a defence.

Counter-Transference — Carl Jung

'He sees all the dangers just as we do, but he still wants to risk it with ΨA' (*F/Fer* 1, 246). Thought-transference represents one internal threat to the body of psychoanalysis. Just before their voyage to America, in June 1909, Freud writes to Jung of another. Discussing the latter's sexual relations with his patient Sabina Spielrein, Freud recognizes such experiences — even if he has 'never been taken in quite so badly' himself (*F/Jun* 230) — and coins a name for them: the counter-transference. No lasting harm is done. One develops a thick skin, *man wird der 'Gegenübertragung' Herr* (F/Jun 231). In practice, analysts and doctors have always needed to develop a thick skin; now the analytic situation acquires a skin of its own in theory. Affects that arise inside it — even the analyst's — are not the same as those outside.

The counter-transference must be resisted, defended against. Jung has risked it with Spielrein, but psychoanalysis cannot. Henceforth analysts must recognize [*erkennen*], monitor [*überwachen*], surmount [*bewältigen*], overcome [*überwinden*], keep down [*niederhalten*], suppress [*unterdrücken*] and generally master [*beherrschen*] the counter-transference in themselves.[13] An endless, even impossible task. When in their private correspondence Ferenczi seeks to celebrate Freud — 'After all, you are ψα in person!' — the latter declines the honour: 'I am also not that ψα superman whom we have constructed, and I also haven't overcome the counter-transference. I couldn't do it, just as I can't do it with my three sons' (F/Fer 1, 220, 221). To protect his psychoanalytic sons — and psychoanalysis — Freud suggests that discussions of counter-transference continue in private. Referring to the very same patient of whose prophecy he had made a New Year's present to Ferenczi at the beginning of 1911, Freud writes to Jung at the end of the year. People say things, things to people they like, things that get back to the master.

> Frau C— had told me [*hat mir (. . .) erzählt*] all sorts of things about you and Pfister, if you can call the hints she drops 'telling' [*Erzählen*]: I gather that neither of you has yet acquired the necessary objectivity in your practice, that you still get involved, giving a good deal of yourselves and expecting the patient to give something in return. Permit me, speaking as the venerable old master [*würdiger alter Meister* — Freud is quoting Jung's words back to him], to say that this technique is invariably ill-advised and that it is best to remain reserved and purely receptive. We must never let our poor neurotics drive us crazy. *I believe an article on 'counter-transference' is sorely needed; of course we could not publish it, we should have to circulate copies among ourselves.* (F/Jun 475–6; italics added)

Freud's promised article on counter-transference never appears — either as a publication or in private. He holds to his reluctance to write about counter-transference in any format. Indeed, he uses the word only four times in print. The first two of those occurrences are in 'The Future Prospects of Psychoanalytic Therapy'. Freud first speaks openly of 'counter-transference' in a meeting of the Vienna Psychoanalytic Society in March 1910, before using the word again in the address he gives in Nuremberg to open the 2nd International Psycho-Analytical

Congress — that is, the forum in which Ferenczi will publicly call for the formation of the IPA. The threat of counter-transference and the body of psychoanalysis are articulated together.

If counter-transference today no longer threatens — and is for many analysts and psychotherapists the very medium in which they work — Ferenczi's understanding of its '"being induced [*Induziertwerden*]" by the patients' has proved more fruitful than any Freudian imperative or indeed fantasy of mastery (*F/Fer* 1, 253). Although she cannot entirely leave the language of 'danger' behind, Paula Heimann much later at the 16th International Psycho-Analytical Congress will stress, 'the analyst's counter-transference is not only part and parcel of the analytic relationship, but it is the patient's *creation*, it is part of the patient's personality'.[14] 'The analyst's counter-transference is an instrument of research into the patient's unconscious' (81). This is perhaps not Freud's line on the counter-transference, but it could be him on the phone: on about the telephone, his mastery slips.

A Ghost?

The telepathic [*telepathische*] process is supposed to consist in a mental act in one person instigating the same mental act in another person. What lies between these two mental acts may easily be a physical process into which the mental one is transformed at one end and which is transformed back once more into the same mental one at the other end. The analogy with other transformations, such as occur in speaking and hearing by telephone, would then be unmistakeable. And only think if one could get hold of this physical equivalent of the psychical act! It would seem to me that psychoanalysis, by inserting the unconscious between what is physical and what was previously called 'psychical', has paved the way for the assumption of such processes as telepathy [*Telepathie*]. If only one accustoms oneself to the idea of telepathy, one can accomplish a great deal with it — for the time being, it is true, only in imagination [*in der Phantasie*]. (*SE* 22, 55)

There is psychoanalysis. And with its institutionalization of the transference come tacitly, even secretly, thought-transference and the counter-transference. If Freud and his colleagues do not speak of the counter-transference after 1915, thought-transference returns after the First World War quietly, insistently. By which time Freud may be a ghost.

On 12 May 1919 he writes to Ferenczi: 'With this news on the 6th of the month, an inhibition in my up to then increased productivity set in. I had not only completed the draft of "Beyond the Pleasure

Principle", which is being copied out for you, but I also took up the little thing about the "uncanny" again, and, with a simple-minded idea [*Einfall*], I attempted a ψα foundation for group psychology' (*F/Fer* 2, 354). In his biography of Freud, Ernest Jones, the most resistant of psychoanalysis's inner circle to the occult, misdates the letter to 6 May, Freud's birthday.[15] Even Jones understands the date's significance. On 6 May 1919 Freud turned 63. As he explored the significance of the numbers 61 and 62 with Jung privately in 1909, Freud now presents them publicly in 1919 in 'The "Uncanny"' as:

> this factor of involuntary repetition which surrounds what would otherwise be innocent enough with an uncanny atmosphere, and forces upon us the idea of something fateful and inescapable when otherwise we should have spoken only of 'chance [*Zufall*]'. For instance, we naturally attach no importance to the event when we hand in an overcoat and get a cloakroom ticket with a number, let us say [just for example!], 62; or when we find that our cabin on a ship bears that number. But the impression is altered if two such events, each in itself indifferent, happen close together (. . .). We do feel this to be uncanny. And unless a man is utterly hardened against superstition, he will be tempted to ascribe a secret [*geheime*] meaning to this obstinate recurrence of a number; he will take it, perhaps, as an indication of the span of life allotted to him. (*SE* 17, 237–8)

On his 62nd, Freud wrote to Ferenczi: 'The nice superstition with the 62 now finally has to be given up. There is indeed no relying on the supernatural!' (*F/Fer* 2, 281). That was the end of his 62nd year, but he had just turned 62. One year on, he is 62 no more, and — against every superstition shared with his intimates over a decade — definitely alive. He signs his next letter to Max Eitingon like a child: 'Freud aet. [age] 63'.[16]

Having outlived his own death, taking up a little thing he started earlier — when he was still alive — the first text he publishes — writing as a ghost — is 'The "Uncanny"'. Its subject is its own event. Working from Hoffmann's celebrated 'The Sandman' through a parade of literary ghosts and spirits, Freud's essay ends with his only reference to a text by Oscar Wilde, 'The Canterville Ghost', the story of what Freud calls 'a "real" ghost', a man who has survived his own death and wants only (once more) to die (*SE* 17, 252). Freud's next significant text, already drafted before his 'death', is published in 1920 with the 'posthumous' addition of the death drive.[17] The last idea he projected in life, *Group Psychology and the Analysis of the Ego*, is in press in April 1921. And then?

Freud is still not dead.

The Secret Committee

The Canterville ghost speaks English. The end of the war heralds not just the arrival of British and American analysands, but also the prospect of public IPA congresses and private Secret Committee meetings. We are finally at the episode this story thought it was about.

Once, in the face of disappointment with Freud's potential heirs ('Ferenczi is running a big risk with the Gedankenübertragung — true or false'), Jones proposed 'that a small group of men could be thoroughly analysed by you, so that they could represent the pure theory unadultered [sic] by personal complexes, and thus build an unofficial inner circle in the Verein and serve as centres where others (beginners) could come and learn the work.'[18] An inner circle — a psychoanalytic body within the body of psychoanalysis — entirely private, a presence without status. Freud responded with delight: 'What took hold of my imagination at once is your idea of a secret council composed of the best and most trustworthy among our men to take care of the further development of ΨA and defend the cause against personalities and accidents when I am no more' (F/Jon 147). The Secret Committee was constituted — without a constitution. A defensive ring around Freud, he linked himself to each member of it with the gift of a signet ring.

Freud and his closest colleagues organized for years against his death — to ensure that psychoanalysis would survive that inevitability — and in 1919 he does not die. A member of the Secret Committee, his friend Anton von Freund, dies in early 1920, as if in Freud's stead — it is the latest 'news' of his terminal illness that Freud refers to in his 12 May 1919 letter to Ferenczi. Freund dies, but Freud and the Secret Committee survive. He has arranged for Freund's ring to be passed to his replacement, but Freund's widow objects. Freud offers Eitingon his own ring instead. Inside the ring of psychoanalysis, Freud no longer wears a ring. Around him circular letters, *Rundbriefe*, carry the inner circle's communications.

The next international congress is postponed, but a secret congress of the Secret Committee is possible. In a November 1920 circular letter Freud's colleague in Vienna, Otto Rank, reports 'a scientific proposal emanating from the Professor', a 'topic for the next Committee meeting': 'whether and what influence it would have on the theory and practice of psychoanalysis to accept the phenomena gathered under the name thought-transference'.[19] Jones's objection — 'chiefly because there are other [themes] of a more psa nature about which I should like to learn' — is the only one, and Freud's proposal is agreed (*Rund* 1, 179). By April 1921 the meeting is set for September in Hildesheim and Braunschweig (perhaps Goslar): there 'we are on the doorstep of the Harz, so could combine visiting the towns with a trip to the mountains' (*Rund* 2, 145). Freud saves his latest scientific communication, 'Some Neurotic Mechanisms in Jealousy, Paranoia and Homosexuality', for the meeting. He takes the material for his principal paper on thought-transference with him when he leaves for his summer holidays in the Tyrol about 15 July. With his family first at the Villa Wassing in Bad Gastein and then at Kurheim in Seefeld, he won't come back to Vienna before leaving for Germany.

The Manuscript

In one set of mountains Freud writes a paper to be delivered in another. Two holidays and two families — one biological and one psychoanalytic — he will carry his thoughts on telepathy between them. Immersed in the topic, he replies in late July to the third request that year to become involved with a publication devoted to the study of occult phenomena. As Jones relates Freud's correspondent later relating Freud's answer, 'If I had my life to live over again I should devote myself to psychical research rather than to psycho-analysis' (Jones 3, 419).[20] What his correspondent does not know is that, after 1919, Freud has a life to live over, and is devoting it to psychical research. On 2 August he begins to write, for an intimate audience. An audience of six, people he likes. He is finally making public in a small way material that he and Ferenczi have been exploring privately for a decade.

The paper is finished on 6 August — and not quite as he wished. Earlier he misplaced his most striking example, his own experience of uncanny coincidences in a single analytic session with a patient he would later call Herr P. He failed to translate his own writing. As he explains in the paper, 'When, while I was at Gastein, I looked out the notes which I had put together and brought with me for the purpose of the paper, the sheet on which I had noted down this last observation was not there, but in its place I found another sheet of indifferent memoranda on quite another topic, which I had brought with me by mistake. Nothing can be done against such a clear resistance' (*SE* 18, 190). In the event, he drafts in another case as his third example. Later, he will write up the original third case, the forgotten one, in a manuscript headed 'Postscript'.

As it is, Freud's paper has no title — the heading at the top of the first page reads only 'Introductory [*Vorbericht*]'. We don't know what day Freud read it on or what town he read it in. We don't know what discussion followed — only that it was animated. We don't know whether anyone else read a paper. We know only that Freud's paper was read aloud and remembered. He half-suggests reading it again at the next public congress, but is dissuaded by Jones and Eitingon. Instead, he returns to its material in other writing. Its second case figures in his short 1925 piece 'The Occult Significance of Dreams'. All four cases (that is, including the forgotten one) appear in the *New Introductory Lectures*. But Freud never returns to publish the original paper.

Instead, it was read aloud and remembered. Eitingon recollects it well enough to ask to borrow the manuscript some time before the middle of February 1925, when Freud writes to the Committee, 'Eitingon has taken with him the manuscript of the secret essay [*des geheimen Aufsatzes*], in which at our meeting in the Harz I derived such analytic confirmations of the telepathic hypothesis' (*Rund* 4, 236). Ferenczi's reply laments the barrier of medical discretion or confidentiality, 'Too bad that the Harz secret essay [*der Harzer geheime Aufsatz*] cannot be published' (F/Fer 3, 205). Between them the paper has become 'the secret essay', one of a succession of names it acquires in the absence of a title. Eitingon's wish to see it published leads him to ask if the patients' authorization — for their secrets to be revealed — could be sought. Impossible, Freud replies. Eighteen months later he asks for the manuscript [*das Harzer Memoire über die Telepathie*] back (F/Eit 1, 485). Eitingon responds that he did have it [*das Harzer Telepathie-Manuskript*] once, when he was wondering if it couldn't be published in *Imago*, but that he returned it shortly afterward: only the date escapes him [*ist mir entfallen*] (1, 488). A fortnight later Freud writes that he has looked for it [*mein okkultes Manuskript*] again in vain in Vienna (1, 492). Eitingon would have returned it in person, and he cannot recall such an event. Could Eitingon please look once more in Berlin? He will continue to search in Vienna, though without much hope: fate will decide its future (1, 492). The secret essay has secreted itself. The transmission of the occult manuscript has been occluded. The fate of the essay in which fate figures so prominently is unknown.

By 1941, that is, shortly after Freud's death — his second death — the ill-fated manuscript must have resurfaced: the editors are able to include it in the *Gesammelte Werke*. They have a title for it too: 'Psychoanalysis and Telepathy [*Psychoanalyse und Telepathie*]' — this despite the word 'telepathy''s not appearing once in the text. And they abridge the text, making the sort of silent cuts and emendations that Freud once told his colleagues would ruin it. Decades later Ilse Grubrich-Simitis and Paul Roazen restore some of the excised material,[21] but even today Freud's secret essay, as delivered to the Secret Committee, remains unpublished, a secret.[22] The manuscript of the 'Postscript', the original third case, the notes for which Freud could not find in Bad Gastein, is even more inaccessible. Strachey, when editing 'Psychoanalysis and Telepathy' in the *Standard Edition*, notes the 'Postscript''s close agreement with the version of the case in the *New Introductory Lectures*: 'it has therefore not seemed necessary to include it here. Any substantial points of difference will be recorded in *Standard Ed.*, 22' (*SE* 18, 176). A story which in 1964 his editorial apparatus to Volume 22 repeats: 'It should be added, however, that since that volume of the *Standard Edition* was published, in 1955, the manuscript has once again unaccountably disappeared' (*SE* 22, 48n.). To judge from the Library of Congress catalogue, its fate remains unknown.

The Paper

The odd thing about the 'Postscript', the original third case — of Herr P., as he is called in the *New Introductory Lectures* — is that Freud ever thought it belonged with his other examples. It presses, but differently. Where the other cases involve soothsayers, wedding rings and sexual relations or desires within tight family circles, the episode with Herr P. concerns English — the language and the literature — and Freud's fellow analysts. Where the others comprise tales narrated by analysands after the fact, its moments happen in analysis itself, indeed in a single analytic session, to Freud. Where they involve patients effectively having their minds read by fortune-tellers, it has the analyst's own mind being read — three times and by a patient. Freud's missed encounter with Frau Seidler in Munich resounds in clear resistance — his resistance to mind-reading, psychoanalysis's resistance to thought-transference. Stories circulate. Manuscripts circulate and go astray. The meeting at which psychoanalysis is to consider the effect of acknowledging thought-transference is not without its own effects.

What is remarkable about the paper Freud reads, an essay about thought-transference at the centre of a congress devoted to the subject, is that none of its three cases explicitly involves thought-transference. Having dismissed all forms of occultism apart from thought-transference, Freud tells of three patients' visits to soothsayers: one works from birth-dates, another from palm prints, and the last from handwriting. Two indeed are those he wrote to Ferenczi of ten years before. Madame Arnold, M. le Professeur and Rafael Schermann in the stories are not mind-readers but fortune-tellers. Where Freud once spoke to Jung of the confirmation of a prophecy in the revelation of a patient's unconscious desire, now he underlines the same prophecy's (of a brother-in-law's death) going unfulfilled.

In the event all three prophecies go unfulfilled — and counterintuitively it is this failure that qualifies them as evidence of thought-transference. In their letters Freud and Ferenczi show no faith in practitioners of the occult; here the fortune-tellers function structurally like the butts of jokes. Freud is interested, rather, in the phenomena of the striking — and strikingly specific — predictions that his analysands report. What matters is not the later coming true (or not) of each prediction, but its power to reveal a current (unconscious) truth. Each prophecy fails accurately to predict a future physical event but is, it turns out, acutely in touch with a present psychical desire. To which each soothsayer has access only by thought-transference. *Es gibt Gedankenübertragung* — the word first occurs in Freud's paper in the assertion of an inference, a conclusion: there is thought-transference (*SE* 18, 184). The fortune-tellers are both mocked and tacitly acknowledged as fellow psychical professionals: they are wild analysts, their prophecies analytic constructions. What matters is not the truth that each soothsayer [*Wahrsager*] speaks, but the storyteller's truthfulness [*die Wahrhaftigkeit des Erzählers*] — the story or prophecy's telling truly (*SE* 18, 183).

Ich glaube an die Wahrhaftigkeit des Erzählers. I believe in the storyteller's truthfulness — the storyteller in the Harz mountains being also Freud, as he narrates three stories of failed prophecies to six colleagues, the circle of those closest to him [*dem Kreise der Nächsten*] (*SE* 18, 180). Of course, before this audience, a fourth failed prophecy silently accompanies his three stories. The storyteller himself is still alive, despite his own repeated prediction that he would die before his 63rd birthday. Freud's paper explores within the confines of psychoanalysis (both theory and institution) not the truth of his prediction of his death but that prediction's power. What carried for more than a decade the wish that he should die in 1919? And whose wish might it be now that he should have died in 1919? The failed prophecy of a telephone number addresses both Freud's personal desire to die and the sons' wishes for their father's death.

For his 65th birthday, four months before their gathering in the Harz mountains, the Secret Committee commissioned a bronze bust of Freud as a present for him. A bust celebrating, memorializing and burying him. Freud did not like sitting for it, but thinking it was for Eitingon, and having taken a liking to the sculptor, acceded: 'So I will sacrifice myself for posterity' (Jones 3, 26). The Secret Committee gave him this 'ghostly [*gespenstisch*] threatening bronze doppelgänger' and he offers them a paper on psychoanalysis and telepathy in return (*F/Fer* 3, 55). The first failed prophecy in it uncovers a murderous wish following the analyst's interpretation of an earlier adventure in the mountains as an attempted murder and suicide. The second unfulfilled prophecy offers the patient as the precondition of its fulfilment an unconscious choice: her being set free from her husband either by his death or by her finding the strength to leave him. The third reveals the analysand's mistress's suicide threats repeating his own earlier suicide attempt. All in their way fit into a story of father and sons, the ghost Freud and his creation psychoanalysis. In 'Psychoanalysis and Telepathy' the boys club of the Secret Committee reaches an impasse — and perhaps its theoretical limit. There will be no agreement within its space of private circulation as to the fate of telepathy or thought-transference within psychoanalysis. And no room either in which to theorize the counter-transference.

Freud closes his paper a little disingenuously: 'You will see that all my material touches only on the single point of thought-induction [*Gedankeninduktion*]' (SE XVIII, 193; translation modified). The switch to 'thought-induction' — what thoughts exactly have been induced here? — goes unexplained (and indeed unnoticed by the translator). The man who has outlived his appointed span concludes, as if speaking to his own memorialization, with a *bon mot*:

Perhaps the problem of thought-transference may seem trivial to you in comparison with the great magical world of the occult. But consider what a momentous step beyond what we have hitherto believed would be involved in this hypothesis alone. What the custodian of Saint-Denis used to add to his account [*Erzählung*] of the saint's martyrdom remains true. Saint Denis is said, after his head was cut off, to have picked it up and to have walked quite a distance with it under his arm. But the custodian used to remark: '*Dans des cas pareils, ce n'est que le premier pas qui coûte.*' The rest is easy. (SE 18, 193)

At the end of his paper a ghostly Freud positions himself as both the martyr and the custodian, the storyteller.[23] His audience he casts as listeners, faithful visitors to the shrine — and Roman soldiers. The rest is easy.

The Journey

In late September 1921 psychoanalysis goes on holiday, discusses telepathy, sends a postcard, climbs a mountain and catches a cold. A legacy from Toni Freund covers all but Freud's expenses. Everyone meets in Berlin on the 20th. Jones develops a head cold the evening he joins the others. Freud finds that Hanns Sachs's being and behaviour have worsened. Their journey starts in Hildesheim. Everything takes place in German. On the 21st, psychoanalysis's inner circle gathers at the Kaiserhof.[24] It seems that they visit the Egyptian museum. They are still in Hildesheim on the 23rd, when they all sign a postcard of the Kaiserhaus to Georg Groddeck. Their next stop is Goslar — or perhaps Hahnenklee outside Goslar. Jones misses some of the sightseeing and tiring walks: his lack of fluency in German is not made easier by his cold. Karl Abraham's original itinerary has been altered. On or before the 26th the group drive from Hahnenklee to Schierke. Some time before the 27th, Eitingon has to go back to Berlin; he sends a telegram to the party at the Hotel Stolberg announcing his safe return. The journey to Schierke by car through the mountains is spoiled by rain and cold. The next day, probably the 27th, the weather must improve, for the group, including Jones, ascends the Brocken, the tallest peak in the Harz, on foot. A mountain walk for Freud, it is also a literary pilgrimage: Faust climbed it with Mephistopheles on Walpurgisnacht. A party of psychoanalysts replaces the gathering witches on the summit. They are lucky enough to see a Brocken spectre, an entirely unghostly apparition. The Secret Committee begins to disperse at 7 on the morning of the 28th. 'It was one of the rare occasions when the whole Committee had the opportunity of meeting together, and the only one when we all spent a holiday together with Freud. It was thus a momentous event' (Jones 3, 85). Happy days. 'How far behind us lies Hildesheim and Schierke' (F/Fer 3, 73).

If no trace of practical thought-transmission survives, there is evidence of the successful transmission of a virus. Starting with Jones, the cold circulates, like psychoanalysis's resistance to thought-transference. And something like the spectre of literature circulates in an extraordinary anecdote. 'Another memory that comes back to me was being on top of a tower that had around the platform an iron rail about the level of one's hips. Freud got us all to lean forward against the rail with our hands behind our backs and our feet well back, and then suddenly to imagine it was not there' (Jones 3, 85). In the event, psychoanalysis does not fall. Jones's story is the more striking for being haunted by the close of 'The Sandman'. In Hoffmann's tale, Nathanael, the troubled protagonist at the head of 'The "Uncanny"'s parade of examples, climbs with his beloved Clara to the gallery atop the lofty tower of the town hall, and attempts to throw her off. She is saved by her firm grip on the iron rail of reality. His own fate is rather different: Coppelius laughs and says, 'Ha, ha — just wait, he'll soon come down by himself.'

In fantasies of suicide — as in 'The Canterville Ghost' or Freud's story of St Denis or indeed his 63rd birthday — the subject survives his or her own death, at least in part. As readers of Jones's story, we might ask what Freud, age 65, leaning out of a tower in the Harz mountains with psychoanalysis, is acting out? the death drive? the first case in his paper's unconscious attempt at murder and suicide? the Secret Committee's unconscious murderous desire towards its creator? his longstanding anxiety that his creation may not survive him? his own being read by 'The Sandman'? Or is this just seven friends on holiday? *Der Zufall*. In English, chance, coincidence and accident are all words of the fall.

The Return of the Counter-Transference

But I have had good reason for asserting that everyone possesses in his or her own unconscious an instrument with which he or she can interpret the utterances of the unconscious in other people. (*SE* 12, 320; translation modified)

At stake in the manuscript, the journey and the meeting is a failure of translation: Freud's failure to translate notes from Vienna to Bad Gastein, his failure to translate his belief in something more than chance into theory, and his failure to convince the Secret Committee to translate thought-transference into psychoanalysis. Five years after their time in the Harz, Freud writes to Jones of his continued private experiments with Ferenczi and Anna — and is again personally convinced. 'If anyone should bring up my Fall [*Sündenfall*] with you, just answer calmly that my acceptance of telepathy [*Telepathie*] is my own affair [*Privatsache*], like my Judaism and my passion for smoking, etc., and that the subject of telepathy is not related to psychoanalysis' (*F/Jon* 597). Beyond the limits of *der Sache*, the cause, the movement, of psychoanalysis, there are *Privatsachen*. Even in the founder. Freud cannot be psychoanalysis in person to Jones because he has not mastered his conviction in the existence of thought-transference. As he could not be psychoanalysis in person to Ferenczi because he had not mastered the counter-transference.

And what of the counter-transference, about which Freud had fallen silent? Something in the analysand's unconscious communicates itself to the analyst's unconscious without the mediation of words or signs. Undoubtedly, it does. But is this communication counter-transference or thought-transference? Freud's promised paper on counter-transference — copies to be circulated among analysts but not published — is never delivered, unless. . .

Unless this is exactly what transpired in the Harz mountains. What if the essay published posthumously — and abbreviated — as 'Psychoanalysis and Telepathy' were indeed the missing paper on counter-transference? And its exploration of *Gedankenübertragung* doubled as a discussion of *Gegenübertragung*? The word 'telepathy' appearing in it no more than 'counter-transference', its title might equally be 'Psychoanalysis and Counter-transference'.

Jones's original idea of an unofficial inner circle proposed that each member of it be analysed by Freud. In the event only Ferenczi was, along with Eitingon and Rank; Jones, in turn, was analysed by Ferenczi. How was Freud to deliver a paper on counter-transference to his own analysands, that is, to the very people in relation to whom he had experienced the counter-transference? The nature of the topic made discussion of it impossible: exploring counter-transference with this audience could only mean publicly exploring the audience itself.

What if, in such circumstances, the secret essay contained a secret beyond that of its audience in the Secret Committee? What if the essay's subject were itself a secret, perhaps at some level even from Freud? What if the essay were a haunted text?

PsiFi?

One analysand of Freud's, also an analyst — from whom the existence of the paper (and the relation of its third case to one of her own patients) was kept secret — seems to have intuited as much. As if by thought-transference, Helene Deutsch's paper 'Occult Processes Occurring during Psychoanalysis' uncannily offers in a few paragraphs a reading of Freud's essay without ever having read it. In spite of its title, her text treats less occult processes than telepathy in analysis and less telepathy than the counter-transference. Published in 1926 — the year after Abraham's death, the year of Rank's departure from psychoanalysis and the year before the Secret Committee's last circular letter — it is the first of what will be a succession of essays by women delivering on Freud's promise of 1911: 'I believe an article on "counter-transference" is sorely needed'. Freud himself could fulfil that need only telepathically.

In September 1921 in the Harz mountains Freud spoke to psychoanalysis, then assembled as a tight male circle. He offered it thought-transference. Some time later, no longer so closed and so male, it accepted the gift — as the counter-transference.

Thought-transference haunts psychoanalysis — as hypnosis does. Both still lie beyond its science of translation. Having fallen out of Freud's writings well before *The Interpretation of Dreams*, hypnosis returns in his 1921 essay *Group Psychology and the Analysis and the Ego* with a vengeance. The return of the theoretically repressed, it figures there as the past of psychoanalysis which never left. In Freud and Ferenczi's correspondence, thought-transference appears as the future of psychoanalysis which will never arrive. Once Sigmund Freud foresaw telepathy as the future medium of psychoanalysis — Sándor Ferenczi's great discovery. An unfulfilled prophecy. As if herself read by an unseen text, Helene Deutsch recasts that prophecy of telepathy as the theory of the counter-transference. Psychoanalysis follows her. And Shoshana Felman translates it from psychoanalysis to literature as the reading effect.

Es F. SF.

NOTES

1 Shoshana Felman, 'Turning the Screw of Interpretation', *Yale French Studies* 55/56 (1977), 94–207; hereafter TSI.
2 Daniel Sibony, 'Hamlet: A Writing-Effect', translated by James Hulbert and Joshua Wilner, *Yale French Studies* 55/56 (1977), 53.
3 'Translation, however, is what psychoanalysis is all about', Felman, 'Foreword', *Yale French Studies* 55/56 (1977), 2.
4 For a crucial engagement with literature and telepathy, see Nicholas Royle, *Telepathy and Literature: Essays on the Reading Mind* (Oxford: Basil Blackwell, 1991) and the essays that follow from it in *After Derrida* (Manchester: Manchester University Press, 1995) and *The Uncanny* (Manchester: Manchester University Press, 2003).
5 If *Literature and Psychoanalysis* is famous for its translation of Lacan to the English-speaking world, its elevation of Freud's 'The "Uncanny"' — to which two-thirds of its authors refer — to the status of canonical text has been no less influential.

6 Josef Breuer, in *The Standard Edition of the Complete Psychological Works of Sigmund Freud*, 24 vols, translated and edited by James Strachey (London: Hogarth Press and the Institute of Psycho-Analysis, 1953–74), 2, 193. Hereafter *SE*.
7 *The Freud/Jung Letters: The Correspondence between Sigmund Freud and C. G. Jung*, edited by William McGuire, translated by Ralph Manheim and R. F. C. Hull (Princeton: Princeton University Press, 1974), 219. Hereafter *F/Jun*.
8 Also quoted in Helene Deutsch, 'Occult Processes Occurring during Psychoanalysis' [1926], translated by George Devereux, *The Therapeutic Process, the Self and Female Psychology: Collected Psychoanalytic Papers*, edited by Paul Roazen (New Brunswick NJ: Transaction, 1992) 223–38; 226.
9 Felman alludes to Jacques Lacan, 'The Freudian Thing' [1956], *Ecrits: A Selection*, translated by Alan Sheridan (London: Tavistock, 1977), 116. For more on the journey to New York — and translation and transference — see my 'Freudian Idiom — A Hotel Chain' *Angelaki* 9:1 (2004), 103–23.
10 Deutsch presciently takes up substantive elements of the correspondence in 1926. The verbal doubling of the two terms goes unnoticed in her referring to thought-transference as 'telepathy' — the latter being the term Freud had used in print in the little he had published on the subject to that point.
11 *The Correspondence of Sigmund Freud and Sándor Ferenczi*, 3 vols, edited by Eva Brabant, Ernst Falzeder and Patrizia Giampieri-Deutsch, translated by Peter T. Hoffer (Cambridge, MA: Belknap–Harvard University Press, 1993–2000), vol. 1, 175. Hereafter *F/Fer*.
12 In the *New Introductory Lectures* Freud suggests that thought-transference 'is so close to telepathy and can indeed without much violence be regarded as the same thing' (*SE* 22, 39). His preference for one word over the other at any moment seems not to be completely determinable by sense, chronology or context. I use 'thought-transference' here, as the term that predominates in both Freud's correspondence with Ferenczi and 'Psychoanalysis and Telepathy' (despite the latter's title).
13 See *SE* 11, 145, and *The Sigmund Freud–Ludwig Binswanger Correspondence, 1908–1938*, edited by Gerhard Fichtner, translated by Arnold J. Pomerans (London: Open Gate Press, 2003) (hereafter *F/Bin*), 112; Ferenczi in *F/Fer* 1, 253; *SE* 11, 145; *F/Jun* 291, *Minutes of the Vienna Psychoanalytic Society*, 4 vols, edited by Herman Nunberg and Ernst Federn, translated by M. Nunberg (New York: International Universities Press, 1962–75), vol. 2, 447, *F/Fer* 1, 221, and *F/Bin* 112; *SE* 12, 164; *F/Fer* 1, 158; Ferenczi in *F/Fer* 2, 99.
14 Paula Heimann, 'On Counter-Transference', *International Journal of Psycho-Analysis* 31:1 (1950), 81–4; 83.
15 Ernest Jones, *Sigmund Freud: Life and Work*, 3 vols (London: Hogarth Press, 1953–7), vol. 3, 426. Hereafter Jones.

16   Sigmund Freud and Max Eitingon, *Briefwechsel 1906–1939*, 2 vols, edited by Michael Schröter (Tübingen: edition diskord, 2004), vol. 1, 155. Hereafter *F/Eit*. All translations from this correspondence are mine.
17   *Psychoanalysis and History* 17:2 (2015).
18   *The Complete Correspondence of Sigmund Freud and Ernest Jones, 1908–1939*, edited by R. Andrew Paskauskas (Cambridge, MA: Belknap–Harvard University Press, 1993), 146. Hereafter *F/Jon*.
19   *Die Rundbriefe des 'Geheimen Komitees'*, 4 vols, edited by Gerhard Wittenberger and Christfried Tögel (Tübingen: edition diskord, 1999–2006), vol. 1, 156. Hereafter *Rund*. All translations from the *Rundbriefe* are mine.
20   Freud would later deny this reply, but Jones as his biographer is pleased to discover a copy of the original letter, a translation of which he announces (Jones 3, 420) that he is publishing in Appendix B — except that Appendix B contains 'Surgical Notes', and nothing, not even a mention, of the letter appears in the appendix devoted to 'Miscellaneous Extracts from Correspondence'.
21   Ilse Grubrich-Simitis, *Back to Freud's Texts: Making Silent Documents Speak* [1993], translated by Philip Slotkin (New Haven: Yale University Press, 1996), 208–13; Paul Roazen, 'Using Oral History about Freud: A Case in His "Secret Essay"', *American Imago* 58:4 (Winter 2001), 793–812; 807–8.
22   As does the identity of two of the four patients. For more details about the third patient, a 'partner' of Ivar Kreuger, and an account of Helene Deutsch's exchange of secrets with Freud, see Roazen above. Maria Torok's speculation that the fourth patient, Herr P. in the 'Postscript', is Sergei Pankejeff, the Wolf-Man, seems unlikely: David Forsyth had already been in analysis for five weeks in 1919 (since 6 October) when Pankejeff re-entered analysis with Freud on 11 November: 'Afterword: What is Occult in Occultism? Between Sigmund Freud and Sergei Pankeiev Wolf Man' [1983], Nicolas Abraham and Maria Torok, *The Wolf Man's Magic Word: A Cryptonomy*, translated by Nicholas Rand (Minneapolis: University of Minnesota Press, 1986), 84–106.
23   Freud misremembers Madame du Deffand's words: '*dans une telle situation* il n'y a que le premier pas qui coûte': *Letters of the Marquise du Deffand to the Hon. Horace Walpole*, vol. 1 (London, 1810), 157.
24   Sources here include: Freud, *Unterdeß halten wir zusammen. Briefe an die Kinder*, edited by Michael Schröter with Ingeborg Meyer-Palmedo and Ernst Falzeder (Berlin: Aufbau, 2010), *Briefwechsel Sigmund Freud–Georg Groddeck*, edited by Michael Giefer with Beate Schuh (Frankfurt am Main: Stroemfeld, 2008) and Freud, 'Briefe an Kata und Lajos Lévy (1918–1926)', edited by Thomas Aichhorn and Michael Schröter, *Luzifer-Amor* 25:50 (2012), 7–61.

Freud's Fictions: Fixation, Femininity, Photography

Elissa Marder

> Literature, in other words, is the language which psychoanalysis uses in order to speak of itself, in order to name itself. Literature is therefore not simply outside psychoanalysis, since it motivates and inhabits the very names of its concepts, since it is the inherent reference by which psychoanalysis names its findings.
>
> Shoshana Felman, 'To Open the Question'

Fixation, a Queer Word

The word 'fixation' immediately evokes psychic rigidity, neurotic or obsessional preoccupations, regressive and/or perverse sexual attachments. In everyday speech, the term 'fixation' gestures allusively to the language of psychoanalysis as it connotes a state of pathological stuckness, an inability to move forward or even to move at all. One often hears, for example, that so-and-so is 'fixated' on this or that person, object or idea. Within psychoanalysis, however, fixation is a peculiarly slippery term. Throughout Freud's writings, the word appears at critical junctures and has several — apparently divergent — meanings. Freud variously uses fixation as a common noun, a proto-metapsychological concept, and a particularly charged rhetorical figure. 'Fixation' designates something at the borders between a concept and a word; it is a word-image-thing that serves as a nodal point for a fluid conceptual field. Freud invokes fixation throughout every period of his psychoanalytic writings, but the concept itself is anything but fixed within psychoanalysis. Moreover, because Freud often appeals to the term 'fixation' when grappling with material that resists his formulations (either because he finds himself confronted with something he doesn't recognize or because it runs counter to his metapsychological models of psychic organization), fixation often operates like a counter-concept that opens up Freud's metapsychology from within. As we shall see, at stake is nothing less than rethinking sexual difference and the temporality of the subject.

In the *Language of Psychoanalysis*, Laplanche and Pontalis describe fixation as 'a mode of inscription of certain ideational contents (experiences, imagos, phantasies) which persist in the unconscious in unchanging fashion and to which the instinct remains bound'.[1] Fixation is both the general term for the primitive mode of psychic inscription and the name for anything that impedes psychic development or that resists the forward movement of time. Because it reactivates traces from the past in the present moment, fixation both arrests time and is a vehicle of time travel. Depending on context, fixation can mean variously the most basic form of psychic writing that is a necessary precondition for any subject formation, an arrest at a particular phase of development, or a prolonged attachment to a primal libidinal object.

Like primal words, fixations operate in two seemingly opposed fashions. They fix time and make it possible for time to be unfixed. Fixation implies temporal arrest, but is also associated with everything within Freud's theory that escapes the confines of development, teleology and linear temporality. It is a principle of regression and futurity, of petrified immobility and contingency — a name both for the primal origin of sexuality and the very word for what shuts sexuality down. Because Freud often appeals to the term 'fixation' to designate events, ideas, images that defy or elude his conceptual framework, his invocations of 'fixation' are often associated with surprising, mysterious and evocative zones within his thinking and writing.[2] As Jacques Lacan intimates in his late seminar 'L'étourdit', fixation is never far from fiction or, as we shall see shortly, from the specific challenges posed to psychoanalysis by female sexuality.[3] Fixation is Freud's first way of describing how the psyche comes into being as a form of idiomatic writing. Fixation destines each psyche to be inflected and marked by the fictions that develop from its primal points of attachment and resistance.

Fixation and Femininity

In Freud's earliest works, fixation is an irreducibly queer word. In the 1905 *Three Essays on Sexuality*, fixation provides Freud with the means to explain that the very meaning of sexuality is that there is no heteronormativity.[4] There, and elsewhere, fixation is associated with male homosexuality and other forms of non-normative sexuality. However, in his late texts devoted specifically to the knotty problems of female sexuality, fixation becomes associated with the stultifying and soul-killing rigidity of femininity. In those later texts, 'fixation' usually refers both to an unresolved lingering identification with, and attachment to, the mother as first love object, and attachment to the clitoris as the active, phallic expression of that attachment. In 'A Child is Being Beaten' (1919), for example, Freud concludes that the beating fantasy has a specific meaning for little girls who remain 'fixated' on their clitoris:

> This phantasy seems to be a relic of the phallic period in girls. The peculiar rigidity which struck me so much in the monotonous formula 'a child is being beaten' can probably be interpreted in a special way. The child which is being beaten (or caressed) may ultimately be nothing more nor less than the clitoris itself, so that at its very lowest level the statement will contain a confession of masturbation, which has remained attached to the content of the formula from its beginning in the phallic phase till later life. (SE 19, 254)

Freud opens his infamous 1931 essay 'Female Sexuality' by establishing a link between sexual development, 'fixation' and time. While he initially presents fixation as a developmental problem stemming from a lingering attachment to the mother and the clitoris that is particularly problematic for little girls, it quickly becomes clear that 'fixation' is a problem *in* time and *of* time more generally. 'Fixation' essentially alters the very temporal structure of the psyche.

> Indeed, we had to reckon with the possibility that a number of women remain arrested in their original attachment to their mother and never achieve a true change-over towards men. This being so, the pre-Oedipus phase in women gains an importance which we have not attributed to it hitherto. Since this phase allows room for all the fixations and repressions from which we trace the origin of the neuroses, it would seem as though we must retract the universality of the thesis that the Oedipus complex is the nucleus of the neuroses. (SE 21, 225–6)

Freud here suggests that, if the discovery of feminine fixations actually threatens the 'universality' of the Oedipus complex, it is not merely on account of the *fact* that the little girl remains attached to the mother for a long time, but rather because the nature of fixations themselves disrupts the ability to produce any normative or normalizing development model at all. Unlike the Oedipus complex, which imposes a universal generic chronology of events (to which presumably each individual can nonetheless respond in a unique fashion), feminine fixations are radically variable and unpredictable. Fixations fix each individual individually and contingently, but they themselves are not fixed in time. Paradoxically, from a temporal perspective, fixations are very fluid. A pre-Oedipal fixation (leading to a conflict with normative heterosexuality and/or femininity) can be revived at any time during a woman's life. The work of fixation is never done.

At this point it starts to become clearer why, having discovered the importance of pre-Oedipal fixations in women (and having then subsequently understood that the primal attachment to the mother is shared by the boy child as well), Freud is now faced with a genuine conceptual impasse. Given the slippery and contingent nature of fixations, he can no longer provide any coherent (universal) narrative of female sexual development. The discovery of pre-Oedipal feminine fixation means that each case of fixation will have to be taken on a case-by-case basis, as there can no longer be a standard chronology for sexual development.[5] Unlike the Oedipus complex, which provides the template for a universal structure, fixation is *not* a complex, but rather a way of describing a mode of predisposition and receptivity to accidental events that always might reverse, arrest or divert predictable developmental patterns. Faced with this uncertainty, Freud turns to the concept of 'femininity' as a means of counteracting the contingency that threatens his universal model of the psyche. In other words, Freud reacts to the unpredictable contingencies of fixation *during* sexual development by establishing 'femininity' as its fixed and predetermined endpoint.

From a conceptual standpoint, then, 'femininity' provides Freud with a (normative) means to fix the non-normative contingencies of fixation. It is precisely because of the *temporal* unpredictability and instability of the feminine castration complex that Freud is compelled to cling to the notion that women are 'destined' to femininity. He needs to posit a fixed *telos* (femininity) in order to counteract the temporal variability that he encounters through his interrogations of female sexuality.

In the late writings, Freud invokes 'fixation' both to describe the mechanisms according to which a girl *fails* to reach femininity and as the sign that she has, in fact, arrived. Indeed, paradoxically, it turns out that the price of arriving at 'femininity' is a total arrest of all psychic and libidinal movement. In this regard, the penultimate paragraph of the lecture called 'Femininity' is simply breathtaking. Here, Freud argues that the enormous psychic labour required of a woman to overcome her fixations so that she can arrive at 'femininity' exhausts all her psychic energy, destroys her capacity for change, renders her incapable of any further psychic development or of reaping any benefits from psychoanalysis. Consequently, once she reaches femininity, she remains permanently fixed and frozen in that deadened state. In a very famous passage, after describing a man of thirty as 'youthful' and open to analysis, Freud goes on to describe the 'feminine' woman thus:

> A woman of the same age, however, often frightens us by her psychical rigidity and unchangeability. Her libido has taken up final positions and seems incapable of exchanging them for others. There are no paths open to further development; it is as though the whole process had already run its course and remains thenceforward insusceptible to influence — as though, indeed, the difficult development to femininity had exhausted the possibilities of the person concerned. As therapists we lament this state of things, even if we succeed in putting an end to our patient's ailment by doing away with her neurotic conflict. (SE 22, 135)

Thus, 'femininity' succeeds only in resolving archaic pre-Oedipal fixations (phallic attachments that come from the past) to the extent that it also succeeds in freezing the future out of existence. We arrive at the perverse conclusion that 'femininity,' which ought to be the ostensible aim and goal towards which a girl's sexual development predestines her, actually destroys the very possibility of a future.

Fixation is the sticking point in all of Freud's attempts to integrate female sexual development into his general theory of universal (male) subjectivity. His attempt to fix the theory of female sexuality via fixation also fails. Instead, Freud's fixation on the connection between female sexuality and fixation opens up psychoanalytic theory to its foundational fictions. And it also exposes that theory to alternative possibilities made possible through fiction.

Freud's Fictions

> Hence, strangely, the only thing I tolerate, that I like, that is familiar to me, when I am photographed, is the sound of the camera.
>
> Roland Barthes, *Camera Lucida*

For the purposes of the discussion that follows, it is interesting to note that there is an eerie resonance between the 1933 portrayal of the fossilized fate reserved for a feminine woman of thirty and Freud's description of the anonymous female protagonist of the obscure case that we are about to explore: 'She was thirty years old, a most attractive and handsome girl, who looked much younger than her age and was of a distinctly feminine type.' These lines come from one of Freud's most brazenly fictive texts – the small and relatively obscure piece of writing from 1915 that goes by the seemingly innocuous title 'A Case of Paranoia Running Counter to the Disease' (*SE* 14). In this pseudo case history, Freud's fixation on the relation between female sexuality and fixation obliges him to confront some of the most intractable and elusive foundational fictions of psychoanalysis. Fiction and fixation come together in this strange case. Freud adopts the voice and the conventions of a fiction writer in order to lay down one of the most primordial (and arguably 'fictive') conceptual building blocks of his theory: the notion of primal phantasies.

Fixation operates at every level of this case. The case is not only *about* 'fixation,' it is also a case *of* multiple instances and modes of fixation. As we shall see, it is not incidental that photography (a medium that arrests time and movement and 'fixes' its living objects into frozen positions) plays such a crucial role in the case. The case, as Freud presents it, is a strange mash-up of different popular literary and photographic genres. It combines features of a gothic ghost story, a fantastic tale, a classic detective story, a romantic thriller and a pornographic photo album. The basic elements of the case are as follows: a lawyer consults Freud because he is concerned about a female client who claims to have been abused by her male colleague and would-be lover. But, as the lawyer harbours doubts about the credibility of her story, he persuades the woman to bring her case to Freud. Here is how Freud first recounts her version of the unsettling events that transpired during her fateful afternoon tryst with her lover:

There they kissed and embraced as they lay side by side, and he began to admire the charms which were now partly revealed. In the midst of this idyllic scene she was suddenly frightened by a noise, a kind of knock or click. It came from the direction of the writing-desk, which was standing across the window; the space between desk and window was partly taken up by a heavy curtain. She had at once asked her friend what this noise meant, and was told, so she said, that it probably came from the small clock on the writing-desk (...). As she was leaving the house she had met two men on the staircase, who whispered something to each other when they saw her. One of the strangers was carrying something which was wrapped up and looked like a small box. She was much exercised over this meeting, and on her way home she had already put together the following notions: the box might easily have been a camera, and the man a photographer who had been hidden behind the curtain while she was in the room; the click had been the noise of the shutter; the photograph had been taken as soon as he saw her in a particularly compromising position which he wished to record. (*SE* 14, 264)

The concept of fixation is central to Freud's interpretation. Recourse to it enables him both to identify the surprising source of the mysterious knocking noises that the woman hears and to explain why she is so alarmed by them. At the end of the case — after several important reiterations of the material in it — Freud triumphantly unveils his solution to the mystery. According to him, the sounds that the woman describes in such vivid detail never happened. There was no external camera clicking noise and no photograph taken by the men on the staircase. The clicking noises come from within her and not from the external world. He infers that her amorous exchange with her lover awakens an archaic and ambivalent erotic attachment to her mother that is expressed as a primal phallic fixation on her clitoris. He then concludes that the clicking and knocking noises that she attributes to the camera in the room emanate, in fact, from her own clitoris. The clicking sounds she hears during her tryst are transmissions from a primal past that are reproduced in her very own black box. Those primal sound images come from an immemorial past and reawaken that past within her as sensations that become transposed into auditory perceptions in the present moment.

Freud's sensational solution to the mystery of the clicking sounds has made this case notorious in certain critical circles. During the 1980s it was discussed widely both within and outside of psychoanalytic circles and was the object of influential readings by analysts and feminist critics alike.[6] It has acquired something of a cult status among feminist theorists in particular. Despite the critical attention that it attracted and the many valuable insights that emerged from the diverse readings that were devoted to it, the case remains relatively unknown in comparison to Freud's other case histories. There is something so irreducibly queer about the case and so decidedly odd about Freud's interpretation of it that calls out for another look. In what follows, I propose a counter-intuitive – and perhaps even perverse – reading of the case to show how the link that Freud establishes between fixation and phantasy can be read as a fantastic, photographic, feminine counterpoint to some of the most normative tendencies in psychoanalysis. Freud's clinical description of how fixation and phantasy work together undermines his own theories about the centrality of castration and the universality of the Oedipus complex and opens up psychoanalysis to the untapped power of its own fictions. Fixation, as we have been suggesting, always moves in two directions at once: it both animates the very source of creativity and serves as the petrifying medium of its destruction.

Before turning to Freud's conceptually suggestive, albeit quasi-pornographic, interpretation of this case, I would like to point out a number of elements surrounding the case that contribute to its singularly peculiar status. For starters — and it is surprising that this fact has rarely been remarked upon — although Freud refers to the woman as a 'patient', she never enters into psychoanalytic treatment with him and he sees her on only two occasions. Although Freud draws significant clinical and meta-psychological conclusions from his all-too brief encounter with this woman, from a clinical standpoint, this case is not real. It is a fictional case: the woman is not Freud's patient; there is no evidence that the scenario that Freud recounts ever really happened; the narrative structure resembles that of a short story. Moreover, this fictional case gives rise to a phantasmatically presented clinical claim about the primal role of primal phantasies in psychoanalysis. The fictional status *of* the case is intimately related to the discovery of primal phantasy *in* the case.

It is important to recall that this pseudo-clinical case, published in 1915, is Freud's first clinical treatment of a woman 'patient' after *Dora*, which was published in 1905. Prior to *Dora*, Freud's most famous clinical cases were virtually all devoted to female hysterics to whom, like Dora, he gave memorable fictional pseudonyms: 'Emma', 'Irma' and so on. After *Dora*, however, all of Freud's famous clinical cases are dedicated to male patients in whom the relationship between castration anxiety and animal phobias figures prominently. These male patients all become known by name (Schreber) or by their clinically descriptive fictional nicknames (for example 'Rat Man', 'Wolf Man' and 'Little Hans'). Aside from the 'Case of Paranoia Running Counter to the Disease', after *Dora* (*SE* 7), there is only one other clinical case that features a woman patient: 'The Psychogenesis of a Case of Homosexuality in a Woman (1920)' (*SE* 18). After *Dora*, no woman patient is referred to by name. But, although the protagonist in the latter case is unnamed, the title of the case allows her to be clearly identified as the 'young homosexual woman'.

The nameless status of the woman in 'The Case of Paranoia Running Counter to the Disease' is somewhat different from

Freud's other unnamed clinical characters, and has somewhat different consequences. This woman's missing name makes it very difficult to refer to her or the case. A name, after all, is a kind of fixation. Freud prefaces the case presentation with a curiously odd disclaimer in which he 'confesses' that he has altered 'the *milieu* of the case in order to preserve the incognito of the people concerned, but (...) altered nothing else' (263). Like a pornographic photograph that is put into circulation at a remove from the original context of its production, the anonymity of the woman at the centre of the case paradoxically enhances and exacerbates the impact of her exposure. It is almost impossible to talk about this case without referring to it by way of Freud's lurid reconstruction of her sexual arousal. In most of Freud's clinical cases, the title of the case (and/or the nickname of the patient) makes it possible to identify, at least provisionally, the conceptual problem that the case is trying to resolve. But this case is quite a bit more complicated in that regard. As its titular designation as a 'counter case' coyly indicates, this case is not simply — or even primarily — about female paranoia at all. As we shall see, female paranoia functions more like a plot device that provides Freud with a narrative frame for one of the knottiest and most fantastic notions in all of psychoanalysis: primal phantasies.

That said, the question of female paranoia does, in fact, provide Freud with his point of departure. His ostensible aim in writing the case is to explain why the specifically feminine manifestation of paranoia that he encounters in this woman apparently contradicts and runs counter to the universal (male) model structure that he had previously derived on the basis of the Schreber case (*SE* 12). In his earlier writings about paranoia, Freud had argued that paranoia can always be explained as a repressed and repudiated homosexual attachment to a figure of the same sex. According to this view, paranoia is always simultaneously a defence against and manifestation of homosexual attachment. Here, however, Freud is obliged to explain why this woman's paranoia expresses itself as a fantasy of persecution by a person of the opposite sex. Throughout the case Freud does a lot of fancy footwork to juggle several different competing — and perhaps even mutually exclusive — explanations to account for the differences between the generic (male) structure of paranoia and its specifically feminine incarnation here. Moreover, as I have already indicated, paranoia may not, in fact, be what this case is essentially about.

Knock Knock (Double Takes)

In order to appreciate the conceptual stakes of Freud's startling explanation of the mysterious knocking sounds and the vertiginous intricacies of the case more generally, we must take a closer look at its narrative structure. The case is virtually unintelligible unless one recognizes that it is, as Naomi Schor aptly puts it, a 'complicated twice-told tale'.[7] Every event recounted in the case happens twice and every act of telling occurs twice. The woman sees Freud twice, she sees her lover twice, she produces two distinct paranoid delusions, and Freud tells the story of her afternoon tryst twice. Moreover, as Freud tends to reverse the temporal order in which he narrates each repeated event, it takes multiple readings of the case in order to figure out which iteration of which event presumably transpired first and why it matters. As we shall see, the representation of each narrative event in the case is often represented prior to, and in lieu of, an earlier, unmarked first iteration that haunts it like a latent primitive, undeveloped photographic negative.

After his initial account of the woman's story, Freud interrupts his own narrative to explain to the reader that he feels compelled to initiate a second meeting with her because he is perplexed and unsatisfied by the apparently heterosexual form of her paranoia:

> My own observations and analyses and those of my friends had so far confirmed the relation between paranoia and homosexuality without any difficulty. But the present case emphatically contradicted it. The girl seemed to be defending herself against love for a man by directly transforming the lover into a persecutor: there was no sign of the influence of a woman, no trace of a struggle against a homosexual attachment. In these circumstances the simplest thing would have been to abandon the theory that the delusion of persecution invariably depends on homosexuality, and at the same time to abandon everything that followed from that theory. (...) But I saw another way out, by which a final verdict could for the moment be postponed. (...) I therefore said that I could not form an immediate opinion, and asked the patient to call on me a second time, when she could relate her story again at greater length and add any subsidiary details that might have been omitted. (265–6)

During his *second* interview with the woman, Freud learns that she had visited her lover not merely once, but twice. Moreover, during the *second* interview with Freud he learns that it is during her *second* tryst with her lover that she first becomes alarmed by the clicking and knocking sounds and concludes that her lover has been taking compromising pictures of her. During the second meeting Freud succeeds in discovering a missing connection, as well as a missing person, that enables him to establish a hitherto unsuspected causal link between the two amorous encounters. Freud elicits the following story from the woman: the day following her first visit to her lover's apartment, while they were both in their shared workplace, she witnessed her lover in intimate conversation with her supervisor, a white-haired older woman, who reminds her of her mother. While watching her lover with the older woman, she has two distressing thoughts: 1) she imagines that the two of them are talking about her and that her lover has betrayed her by exposing her relationship with him to the disapproving supervisor; 2) she imagines that the two of them are having — or have had — an affair with one another. Freud describes this scene as the woman's 'first delusion' and postulates that it constitutes a first iteration of the delusion that recurs, in inverted form, in the subsequent scene with her lover.

Although Freud does not comment specifically on this fact, it is striking that the woman's two distressing thoughts place her in two opposed — but equally unbearable — positions in the scene that she observes. She imagines herself both as the very object and focus of the couple's shared gaze and she imagines herself as being radically excluded from the scene by their exclusive interest in one another. In the first instance, she sees herself as too present — shamefully exposed — whereas, in the second instance, she sees herself as reduced to nothing. But the fact that in both instances she appears to be looking for traces of the presence or absence of her own image lends a photographic quality to this scene. She is both inside and outside the picture she watches and records. The scene is one of photographic fixation. In watching it, she takes a mental picture and she herself becomes transfixed by the image she produces. Her fixation on the scene and her doubled position in the scene is simultaneously paranoid and photographic. Moreover, as Freud's reading implies, the woman only becomes fixated on this scene because she was already fixated. This scene recalls and reactivates an earlier and much more primal scene of fixation.

The apparition of the white-haired woman in this reconstructed scene tells Freud everything he needs to know. On the basis of this new addition to the woman's story, he finds the missing evidence of the homosexual attachment for which he had been looking to support his theory regarding the essential link between homosexuality and paranoia. The image of the white-haired woman that emerges between the two encounters prompts Freud to disclose the enduring latent presence of a triangular, quasi-Oedipal scenario that is imprinted in her, is triggered by her observation of her lover with her supervisor and subsequently motivates her complicated extrasensory experiences during her second encounter with her lover. The white-haired woman is herself only a spectral reproduction of a far more ghostly phantom figure: an archaic image of the mother on whom the young woman remains fixed. It is this ancient fixation on a prehistoric maternal imago that is reawakened during the love scene.

Her love for her mother had become the spokesman of all those tendencies which, playing the part of a 'conscience', seek to arrest a girl's first step along the new road to normal sexual satisfaction – in many respects a dangerous one; and indeed it succeeded in disturbing her relation with men. (...)

When a mother hinders or arrests a daughter's sexual activity, she is fulfilling a normal function whose lines are laid down by events in childhood, which has powerful, unconscious motives, and has received the sanction of society. It is the daughter's business to emancipate herself from this influence and to decide for herself on broad and rational grounds what her share of enjoyment or denial of sexual pleasure shall be. If in the attempt to emancipate herself she falls a victim to a neurosis it implies the presence of a mother-complex which is as a rule overpowerful, and is certainly unmastered. The conflict between this complex and the new direction taken by the libido is dealt with in the form of one neurosis or another, according to the subject's disposition. The manifestation of the neurotic reaction will always be determined, however, not by her present-day relation to her actual mother but by her *infantile relations* to her *earliest image* of her mother. (267–8; my emphasis, EM)

By uncovering a repressed primal homosexual attachment to the archaic mother in the woman, Freud simultaneously argues on the one hand that the counter case is not really a counter case because it confirms his conviction about the structural link between paranoia and homosexuality, while on the other he also maintains that because homosexual attachment to the mother plays such a determining role in female sexuality more generally, female paranoia takes a fundamentally different form from male paranoia. But there is still a problem with Freud's attempt to make this counter case conform to the generic male model. Although Freud's discovery of the latent homosexual attachment to the white-haired mother surrogate allows him to find an *expression* of paranoia analogous to the earlier generic masculine model (projection), the *source* of the paranoia in the woman is derived from two points of fixation: her un-relinquished infantile attachment to her (phallic) clitoris, and her ambivalent fixation on her mother. In this version of paranoia, the relation to the mother is key as she occupies two divergent roles: she is both the primary object of love and the persecutory and inhibiting obstacle to its gratification. By working both the homosexual/persecution angle and the mother/clitoris fixation angle, Freud has it both ways. The counter case both confirms his *general* theory about paranoia while the specifically feminine aberrations in the case provide him with new material and a way of unveiling a surprising new concept. It is here, in the margins of this marginal counter case, that Freud first introduces the concept of the primal phantasy. He then uses this case as the supporting clinical reference point for all his subsequent explanations of primal phantasies and their relation to primal scenes.

The Mother's Eye

Also in the case of the supposed camera, I am reminded of the mother's eye, which like God's eye 'sees everything', which has always seen the child all alone naked and stripped, and now sees it in this state with the man.

Letter from Lou Andreas Salomé to Freud, 15 March 1916

In the penultimate pages of the case, Freud recounts the knocking scene for the second time. Adopting a narrative voice similar to that of a detective who has meticulously reconstructed the scene of a crime in order to expose the identity of the culprit, in this second reiteration, Freud supplements his earlier version of the story with a new interpretation of the evidence already presented.

Lying partly undressed on the sofa beside her lover, she heard a noise like a click or beat. She did not know its cause, but she arrived at an interpretation of it after meeting two men on the staircase, one of whom was carrying something that looked like a covered box. She became convinced that someone acting on instructions from her lover had watched and photographed her during their intimate *tête-à-tête*. I do not for a moment imagine, of course, that if the unlucky noise had not occurred the delusion would not have been formed; on the contrary, something inevitable is to be seen behind this accidental circumstance, something which was bound to assert itself compulsively in the patient, just as when she supposed that there was a *liaison* between her lover and the elderly superior, her mother-substitute. Among the store of unconscious phantasies of all neurotics, and probably of all human beings, there is one which is seldom absent and which can be disclosed by analysis: this is the phantasy of watching sexual intercourse between the parents. I call such phantasies – of the observation of sexual intercourse between the parents, of seduction, of castration, and others – 'primal phantasies'; and I shall discuss in detail elsewhere their origin and their relation to individual experience. The accidental noise was thus merely playing the part of a provoking factor which activated the typical phantasy of overhearing which is a component of the parental complex. (269)

Freud here derives an ostensibly *universal* primal phantasy (the desire to watch parental coitus that gives rise to curiosity regarding all of the sounds that are associated with adult sexuality)[8] from the specifically feminine particularities of this case via three points of fixation: fixation on the clitoris, fixation on the mother, and fixation by a photographic image. As we have seen, the arousal of the clicking clitoris revives a sexual fixation on the mother and awakens the woman's ambivalence about the duplicity of the maternal figure. Because the mother is both the object of love and the source of prohibition against love, the woman's sexual arousal is simultaneously experienced as an arresting inhibition: she thus 'hears' an internal voice (the clicking noise) that then triggers the production of the paranoid fantasy about being photographed.

Freud's substantiation of the existence of this universal archive of 'primal phantasies' via the clicking clitoris ultimately hinges upon his contention that the source of the sounds that the woman hears come entirely from a reactivated infancy that remains preserved within her rather than from any actual object in the world. Although Freud initially proposes that her delusion *could* have been triggered by a random, contingent, accidental noise that she retroactively attributes to the sound of a camera held by the two men on the landing, he ultimately stakes his entire argument on the claim that that there was never any external noise at all. The noise she hears, like the sounds of a seashell, are transmissions from a time before time that passes through her. Despite his denial of any real, accidental, noise, Freud's reading depends nonetheless on an implicit primal association between the ticking of a clock, the clicking of a camera shutter and the proto-photographic properties that he ascribes to the woman's clitoris.

It bears mentioning that this entire 'counter case' functions like a feminine photographic supplement to Freud's famous *Wolf Man* case.[9] The derivation of 'primal phantasies' here is directly related to his derivation of the 'primal scene' in the *Wolf Man* case history. The two cases are inverted images of one another and they demand to be read through one another. Whereas 'The Case of Paranoia Running Counter to the Disease' is devoted to female sexuality and primal phantasies, in *Wolf Man* castration and animal phobias are essential to Freud's reconstruction of the primal scene. It is also striking that, in *Wolf Man*, Freud invokes this case — and the concept of 'primal phantasies' more generally — to account for some discrepancies in his own clinical material about castration and sexual difference. After laboriously proving that the primal scene witnessed by the Wolf Man was a real lived experience rather than an imagined phantasy, in the famous closing passages of the case Freud famously leaves open the possibility of a convergence between the actual primal scene witnessed by the Wolf Man and the primal phantasies that undergird that real scene. More specifically, in that case history, despite the clinical evidence that women are the bearers of the threat of castration, Freud invokes the concept of 'primal phantasies' (at the expense of his own clinical evidence) in order to explain why animal phobias must always be a reflection of fear of castration by the father and not the mother.

In this case, however, unlike the primal scene that Freud describes in the *Wolf Man* case history, there is strictly *nothing* in the content of the woman's primal phantasy or in the paranoid delusion of the clicking clitoris by which that phantasy is transmitted that relies upon or reflects any psychic knowledge of sexual difference or castration. Indeed, one of the most fascinating aspects of this case is how thoroughly its depiction of fixation undermines all attempts to fix anything like sex or gender. For our purposes, however, it is sufficient to note that both primal phantasies and primal scenes are temporally un-locatable events that *structure figuration* without being themselves *accessible to figuration*. They are, by their nature, both un-documentable and unverifiable. In *Wolf Man*, the ostensibly 'real' primal scene makes itself known through a dream. Here, primal phantasies make themselves known by the way they knock knock on the doors of the psyche.

According to Freud's analysis, the paranoid photographic fantasy enables the woman to reconcile her regressive infantile sexual fixation on the mother with her (apparently) progressive heterosexual object choice. In other words, the photographic properties of her paranoid projection make it possible for her to live simultaneously in two times, with two different love objects. That said, it is not exactly clear that the woman is ever present at the scene as a woman or that the man ever occupies the position of a man for her. For this reason, this counter case still runs counter to Freud's attempt to assimilate it back into the generic model of paranoia based on homosexuality. Homosexuality loses all meaning in the context of this case as nothing in it permits us to ascribe the fixed sex or gender classifications that would allow us to classify the mode of attachment here as either homosexual or heterosexual.

Further, if we take a closer look at Freud's fixation on the clitoris, we find that it is a trace of the infantile phallic sexuality that is, for Freud, common to children of both sexes. In this sense, the pre-genital phallic clitoris is neither masculine nor feminine. It has no sexual relation to anything other than itself and its first others. Like the navel to which it bears some figural relation, it is a nodal trace of a primal attachment to the mother. The clitoris functions like a bell or a clock that recalls the mother's voice and eye.

The Photographic Medium: Freud, Photographer

At the end of this short case, which is something like a literary snapshot, Freud makes a series of somewhat odd concluding claims. In the penultimate paragraph, he suggests that it was only with the help of the paranoid delusion that his woman patient became able to desire a man at all. He then attempts to transpose the lessons learned from this 'counter' case about the specificity of feminine fixations back into a universal (and explicitly male) metapsychological paradigm. On the basis of this paranoid woman's counter example, he suggests that regressive fixations can, paradoxically, produce unusual and unpredictable forms of psychic movement. Thus, although the case concludes on the word 'fixation', which he there defines as 'manifestation of very early linkages — linkages which it is hard to resolve — between instincts and impressions and the objects involved in those impressions' that 'have the effect of bringing the development of the instincts concerned to a standstill' (272), Freud also ventures the paradoxical thought that the fixations of female sexuality and the fantasies that accompany them might be able to produce a more fluid way of thinking about the time of the subject more generally.

As we have seen, photography is not only the (presumably imagined) medium of the paranoid scenario *within* the case, it also determines the representational form *of* the case as well. On the basis of a story that he hears from the woman's lawyer, Freud produces a picture of her that exposes her sexual 'fixation' in order to demonstrate via that fixation (the clicking clitoris) that she herself has reproduced a photographic image of a universal primal phantasy.

It is Freud who becomes the imaginary photographer in this case. He talks about the woman with his lawyer friend, and then becomes fixated on exposing the scene that is developed and revealed through his reproduction of it. Freud's revelation of the 'clicking clitoris' exposes the body of his patient twice, in two times: his narration exposes the sex scene she had wanted to hide and, going further, produces a (quasi-pornographic) mental image of her aroused genitals on the basis of her (maybe not so paranoid?) fantasy that some men were talking about her and were planning on taking pictures of her exposed body. His interpretation performatively transforms her delusional auditory perceptions into a memorable photographic trace of her body in the very act of lovemaking. In this way, Freud becomes an actor in the scene that he is describing. He takes up the position of the male witness or the mother's eye. He photographically reproduces a scene of primal phantasy to which the reader then becomes privy.

But, if he is the photographer, her clicking clitoris is the camera that not only exposes the convolutions of her sexual life, but also serves as a transmitter of timeless fictions that it both records and reproduces. This prosthetic technological recording device re-produces images — in the present — of phantasies that, according to him, come from a prehistoric phylogenetically transmitted primal past.

Freud's reading presupposes that the primal image that he asks us to see or to hear cannot be reduced simply to biological sexual arousal even if it is also that as well. One of the most interesting things about this case is that the clicking clitoris cannot be understood as a body part in any simple sense. Sexual arousal is an effect rather than a cause of the structure proposed here. Throughout Freud's writings the clitoris is a dangerous supplement, a figure for the first knob or knot on which the primal attachments are fixated, a transmitter of images, sounds, neither purely imagined nor experienced. Relic from a time before time, the clicking clitoris keeps time out of joint.

Moreover, the uncanny extrasensory perceptions produced by her body part become the delivery device for his theory. In a chiasmic reversal, her delusional story becomes the basis for his theory of phantasy. Her fixation produces his phantasy; his fixation reproduces her phantasy. Freud's undeniably salacious photographic demonstration is not simply reducible to a desire to titillate or further evidence of his problematic treatment of women. Something stranger is at work. In the association he produces between the clock/camera sounds and the clitoris, he implicitly and irrevocably introduces a truly enigmatic, contingent, prosthetic, fantasmatic and temporally unstable dimension into his evolving theory of sexuality and subjectivity. After this case, despite his best efforts, Freud will systematically fail to produce a normative narrative of female sexuality. And although Freud attempts to appropriate the clicking clitoris to fix an image of the primal phantasies as a universal norm, the case itself provides a literary counterargument to that claim. Fixation is the primal node of figuration itself that sends his entire theory of sexuality veering.[10]

NOTES

1 Jean Laplanche and Jean-Bertrand Pontalis, *The Language of Psychoanalysis*, translated by Donald Nicholson-Smith (New York and London: W. W. Norton & Company, 1973), 162.
2 For a brilliant treatment of the importance of this word in Freud's writings, see Forbes Morlock's 'Freudian Idiom', *Angelaki: Journal of the Theoretical Humanities* 9:1 (2004), 103–23.
3 Steven Miller has pointed out to me that, in 'L'étourdit', Jacques Lacan coins the portmanteau word 'fixion' (a cross between fixation and fiction). See *Autres écrits* (Paris: Editions du Seuil, 2001), 482–3.
4 Sigmund Freud, *The Standard Edition of the Complete Psychological Works of Sigmund Freud* (hereafter *SE*), 24 vols, translated and edited by James Strachey, in collaboration with Anna Freud, assisted by Alix Strachey and Alan Tyson (London: The Hogarth Press and the Institute of Psycho-Analysis, 1953–74): here *SE* 7, 123–245.
5 Although Jean Laplanche does not specifically focus on fixation, his discussion of the singularity of the castration complex in the girl child (as opposed to the 'universal' status of the complex in the little boy) has influenced the arguments presented here. See *Problématiques II* (Paris: Presses universitaires de France, 1980).
6 Some of the most important treatments of the case were by analysts Jean Laplanche and Jean-Bertrand Pontalis, 'Fantasy and the Origins of Sexuality', *The International Journal of Psycho-Analysis* 49 (1968) and Guy Rosolato, 'Paranoia et scène primitive', *Essais sur le symbolique* (Paris: Gallimard, 1985), 199–241. For feminist readings of the case, see Naomi Schor's 'Female Paranoia: The Case for Psychoanalytic Criticism', *Yale French Studies* 62: *Feminist Readings: French Texts/American Contexts* (1981), 204–19; Mary Ann Doane, *The Desire to Desire: The Woman's Film of the 1940s* (Bloomington: Indiana University Press), 1987; and Patricia White, 'Female Spectator, Lesbian Specter: "The Haunting"' in *Inside/Out: Lesbian Theories, Gay Theories*, edited by Diana Fuss (New York: Routledge, 1991), 142–72. More recently, the case has been taken up by Judith Halberstam in *Skin Shows: Gothic Horror and the Technology of Monsters* (Durham, NC: Duke University Press, 1995), Mladen Dolar, *A Voice and Nothing More* (Cambridge: MIT

Press, 2006) and Sianne Ngai, *Ugly Feelings* (Cambridge, MA and London: Harvard University Press, 2007).

7 See Schor, 'Female Paranoia', 208.

8 See Laplanche and Pontalis, 'Fantasy'. In his later work, Laplanche builds on this early reading of the case to ground his later claims regarding 'enigmatic signifiers' and a generalized theory of seduction; see, in particular, *New Foundations for Psychoanalysis*, translated by David Macey (Cambridge, MA and Oxford: Basil Blackwell, 1989). Although I am greatly indebted to Laplanche's writings about the importance of fantasy, I am not convinced that he adequately accounts for the way questions of sexual difference inflect the very material that forms the basis for primal phantasies.

9 For a related reading of the photographic properties of the primal scene in the *Wolf Man*, see 'The Sexual Animal and the Primal Scene of Birth' in my book *The Mother in the Age of Mechanical Reproduction: Psychoanalysis, Photography, Deconstruction* (New York: Fordham University Press, 2012), 53–76.

10 This reference is a nod to Nicholas Royle's book *Veering: A Theory of Literature* (Edinburgh: Edinburgh University Press, 2011). The following passage on 'Nodism' was important to my thinking from the beginning: 'Nodism is a practice of reading that takes its orientation from a single word, phrase, or syllable in a work of literature. (...) It is a dreamy word, no doubt, and dreams are strangely knotty, as Freud saw. If you want to explore nodism, then, it helps to have a slightly dreamy disposition, or at least an interest in the oneiric' (210–11).

The Function and Field of Scansion in Jacques Lacan's Poetics of Speech

Isabelle Alfandary

Scansion is a device that has been famously introduced and theorized by Jacques Lacan as key to the practice of psychoanalysis. My contention in what follows is that scansion is anything but a detail in Lacan's theory and practice of analysis: it compels us to reconsider Lacan's supposedly metaphysical rapport to so-called 'full speech' as has been argued by Jacques Derrida in *The Post Card*.[1] Basing the analytic practice on a poetic device and a prosodic gesture deeply affects Lacan's conception of speech. Taking up the notion of scansion in Lacan's work brings us to one of the premises of his teachings, especially in the form they take right from the early seminars where the notion makes a premature entry into his lexicon. If not immediately thematized, scansion indeed emerges very early on in Lacan's work. It is interesting to follow its occurrences in the script of the seminar: it makes a premature and glaring entry on to the seminar scene, contemporaneous with the advent of the symbolic function, only to fade away just as quickly and reappear finally near the conclusion in the last moments of the seminar — as if scansion, having come about in its relation to the symbolic, were returning into the realm of the Real. Scansion is to be deduced logically right from the first seminars on the symbolic order, the heteronomy of which Lacan postulates, affirming that '[n]o prehistory allows us to efface the cut brought about by the heteronomy of the symbolic'.[2] But the cut actualized by the scansion, from which it proceeds, even if it is not simply a cut, as I will attempt to show, must be linked back to what Lacan, not long after his seminar on 'The Purloined Letter', conceives as being 'located outside of man, [which] is the very notion of the unconscious' (*Ecrits*, 393). In the seminar on 'The Non-Dupes Wander' ('Les non-dupes errent') (1974), scansion is explicitly tied to the repetition automatism brought to light by Freud in *Beyond the Pleasure Principle*. The child's playing with the spool of thread gives this scansion its structure (*Ecrits*, 497).

In so far as it engages time as well as the signifier, the signifier in its relationship to time, its sequence, its phrasing, its measure, scansion turns out to be one of the pivots of the technique of cure, at the exact articulation between theory and psychoanalytical practices, inseparable from the process of transference:

> It is an operation whose fundamental outlines are found in psychoanalytic technique. For it is insofar as the analyst intervenes by scanding [*sic*] the patient's discourse that an adjustment occurs in the pulsation of the rim through which the being that resides just shy of it must flow. The true and final mainspring of what constitutes transference is the expectation of this being's advent in relation to what I call 'the analyst's desire', insofar as something about the analyst's own position has remained unnoticed therein, at least up until now. This is why transference is a relationship that is essentially tied to time and its handling. (*Ecrits*, 716)

Scansion is a term used in prosody, which undoubtedly was not chosen at random by him who long before sitting on school benches learned how to scan the verses of Greek and Latin authors. Grounded in the most ancient times, the rules of scansion were handed down, uninterrupted, from generation to generation of poets and students. It relies on the existence of meter, whose structure it brings to light through the action of scanning. Scanning turns out to be a gesture of a very particular kind: through an action, which involves minimal intervention — usually the inscription of a mark, or the vocal realization of a measure or of an accent — is revealed, discerned, a rhythm subtended by what poeticians call an alternation of positions, an alternation of long or short positions (or of stressed or unstressed positions for languages like English that use an accentual meter). Scanning is thus bringing to light a hidden rhythm, making one hear a tempo, which at first is indiscernible, but works silently without saying its name.

There is, however, nothing mechanical about scanning. Accentuating consists in making a decision whose prosodic nature carries with it an implicit hermeneutics, and whose method of recognition is necessarily unstable. Every instance of prosody involves an indispensable licence: in order to correctly scan a verse, textbooks affirm, one must exercise one's judgement and choose what to accentuate. The rules that govern scansion in each language, if indeed they exist, leave it to the reader/listener to make discrete, exquisite and timely decisions that disambiguate a point of speech. In his essay

'Closing Statement: Linguistics and Poetics', Roman Jakobson writes: 'Far from being an abstract, theoretical scheme, meter — or in more explicit terms, *verse design* — underlies the structure of any single line — or, in logical terminology, any single *verse instance*. Design and instance are correlative concepts'.[3] The action of scanning is thus connected to the action of reading, halfway between performance and interpretation.

Scansion resembles a modality of punctuation; it is the punctuation of rhythm. Scansion comes back to accentuate by means of a cut. If one had to retain but one mark of punctuation in order to characterize the style of scansion proper to Lacan, one would hesitate between the long dash that interrupts without further ado, the hyphen that opens up an interval within a word, that separates it, splits it into two, and this sub-graphic notation that is the tonic accent, that does not itself belong to the utterance, but is added on top of it, is superimposed on it, in the manner of a tracing paper or an annotated musical score — an accent that manifests itself graphically, in the shape of a typographical accent or a cross.

But rhythm as the condition of possibility of the involvement of meaning is not itself the meaning. It is this gap between meaning and rhythm that scansion actualizes, more so, in fact, than it signals it. Traditionally, a critical function is conferred on scansion: that of disambiguating meaning. In *Rhetoric*, Aristotle deplores the flawed punctuation in some of Heraclitus' fragments:

> It is a general rule that a written composition should be easy to read and therefore easy to deliver. This cannot be so where there are many connecting words or clauses, or where punctuation is hard, as in the writings of Heraclitus. To punctuate Heraclitus is no easy task, because we often cannot tell whether a particular word belongs to what precedes or what follows it. Thus, at the outset of his treatise he says, 'Though this truth is always men understand it not', where it is not clear with which of the two clauses the word 'always' should be joined by the punctuation.[4]

If for Aristotle the ambiguities caused by the absence of punctuation are to be proscribed, and the significance of the adverb 'always' to be elucidated, it is mostly by resorting to the rules that govern scansion that such a semantic decision may be taken. In 'The Function and Field of Speech and Language in Psychoanalysis', a lecture delivered in 1953 on the topic of 'Empty Speech and Full Speech in the Psychoanalytic Realization of the Subject', Lacan introduces scansion as the means to a cure that he deems inseparable from the analyst's art:

Let us focus instead on the *hic et nunc* to which some analysts feel we should confine the handling of analysis. (...)

The analyst's art must, on the contrary, involve suspending the subject's certainties until their final mirages have been consumed. And it is in the subject's discourse that their dissolution must be punctuated.

Indeed, however empty his discourse may seem, it is so only if taken at face value — the value that justifies Mallarmé's remark, in which he compares common use of language to the exchange of a coin whose obverse and reverse no longer bear but eroded faces, and which people pass from hand to hand 'in silence'. This metaphor suffices to remind us that speech, even when almost completely worn out, retains its value as a *tessera*.

Even if it communicates nothing, discourse represents the existence of communication; even if it denies the obvious, it affirms that speech constitutes truth; even if it is destined to deceive, it relies on faith in testimony.

Thus the psychoanalyst knows better than anyone else that the point is to figure out [*entendre*] to which 'part' of this discourse the significant term is relegated, and this is how he proceeds in the best of cases: he takes the description of an everyday event as a fable addressed as a word to the wise, a long prosopopœia as a direct interjection, and, contrariwise, a simple slip of the tongue as a highly complex statement, and even the rest of a silence as the whole lyrical development it stands in for.

It is, therefore, a propitious punctuation that gives meaning to the subject's discourse. This is why the ending of the session — which current technique makes into an interruption that is determined purely by the clock and, as such, takes no account of the thread of the subject's discourse — plays the part of a scansion which has the full value of an intervention by the analyst that is designed to precipitate concluding moments. Thus we must free the ending from its routine framework and employ it for all the useful aims of analytic technique (*Ecrits*, 208–9; my underlining).

This passage articulates the logic that subtends Lacanian scansion conceived as 'propitious punctuation' and which leads Lacan to turn scansion into an element central to the analytical technique on modes that range from the repetition of an utterance by the analyst to the interruption of the session on a verbal sequence. One must add without delay, to paraphrase Heidegger's famous formula, that the essence of this element of psychoanalytical technique is that there is absolutely nothing technical about it. The very famous and violently decried 'variable-length session' that caused the author certain setbacks which had a lasting effect on his institutional trajectory[5] finds in scansion its logical justification, its poetic reason. Scansion allows the subject to hear, to *realize* — literally — to render real, 'palpable', to borrow Jakobson's term, stemming from the reality of the cut, his position of imaginary grasping in relation to this regime of speech in cure that Lacan calls empty speech (*Ecrits*, 211). In this regard, scansion acts as a lever, and this is what establishes it as a means to a psychoanalytic act: the accentuation carried out by the act of scanning causes — anything but mechanically, or magically — full speech to occur in empty speech.

In his Rome address, he reports a previously unseen experience of the cure of a typical obsessive:[6]

> The subject's resistance may become completely disconcerted. From then on, his alibi — hitherto unconscious — begins to unveil itself to him, and we see him passionately seek the why and wherefore of so much effort. I would not say so much about it if I had not been convinced — in experimenting with what have been called my 'short sessions', at a stage in my career that is now over — that I was able to bring to light in a certain male subject fantasies of anal pregnancy, as well as a dream of its resolution by Caesarean section, in a time frame in which I would normally still have been listening to his speculations on Dostoyevsky's artistry. In any case, I am not here to defend this procedure, but to show that it has a precise dialectical meaning in analytic technique. (*Ecrits*, 259–60)

For Lacan, scansion is deduced from clinical practice, from the analyst's intervention, whose inextricable fabric of clinical as well as institutional effects he was far from having anticipated. Scansion first and foremost fulfils a maieutic function, of an undoubtedly metaphysical ascendance — that of 'bringing to light' the content of the unconscious fantasy. Far from seeking to make it first the keystone of his practice, or from defending it to and against everyone, Lacan justifies in 'The Function and Field of Speech and Language in Psychoanalysis' the heuristic value of this technical point. In 1966, with the publication of *Ecrits*, he returns to the 'Rome Discourse' adding a note that marks the importance of the clinical as well as institutional — ethical — stake of the said technique: '(Added in 1966:) Whether a chipped stone or a cornerstone, my forte is that I haven't given in on this point' (268).

The function of scansion is to accentuate a 'part' of the subject's discourse to make it resonate, to isolate a signifier, to make it audible through its material and phonemic plasticity in its irreducible ambiguity, its phonic texture: in so doing, the analyst masters the 'ending' (*chute*) that he brings forward. This ending, which is not without resemblance to the punch line constitutive of the joke, is an ending whose value is the sublation of the signifier. The effect of sense — the ambiguity with which sense is weaved and which is to be experienced as a result of scansion — is constituted retrospectively by a cut first suspended from non-sense (*hors-sens*), from an undecidability of meaning that prohibits or inter-dicts (*inter-dit*) the subject, and, if need be, moves him with respect to his speech, gives him a glimpse of the gap that separates him from himself so long as he is talking: in so far as the signifier falls and befalls him.

Lacan argues that, without the 'duplicity' that scansion possibly brings to light, the determinism of the Freudian unconscious would be inconceivable: 'This is so clearly Freud's doctrine that there is no other meaning to give to his term *overdetermination*, or to his necessary requirement that for a symptom to occur there must be at least a duality, at least two conflicts at work, one current and one old. Without this fundamental duality of signifier and signified, no psychoanalytic determinism is conceivable'.[7] What scansion plays on is precisely the possibility for the signifier to open on to more than one signified, for the spoken chain to make audible in an encrypted form — that scansion untangles — one or several hidden signifier(s): '[W]hat is at stake in analytic discourse, is always the following — you give a different reading to the signifiers that are enunciated (*ce qui s'énonce de signifiant*) than what they signify'.[8] For this reason, the analyst must not balk at anorthography: on the contrary, he must count on its possibility. This is the very structure of the relationship that connects (as much as it disconnects) signifier and signified, what Lacan calls 'the evasion of sense', from which scansion, thwarting the logic of signification through the untimely interruption it represents in the chain of sense, proceeds.

In the praxis of cure, scansion fulfils what Lacan calls 'the function of the signifier':

But notwithstanding this, are we now at the level of the function of the signifier? In a thermoelectric machine supported by feedback the signifier is not employed. Why not? Isolating the signifier as such requires something else which, like any dialectical distinction in the first instance presents itself in a paradoxical manner. There is appropriate use of the signifier whenever, at the level of the receiver, what is important is not the effect of the content of the message, nor the triggering in the organ of a given reaction due to the appearance of a hormone, but this — that at the message's point of arrival one makes a note of it. (*Psychoses*, 188)

Thus practised, scansion redoubles the function of the signifier, relies on its very structure to isolate it. In this sense, it does not first nor essentially focus on the signification of the utterance (*énoncé*) ('the content of the message'), but rather on the sense of the enunciation (*énonciation*). Through scansion, the analyst 'makes a note of [the message]', becomes 'receiver', to be understood in both the organic and the communicational senses of the term, in the manner in which the symptom, taking into account its genesis, may be understood by the subject as the signifier's acknowledgement of receipt. 'What do symptoms result from, if it's not from the human organism's being implicated in something that is structured like a language, whereby such and such an element of its functioning will come into play as a signifier? (...) Hysteria is a question centred on a signifier that remains enigmatic as to its meaning' (*Psychoses*, 190). In transference, the analyst becomes the receiver of the signifier, drifting and allowing some of its resulting effects, otherwise repressed, to be projected on to his/her person. In order to do that, its isolation, made possible by scansion, is indispensable to a clinic that has the signifier in its line of sight: 'It's the acknowledgment of receipt [*l'accusé de réception*] that is essential to communication insofar as it is not significant, but signifying' (*Psychoses*, 188). The analyst's acknowledgement of receipt does not stem from a moral premiss, but from a clinic of the subject, from putting into practice what Lacan calls 'proper use of the signifier'. Through his thesis of the primacy of the signifier and its proper use, Lacan definitively breaks away from Saussure whose founding of the sign theory is hence defeated: 'Indeed, it isn't as all or nothing that something is a signifier, it's to the extent that something constituting a whole, the sign, exists and signifies precisely nothing. This is where the order of the signifier, insofar as it differs from the order of meaning begins' (*Psychoses*, 189). Deriving from Saussure's theory of 'the opposition between the signifier and the signified' that he shatters to pieces by means of the primacy of the order of the signifier, Lacan argues for the disjunction and the asymmetry of the orders of the signifier and the signified, and puts an end to the reassuring Saussurean parallelism of the 'famous schema of the two curves'.[9]

No more than the outcome of throwing a die may be postulated can the good fortune of scansion be decreed: if it falls under an implacable logical necessity which is that of the unconscious, scansion, which virtually cannot be calculated, produces effects that come to light only afterwards (*après-coup*). This action that presupposes cutting-off makes sense (fall), and 'gives its sense to the discourse of the subject', as a result of an untimely and interpretative process. Scansion enables the tuning into the text of the unconscious. In the postscript to the published version of Seminar XI, Lacan elaborates on what the analyst's work of reading involves: 'Where it is our duty to interpret, it wouldn't be bad, to begin with, if "reading" were heard and understood for what it means. May speech be the place where what is said is not to be read — this is what startles the analyst, past the aha moment where he, like a roly-poly toy, tumbles to give himself up to listening until he can no longer stand up'.[10]

Weft of Discourse

Scansion falls under what Lacan calls the 'weft' (*trame*) of discourse that it tears and spaces out: it is the punctuation of the weft, on the very surface of the weft, which is to be understood at once as the continuum of the 'signifying chain', 'the continuity of the signifier' (*Psychoses*, 263), as well as in its textile sense — text, fabric — taken from Freud's dream intertext in *Traumdeutung*: 'The unconscious is fundamentally structured, woven, chained, meshed, by language' (*Psychoses*, 119). The incomparably famous quilting point, indeed, the true *punctum*, of Lacan's work, that he borrows from the upholsterer — who serves as a counterpoint to the figure of the Goethian weaver that Freud mentions — in order to represent the function of the signifier, is to be understood as the punctuation of the weft under the action of the needle:[11] 'Everything radiates out from and is organized around this signifier, similar to these little lines of force that an upholstery button forms on the surface of material' (*Psychoses*, 268).

Lacan delivers a rhetorical reading of Freudian processes of condensation and displacement as metaphor and metonymy,[12] systematizing, in the shape of an inventory of tropes, the formalization of the unconscious first undertaken by Freud in *The Interpretation of Dreams*:

Periphrasis, hyperbaton, ellipsis, suspension, anticipation, retraction, negation, digression, and irony, these are the figures of style (Quintilian's *figuræ sententiarum*), just as catachresis, litotes, antonomasia, and hypotyposis are the tropes, whose names strike me as the most appropriate ones with which to label these mechanisms. Can one see here mere manners of speaking, when it is the figures themselves that are at work in the rhetoric of the discourse the analysand actually utters? (*Ecrits*, 433)

The goal of this *gradus ad Parnassum* he engages in and that he extends to figures of prosody is to account for the unconscious structured like a language which responds to tropes that are strictly established, logically constructed and articulated among themselves — rhetoric being the very structure of the unconscious as language, and not a mere manner of speaking. In the seminar on *The Psychoses*, Lacan elaborates on the intimate relationship that ties the mother tongue to the unconscious of the subject who speaks it, the symptom to the system of the signifier:

> A system of signifiers, a language, has certain characteristics that specify the syllables, the usage of words, the locutions into which they are grouped, and this conditions what happens in the unconscious, down to its most original fabric. If the unconscious is as Freud depicts it, a pun can in itself be the linchpin that supports a symptom, a pun that doesn't exist in a related language. (119)

In arguing that the unconscious is structured like a language, Lacan merely draws linguistic conclusions from Freud's discoveries by translating them into tropes of rhetoric. There is more here than an attempt to justify: this point of rhetoric is crucial to Lacan's teaching. It is from this point that his return to Freud is supported; it is from this point that his discourse takes a turn towards a more poetic conception:

> When Freud tells us about the unconscious, he does not say that it is structured in a certain way. And yet he says it, insofar as the laws that he puts forward — the laws of composition of this unconscious — exactly coincide with the some of the most fundamental laws of composition discourse. Furthermore, in the unconscious's mode of articulation are lacking all kinds of elements that are involved in our common discourse: causal links, he will say, with respect to the dream or negation, only to correct himself immediately afterwards and show us how causality is expressed in some other way in the dream. There you have it: the field already identified, defined, circumscribed, explored, or even ploughed by Freud. This is where we return in our attempt to formulate — to go further — to formalize what we have just called the primordial structural laws of language.[13]

For Lacan, the reason why the analyst must have an understanding of rhetoric is that his listening, his understanding is ultimately a mode of analysis that cannot ignore the parts of discourse that rhetoric teaches. To return to the passage quoted earlier, Lacan explicitly casts the analyst's work in linguistic terms:

> [T]he point is to figure out [*entendre*] to which 'part' of this discourse the significant term is relegated, and this is how he proceeds in the best of cases: he takes the description of an everyday event as a fable addressed as a word to the wise, a long prosopopœia as a direct interjection, and, contrariwise, a simple slip of the tongue as a highly complex statement, and even the rest of a silence as the whole lyrical development it stands in for. It is, therefore, a propitious punctuation that gives meaning to the subject's discourse. (*Ecrits*, 209)

Scansion is part of the logic of what Freud calls in 1912 'free-floating attention', 'gleichschwebende Aufmerksamkeit' — and Lacan remarks that attention is explicitly said to be 'equally' floating, and in no way fluctuating (*Ecrits*, 394) in it. The analyst must not favour any element of the patient's discourse in order to pinpoint 'the significant term'. The suspension of deliberation that 'free-floating attention' implies is only a condition of subjective passivation for a puncturingly sharp, punctuating listening of the signifier, for a listening in the guise of a performance that I propose to qualify as poetic in so far as it presupposes a rhetorico-phonetico-enunciative translation in the wake of the one developed by Freud in *The Interpretation of Dreams*. The analyst's 'extra ear'[14] implies a listening in translation that is inseparable from a poetic know-how, a know how to undo, from a *poeîn*, from a genre, from a gesture that remains to be invented:

> May one of your ears become as deaf as the other one must be acute. And that is the one that you should lend to listen for sounds and phonemes, words, locutions, and sentences, not forgetting pauses, scansions, cuts, periods, and parallelisms, for it is in these that the word-for-word transcription can be prepared, without which analytic intuition has no basis or object. (*Ecrits*, 394)

Facts of Prosody

Expanding on Freud's 'fact[s] of syntax' ('fait[s] de syntaxe')[15], as Lacan superbly formulates it, the latter adds what I take to be 'facts of prosody'. Between syntax and prosody, there is but one line that Lacan crosses, that he allows himself to cross from the properties of the signifier. It is because 'a dream has the structure of a sentence' (*Ecrits*, 221) that the psychoanalyst, as conceived by Freud, could not do without knowledge from the liberal arts. Enumerating Freud's list and taking over from it, Lacan invokes several disciplines with the aim to perfect and hone the formation of the analyst:

> The list of disciplines Freud considered important sister sciences for an ideal Department of Psychoanalysis is well known. Alongside psychiatry and sexology we find 'the history of civilization, mythology, the psychology of religions, literary history, and literary criticism' (…) For my part, I would be inclined to add: rhetoric, dialectic (in the technical sense this term takes on in Aristotle's *Topics*), grammar, and poetics — the supreme pinnacle of the æsthetics of language — which would include the neglected technique of witticisms. While these subject headings may sound somewhat old-fashioned to certain people, I would not hesitate to endorse them as a return to our sources. (*Ecrits*, 238)

With this proposition, and singularly, poetics conceived in the Hegelian tradition of aesthetics as 'supreme pinnacle of the aesthetics of language', Lacan intends to return to the author of *Traumdeutung* whose rhetorical base he recalls:

> What is important is the version of the text, and that, Freud tells us, is given in the telling of the dream — that is, in its rhetoric. Ellipsis and pleonasm, hyperbaton or syllepsis, regression, repetition, apposition — these are the syntactical displacements; metaphor, catachresis, antonomasia, allegory, metonymy, and synecdoche — these are the semantic condensations; Freud teaches us to read in them the intentions — whether ostentatious or demonstrative, dissimulating or persuasive, retaliatory or seductive — with which the subject modulates his oneiric discourse. (*Ecrits*, 221–2)

In invoking poetics, Lacan is not randomly choosing a discipline. He is not even expressing his taste for poetry — that of T. S. Eliot, for instance, a few lines of which he quotes in his Rome speech. Unlike Jakobson, Lacan does not separate poetics from linguistics.[16] Like Jakobson, he understands 'poetics' as the function of language that is centred on the message itself:

> The set (*Einstellung*) toward the MESSAGE as such, focus on the message for its own sake, is the POETIC function of language. This function cannot be productively studied out of touch with the general problems of language, and, on the other hand, the scrutiny of language requires a thorough consideration of its poetic function. Any attempt to reduce the sphere of poetic function to poetry or to confine poetry to poetic function would be a delusive oversimplification. Poetic function is not the sole function of verbal art but only its dominant, determining function, whereas in all other verbal activities it acts as a subsidiary, accessory constituent. This function, by promoting the palpability of signs, deepens the fundamental dichotomy of signs and objects. (CS, 356)

Poetics is not the attribute of a single literary genre:

> The case of linguistics is subtler as it must take into account the difference between the enunciated and enunciation, that is, the impact of the subject who speaks as such (and not of the subject of science). This is why linguistics revolves around something else — namely the battery of signifiers, whose prevalence over signification effects must be ensured. Here too antinomies appear, scaled to the extremism of the position adopted in object selection. What is clear is that one can go very far in the elaboration of the effects of language, since one can construct a poetics that owes no more to references to the mind of the poet than to its incarnation. (*Ecrits*, 730–1)

What can be regarded as a poetics of speech in Lacan's work stems from the discovery of 'the difference between the enunciated and enunciation'. The difference in question that post-Saussurean linguistics translates is to be deduced from Freud's discovery of the unconscious, from the difference that the hypothesis of the unconscious itself carries.

On reading the definition proposed by Jakobson, one understands why Lacan retained poetics as the queen of 'sister' disciplines: the 'messages' of the unconscious, in so far as it is structured like a language, are akin to code, to what Jakobson defines as the 'palpability of signs'. In affirming the primacy of the signifier,[17] Lacan explores a bit more what Jakobson calls the 'fundamental dichotomy of signs and objects'.[18] This is not surprising from the moment that one of the keystones of cure lies in the poetic notion — if indeed there is one — of scansion.[19] In the session dedicated to the seminar on *The Psychoses*, where Lacan resorts to the metaphor of the quilting point in order to account for the articulation from the signifier to the signified, he defines scansion as that 'which plays on the properties of the signifier, with the implicit questioning that scansion contains and which extends to coercion' (*Psychoses*, 260). Poetry is not alone in holding poetic function as 'dominant, determining': this function ends up being essential even in unconscious activity. The Lacanian poetic inflection of what was Freud's rhetorical approach relies on the Jakobsonian conception of poetics as belonging wholly to the field of linguistics. The poetics that Lacan elevates to the status of a discipline indispensable to psychoanalytic experience is conceived as 'an exact knowledge of the order proper to the signifier and its properties'.[20]

Because of his poetic inclination, Lacan tends to treat the Freudian sentence in one utterance that through its structure and materiality resembles a line of poetry:

We must thus take up Freud's work again starting with the *Traumdeutung* [*The Interpretation of Dreams*] to remind ourselves that a dream has the structure of a sentence or, rather, to keep to the letter of the work, of a rebus — that is, of a form of writing, of which children's dreams are supposed to represent the primordial ideography, and which reproduces, in adults' dreams, the simultaneously phonetic and symbolic use of signifying elements found in the hieroglyphs of ancient Egypt and in the characters still used in China. (*Ecrits*, 221)

The poetician-analyst's adage could be formulated as follows: there's no rhyme without a reason coming from the formations of the unconscious. Erik Porge rightly reminds us: 'If it is not random, it is for a reason. Which reason? The reasonance, that which reasons and resonates, according to Francis Ponge's word that Lacan borrows and goes so far as to ask: "That which reasonates is the origin of the *res* that reality is made of?"[21]

In *The Post Card*, Jacques Derrida famously criticized Lacan for his phonetic and logocentric shift of Freud's conception of the unconscious.[22] If, however, one stops at scansion, and at the cardinal place it holds in the apparatus of the Lacanian cure, its phonemic support is more ambiguous and more uncertain than it seems at first — if only because, with Jakobson, it can be argued that '[n]o doubt, verse is primarily a recurrent "figure of sound". Primarily, always, but never uniquely' (CS, 367). Scansion cannot merely be reduced to what the linguist calls the 'phonetic isolationism' that Derrida deplores: not belonging to the speech that it disappropriates as a result of the re-mark from which it proceeds, it in effect shuffles the cards of speaking and writing, and becomes part of an economy of the absolutely singular mark, of what I will risk calling a speech *in writing*.

NOTES

1 Jacques Derrida, *The Post Card: From Socrates to Freud and Beyond*, translated by Alan Bass (Chicago: University of Chicago Press, 1987)
2 Jacques Lacan, *Ecrits*, translated by Bruce Fink (New York and London: W. W. Norton, 2007), 392. Hereafter abbreviated as *Ecrits*.
3 Roman Jakobson, 'Closing Statement: Linguistics and Poetics' in *Style in Language*, edited by Thomas Sebeok (New York and London: The Technology Press of MIT and John Wiley & Sons, 1960), 364. Hereafter abbreviated as CS.
4 Aristotle, *Rhetoric,* translated by W. Rhys Roberts (New York: Cosimo, Inc., 2010), 128.
5 Lacan had to explain himself on this practice to the Société psychanalytique de Paris (SPP) (Paris Psychoanalytical Society) on four different occasions from 1951 (when he was urged to restrict himself to the commonly held standard) to 1953. This point about technique certainly impacted the 1953 split that led Lacan, then President of the Paris Psychoanalytical Society, followed by Lagache, Dolto and Favez-Boutonier, to resign from the SPP and create the Société française de psychanalyse (SFP) (French Psychoanalytic Society). The same year, he was notified by the secretary of the International Psychoanalytic Association (IPA) that he was considered as having resigned. In a letter written on 14 July 1953 to Rudolph Loewenstein, Lacan's analyst from 1932 to 1938, he talks about the significance of variable-length sessions,

especially in didactic cures in order to limit rationalizations that amount to resistance.
6   The fantasy reported by Lacan is a distant echo of the fantasies of Freud's 'Rat Man'.
7   Jacques Lacan, *The Psychoses: The Seminars of Jacques Lacan, Book III: 1955–1956*, translated by Russell Grigg, edited by Jacques-Alain Miller (New York and London: W. W. Norton, 1993), 119. Hereafter abbreviated as *Psychoses*.
8   Jacques Lacan, *On Feminine Sexuality: The Limits of Love and Knowledge (1972–1973)*, translated by Bruce Fink, edited by Jacques-Alain Miller (New York and London: W. W. Norton, 1999), 37.
9   'The opposition between the signifier and the signified lies, as you know, at the basis of Ferdinand de Saussure's linguistic theory. It has been expressed in the famous schema of the two curves. At the upper level Saussure locates the series of what he calls thoughts — without the slightest conviction, since his theory consists precisely in reducing this term to that of the signified insofar as it is distinct from both the signifier and the thing — and he insists above all upon the aspect of amorphous mass. It's what, for our part, we shall provisionally call the sentimental mass of the current of discourse, a confused mass in which appear units, islands, an image, an object, a feeling, a cry, an appeal. It's a continuum, whereas underneath is the signifier as a pure chain of discourse, a succession of words, in which nothing is isolable' (*Psychoses*, 261).
10 Jacques Lacan, *Les quatre concepts fondamentaux de la psychoanalyse* (Paris: Seuil, 1973), 252; my translation.
11 'Whether it be a sacred text, a novel, a play, a monologue, or any conversation whatsoever, allow me to represent the function of the signifier by a spatializing device, which we have no reason to deprive ourselves of. This point around which all concrete analysis of discourse must operate I shall call a quilting point. When the upholsterer's needle, which as entered at the moment of *God found faithful in all his threats*, reappears, it's all over, the chap says, I'm going to join the faithful troops. Were we to analyse this scene as a musical score, we should see that this is the point at which the signified and the signifier are knotted together, between the still floating mass of meanings that are actually circulating between these two characters and the text' (*Psychoses*, 267–8).
12 In the seminar *The Psychoses*, after having analysed Hugo's metaphor 'His sheaf was neither miserly nor spiteful', and after having introduced his other rhetoric that is the metonymy, Lacan declares: 'In general what Freud calls condensation is what in rhetoric one calls metaphor, what he calls displacement is metonymy. The structuration, the lexical existence of the entire signifying apparatus, is determinant for the phenomena present in neurosis, since the signifier is the instrument by which the missing signified

expresses itself. It's for this reason that in focusing attention back onto the signifier we are doing nothing other than returning to the starting point of Freudian discovery' (221).
13 Jacques Lacan, *Les Formations de l'inconscient* (Paris: Seuil, 1998), 66. My translation.
14 'Let us note, moreover, that the third ear, which I used to deny the existence of the uncertain beyond of an occult sense, is nevertheless in fact the invention of an author, Theodor Reik, who is rather sensible in his tendency to adapt himself to a realm that is shy of speech. But what need can an analyst have for an extra ear, when it sometimes seems that two are already too many, since he runs headlong into the fundamental misunderstanding brought on by the relationship of understanding? I repeatedly tell my students: "Don't try to understand!" and leave this nauseating category to Karl Jaspers and his consorts' (*Ecrits*, 394).
15 'But in order to obviate any misunderstanding, let me make it clear that this register of truth must be followed to the letter [*à la lettre*]; in other words, symbolic determination, which Freud calls overdetermination, must be considered first as a fact of syntax, if one wishes to grasp its analogical effects' (*Ecrits*, 391, translation modified).
16 'Insistence on keeping poetics apart from linguistics is warranted only when the field of linguistics appears to be illicitly restricted, for example, when the sentence is viewed by some linguists as the highest analysable construction or when the scope of linguistics is confined to grammar alone or uniquely to nonsemantic questions of external form or to the inventory of denotative devices with no reference to free variations' (CS, 352).
17 'And not only does the signifier play a big role there as the signified does, but it plays the fundamental role. In fact, what characterizes language is the system of signifiers as such' (*Psychoses*, 119).
18 'The supremacy of the poetic function over the referential function does not obliterate the reference but makes it ambiguous' (CS, 371).
19 The entire second half of Roman Jakobson's essay on 'Linguistics and Poetics' is dedicated to the comparative analysis of types of versification, especially in English and Russian meters, and reads as a well-reasoned treatise on scansion.
20 'The signifier doesn't just provide an envelope, a receptacle for meaning. It polarizes it, structures it, and brings it into existence. Without an exact knowledge of the order proper to the signifier and its properties, it's impossible to understand anything whatsoever, I don't mean about psychology — it suffices that one restrict it in a certain way — but certainly about psychoanalytic experience' (*Psychoses*, 296–7)
21 Erik Porge, 'L'insaisissable objet du savoir dans l'analyse', *Essaim* 30 (2014), 21. My translation.
22 Derrida, *The Post Card*.

Small Experimental Action

SARAH WOOD

> ... 'the literary thing' is an act to come ...
> Shoshana Felman[1]

> ... Thinking is an experimental action carried out with small amounts of energy, in the same way as a general shifts small figures about on a map before setting his large bodies of troops in motion.
> ... Sigmund Freud[2]

First, there has to be this movement that is a movement of separation. To write, or read, one must become smaller and *act alone*. I am relying on you to understand that this is not, or not only, a naive remark. I am relying on something about reading that is able to turn and be turned, turning over and turning on unforeseen inscriptions, forms of agency, types of action and other emergent effects.

To think about why, and how, literature and psychoanalysis matter today, it might be important to loosen hold on the names and the institutions that correspond to them, and risk going for a more rigorously unreliable form of knowledge-production. If, as the introduction to this *Open Questions* volume puts it, 'literature and psychoanalysis begin with an engagement with that which one can never master or go beyond', then I will have to go some of the way *by coracle*. The voyage of the coracle from Robert Louis Stevenson's *Treasure Island* suggests a certain mode of thinking. To go by coracle may mean having to abandon agency and be directed by the winds, the movements of the sea, as if by chance or fortune. As Shoshana Felman has said: 'reading is rather a risky business whose outcome and full consequences can never be known in advance'.[3] Polemic, manifesto, debate, making a case, critique, teaching — these are all something different, requiring the making and taking of positions. Reading is, at least in some ways, a smaller deal, and a different commitment. For example, to 'tune into the forms of resistance present in the text', as Felman suggests we do in *What Does a Woman Want*, tends to displace the grander ambitions of critical reading (6). These may include the wish to identify, elaborate and appropriate as knowledge a scene on which reading appears, or can be made to appear. The attunement necessary to read requires susceptibility, flexibility, sensibility and an interest in chance as well as in the rigour of reading. It involves something like going into unknown and unconquerable territory. (The territory cannot be taken because language does not *belong*. Derrida notes language's 'curious tendency', as a system of marks, to 'increase simultaneously the reserves of random indeterminacy and the powers of coding or overcoding, in other words, of control and self-regulation'.[4]) These are some of the reasons why this essay is called 'Small Experimental Action' — a phrase derived from Freud's account of thinking. The name draws attention to *thinking* as an experimental action, and because it is also the name of a piece of writing it draws attention to *writing* as an experimental action, and because it is concerned with reading literary and psychoanalytic texts it draws attention to *reading* as an experimental action. Who performs these acts? you may wonder. To think about that, I will draw on some of the things Freud says about *das Ich*, the I, or the ego.

Early in *Jacques Lacan and the Adventures of Insight*, Felman describes an untroubled and, as it turned out, transformative first reading of Lacan's *Ecrits*. She read the text, I would say, in curiosity: 'without fighting with it, without trying to appropriate it as a piece of academic information. (...) It appealed to me in the way literature appeals to me.'[5] It's a big book, the *Ecrits*, but you notice in her account the lightness of the experience as well as the depth and lastingness of the reading effect.

The coracle's lightness is one of its advantages. The narrator of *Treasure Island*, who as a boy heard about it, and found it, and took it, and from whom I take it today, notices this: 'The thing was extremely small, even for me'.[6] When you are small enough to fit in a coracle, you may be too young to know exactly what it is. At first it's just 'Ben Gunn's boat' (120). The boat is 'home-made' and doesn't receive a name straight away. The word 'coracle' arrives afterwards. Jim Hawkins explains he had:

not yet seen a coracle, such as the Ancient Britons made, but I have seen one since, and I can give you no fairer idea of Ben Gunn's boat than by saying it was like the first and worst coracle ever made by man. But the great advantage of the coracle it certainly possessed, for it was exceedingly light and portable. (*TI*, 120–1)

Even when it does get a name, and some history, the coracle is strange. Its roughness is associated with its unprecedentedness. There even seems to be a kind of mad excellence in its being so badly made. Such a bad example may not even *be* one. It is both new and ancient, at least initially only accessible through language's capacity to give an idea, to refer to the unknown by means of the known, to transfer. What it is, what it can do, this not-even-a-coracle, has to be read, learned, even divined. You have to get on board. In this respect, and Stevenson's rhyming 'first' and 'worst' encourages me to say it, the coracle is like an oracle. It is aphoristic and, as I hope to show, one must obey, one must decipher its violent or more subtle teachings. It comes without instructions and you learn its ways partly by means of enactment, as in reading, as if it were something at the edge of language and of experience, inviting us to take a chance on it or in it. The etymology of 'coracle' dissolves into speculation, but the word may or may not derive from Latin *corium*, meaning skin, hide or leather — which it was largely made of — and thence from Greek χόριον, the membrane (or caul) enclosing a foetus, the inside of an egg, intestinal membrane, sometimes used as sausage-casing, or the skin of the eye. Perhaps first of all the coracle asks its passenger to surrender and be passively carried along.

What might this have to do with psychoanalysis, this borrowed, 'rude lop-sided framework' of wood covered in 'goatskin, with the hair on the inside' (*TI*, 120)? It has skin, is partly skin. This makes it a figure for the ego Freud describes as being 'like an external, cortical layer of the id'.[7] Didier Anzieu's work on this Freudian skin ego is well known.[8] I am drifting into analogy. This is part of my small experimental action. What does it mean to say, 'I commit myself to words', as if the enterprise began there? Am I thinking or just reading? Freud, who was interested in analogy as well as quite frequently using analogies, says in 'Anxiety and Instinctual Life': 'analogies, it is true, decide nothing, but they can make one feel more at home' (*AI*, 72). He was never more uncannily funny than in the *New Introductory Lectures*.

Like all made things, the coracle carries traces of violent processes (lopping, skinning, turning that skin inside out). It has features that would make it possible for someone to sit in the coracle and move it: 'one thwart, set as low as possible, a kind of stretcher in the bows, and a double paddle for propulsion' (*TI*, 120). These make it more rigid. It promises to be useful for the onward movement of the narrative and the advancement of the purposes of the book's young hero: 'to slip out under cover of the night, cut the *Hispaniola* adrift, and let her go ashore where she fancied' (*TI*, 121). Slipping out and cutting adrift are characteristic moves for Jim Hawkins himself. He constantly, one might say compulsively, escapes — slips off, without analysis. He's not interested in power or gold. Here he goes with the tide, through the night from 'How My Sea Adventure Began' to 'The Ebb-tide Runs', and on to singlehanded symbolic victory in 'I Strike the Jolly Roger'. Throughout the book, Jim's adventures accommodate alliances and betrayals, fearless moral stands and more ambiguous sympathies. Sometimes he has to hide and sometimes he fights. A few times he acts on impulse. Everything contributes to staying afloat and continuing the Treasure Island voyage.

Perhaps we should pick up the story itself here, from the moment Jim Hawkins says goodbye to his mother. At Bristol, Jim's party, led by local worthies Dr Livesey and Squire Trelawney, finds the ship *Hispaniola* and a captain to sail her. They also, with suspicious ease, come across an immensely charismatic one-legged ship's cook, Long John Silver. Jim likes this man and is flattered by his attention. Silver quickly gathers a dodgy-looking but apparently compliant crew and off they all go to sea. As they near the island, Jim, sleeping in an apple barrel (a proto-coracle, I would say), wakes to overhear Silver and the crew plotting to mutiny and take the treasure. He tells the Captain, the Doctor and the Squire, and because they are outnumbered they decide to go along with the deception until after the treasure has been found.

When the ship nears Treasure Island, Silver and the would-be mutineers go ashore. So, on an inexplicable 'mad' impulse, does Jim (*TI*, 72). He stays clear of the mutineers but meets Ben Gunn, a crazy marooned ex-pirate, who agrees to help him in return for a share of the treasure and passage home. In a section narrated by the Captain, we hear how he, with the Doctor, the Squire and a few loyal men, come ashore and occupy an abandoned stockade on the island. The remaining crew still on the *Hispaniola* raise the pirate flag. A number of mutineers are killed in an attack on the stockade and there is death and injury on the Captain's side as well. Then, driven by disgust at the confined and now corpse-strewn stockade, and envy of the Doctor, who has gone off into the woods to find Ben Gunn, Jim suddenly runs off into the island a second time. He finds the coracle, gets out to the *Hispaniola* under cover of darkness, and cuts the ship loose.

The ship and the coracle are at the mercy of the tides and currents, and Jim spends the rest of the night afloat and adrift. Then the coracle is carried near to the ship once more and Jim leaps aboard, at which point the coracle breaks up and disappears into the water. He manages to capture the ship and agrees with one remaining wounded pirate, Israel Hands, that they will cooperate to reach land. They successfully beach the ship, then Hands tries to kill Jim but dies in the attempt.

Jim goes ashore to find that Silver and his men have captured the stockade. Silver stops the pirates from killing Jim who is kept as a hostage. Jim is surprised to learn that Dr Livesey has handed over the treasure map to the pirates. They take Jim and go to get the treasure. They find the place but the treasure is gone, and at this point the Captain, the Doctor and the Squire lead a successful ambush on the disappointed and divided pirate party. Ben Gunn had found and moved the treasure years before. Jim and his friends head home with the treasure, leaving three surviving pirates on the island. Silver is taken on the ship but escapes during a stop-off in Spanish America. Once Jim reaches home, he determines never to return to Treasure Island.

Treasure Island is a narrative that invites identification in the heroic mode Freud sketches in 'Creative Writers and Day-Dreaming':

> The feeling of security with which I follow the hero through his perilous adventures is the same as the feeling with which a hero in real life throws himself into the water to save a drowning man or exposes himself to the enemy's fire in order to storm a battery. It is the true heroic feeling, which one of our best writers has expressed in an inimitable phrase: 'Nothing can happen to me!' It seems to me, however, that through this revealing characteristic of invulnerability we can immediately recognize His Majesty the Ego, the hero alike of every day-dream and of every story.[9]

Critical narratives and arguments have their heroes and heroic identifications too. They arise because there are so many hidden fears in reading. The most unheard-of and ego-troubling events are the ones that take place in language itself, and most critical reading reduces these events to meaning-producing processes. But hermeneutically driven reading has little or nothing to say about the indifferent energies of language in which, and by means of which, we try to find something of ourselves and the meanings that are acceptable to us. What if the recognition of inscription were the true cataclysm — the dislodging of the intuitive, reflecting, questioning, speculating 'I' and the exposure of its partial and contingent relation to the winds and tides of indifferent script? To read or write we need language. We need to identify ourselves fantasmatically in a relation to a language. We need to be carried in its mad linear rushes and to be taken along in its movement towards an otherness that, but for this movement and what it engenders in us, might escape us entirely.

The coracle has the openness of an ear. It might be said to follow the movements of the sea with free-floating attention.[10] The analyst Michael Eigen, writing about the treatment of psychosis, describes a 'mysterious lack of imposition' that might arise in psychoanalytic listening. He distinguishes between listening and making-sense. What Eigen tries to do for a psychotic patient, literature can do for us. Everyone needs something of this kind of rather simple, difficult, uncluttered listening:

> The psychotic hears but does not listen. He is overwhelmed by shouts from within that seem to come from everywhere. He needs someone to listen, not simply to make sense out of it all. Sense is cheap (sense is good, precious, but meanings galore swim in psychic seas). Beyond various psychic contents or meanings, he needs to see that someone can listen, that listening exists, in however faulty a mode. He needs to come to believe in listening. Passivity is important. It means, for moments, one is not trying to impose anything on anyone else or on oneself, and in that mysterious lack of imposition, things start to fall into place.[11]

The passivity of reading for pleasure might be seen as no longer simply opposed to critical rigour, but as a necessary element in reading's practical acknowledgement of the text as something other than a vehicle of sense.

Between one chapter and the next, that is between the sentence when Jim 'came to the edge of the retreating water, and wading a little way in, with some strength and dexterity, [sets his] coracle, keel downwards, on the surface' and the one when he signals that he will, in due course, be safely 'done with her', the coracle begins to take the anthropomorphic feminine pronoun traditionally given to boats:

> The coracle — as I had ample reason to know before I was done with her — was a very safe boat for a person of my height and weight, both buoyant and clever in a seaway; but she was the most cross-grained, lopsided craft to manage. (*TI*, 122)

Stevenson insisted *Treasure Island* was 'for boys; no need for psychology or fine writing; and I had a boy [his stepson Lloyd Osbourne, but also young RLS himself] at hand to be a touchstone. Women were excluded.'[12] It's a strangely lopsided and questionable preference of Stevenson's, at least on the face of it, but I am determined to take it lightly and go along for the ride. Stevenson is getting away from certain assumptions and trivial identifications surrounding psychology, literary language and their supposed universality. Empirical and apparently arbitrary starting points are necessary to inaugurate literary, psychoanalytic, literary-theoretical and other kinds of writing-invention. Stevenson was good friends with Henry James, and I also wonder whether he was running in the opposite direction from James's intense creative preoccupations with psychology, fine writing and women. Freud had his own tendency to follow the boy. Hélène Cixous has noted that specificity and refused to be excluded by it: 'I'm interested in the boy; that's psychoanalysis: to be interested in the boy, it starts like that. It starts with Freud being interested in the little Freud, in the boy Freud, and then in other little boys.'[13] The compelling identifications that fiction and other forms of writing can command have to start somewhere, but they don't end there. One gets *interested* and at that point the coded distinctions between fictional narrative, psychoanalytic or literary theory, like those between boy and woman, are revealed as somewhat unreal.

And it is true that the feminine coracle is neither girl, mother nor wife, nor any other kind of woman. It knows how to carry itself in and be carried by the sea, and once it is carrying Jim, he has to go, physically and therefore in his thinking, with the way the coracle moves and is moved. The pronouns suggest an ambiguous transport of sexual difference — one that initially looks more like a chance effect of language than an index of social relations. 'She', like Necessity, who is also feminine, teaches Jim about safety, fear, indirection and being carried, but there's no intention, no lessoning there:

> Do as you please, she always made more leeway than anything else, and turning round and round was the manoeuvre she was best at. Even Ben Gunn himself has admitted that she was 'queer to handle till you knew her way'. Certainly I did not know her way. She turned in every direction but the one I was bound to go; the most part of the time we were broadside on, and I am very sure I never should have made the ship at all but for the tide. By good fortune, paddle as I pleased, the tide was still sweeping me down; and there lay the Hispaniola right in the fair way, hardly to be missed. (*TI*, 122)

She turns: one of the coracle's moves is like that of a trope. This turning makes her a figure for the figural dimensions of writing, dimensions that have to do with direction, movement and formation rather than discursive meaning. She brings Jim magically (magically, because safely) close to forces more ancient than the Ancient Britons, more ancient than language. The coracle has a lot in common with *khōra*, as described by Plato in the *Timaeus*. *Khōra* appears in all sorts of ways, Plato says:

> that wet nurse of becoming, being liquefied and ignited and receiving the shapes of earth, and air, and suffering all the other affections that follow along with these, appears in all sorts of ways to our sight. And because she's filled with powers neither similar nor equally balanced, in no part of her is she equally balanced, but rather, as she sways irregularly in every direction, she herself is shaken by those kinds and, being moved, in turn shakes them back; and the kinds, in being moved, are always swept along this way and that and are dispersed — just like the particles shaken and winnowed out, by sieves and other instruments used for purifying grain: the dense and heavy are swept to one site and settle, the porous and light to another. So too, when the four kinds are shaken by the recipient, who, being herself moved, is like a sieve.[14]

The coracle doesn't have holes like a sieve, but she does have a filtering function. Her properties and proportions make her suitable only for single passengers capable of smallness, lightness and the risks involved in becoming.

Adrift for a long time, lying in the bottom of the coracle, Jim is eventually surprised by 'how easily and securely my little and light boat could ride' (TI, 127). It's as if he is out there for fun. Riding, here as elsewhere, describes the movement of reading and writing that is transported by the text, moving with the forces that gather there. The way the coracle moves is reminiscent of Freud's remarks about the ego's relation to the id: 'Often a rider, if he is not to be parted from his horse, is obliged to guide it where it wants to go; so in the same way the ego is in the habit of transforming the id's will into action as if it were its own' (*EI*, 25). Freud is using a familiar human example, the figure of rider and horse, and the language here may be psychological ('habit', 'will') but the analogy describes a movement that is neither habitual, voluntary nor psychological. It is not even human or animal in any recognisable sense.

The coracle is very responsive to small movements, so that there are unintended consequences even to sitting up in it:

> I began after a little to grow very bold, and sat up to try my skill at paddling. But even a small change in the disposition of the weight will produce violent changes in the behaviour of a coracle. And I had hardly moved before the boat, giving up at once her gentle dancing movement, ran straight down a slope of water so steep

that it made me giddy, and struck her nose, with a spout of spray, deep into the side of the next wave. (*TI*, 127)

Jim is very frightened but still peeps out and studies the coracle's movement, even as he floats in it, alone and on a heavy sea — as one might read a text, or as one might in one's life observe a repetition that remains irresistible, or as a psychoanalyst might listen:

> I was drenched and terrified, and fell instantly back into my old position, whereupon the coracle seemed to find her head again, and led me as softly as before among the billows. It was plain she was not to be interfered with, and at that rate, since I could in no way influence her course, what hope had I left of reaching land?
>
> I began to be horribly frightened, but I kept my head, for all that. First, moving with all care, I gradually baled out the coracle with my sea cap; then getting my eye once more above the gunwale, I set myself to study how it was she managed to slip so quietly through the rollers.
>
> I found each wave, instead of the big, smooth, glossy mountain it looks from shore, or from a vessel's deck, was for all the world like any range of hills on the dry land, full of peaks and smooth places and valleys. The coracle, left to herself, turning from side to side, threaded, so to speak, her way through these lower parts, and avoided the steep slopes and higher, toppling summits of the wave.
>
> 'Well, now', thought I to myself, 'it is plain I must lie where I am, and not disturb the balance; but it is plain also, that I can put the paddle over the side, and from time to time, in smooth places, give her a shove or two towards land'. No sooner thought upon than done. (*TI*, 127–8)

The coracle threads and rides (*reads* and *writes*, I would like to say) across the various and complex surfaces of each wave, close enough to let Jim observe. The coracle is 'safe' and moves 'easily and securely' through moments of fear. The proof of this safety is given by the narration itself, and in the cognitive effects it produces. We know for example that Jim lived to see a coracle, and was thus able to gather into comparable and narratable form the experiences of not-knowing, passive drifting, failed and more successful action — under the heading of something like a human relationship with a named entity whose movements he can study. He is to this extent a schoolboy, a student who learns that the forces of wind and tide that threaten him have the power to save him.

Literature and psychoanalysis both offer a new relation to fear. In 'Turning the Screw of Interpretation', Shoshana Felman quotes Henry James admitting to being afraid — politely afraid of his inability to comment on the meaning of his own writing: 'in truth I am afraid

(...) that I somehow can't pretend to give any coherent account of my small inventions "after the fact"' (Letter to F. W. Myers, quoted in WM, 245). And, in *The Turn of the Screw*, Felman suggests, fear is a side effect of a certain way of thinking about reading — of the thought of what the governess takes to be 'a dynamical relation between seeing and knowing, a conversion of the fact of seeing into the fact of knowing' (WM, 200–1). Felman associates seeing and not-seeing with an ambiguity 'inherent in the very essence of the act of seeing', and quotes the governess, who articulates how acting on a certain kind of wish to know what it is that one sees, to decipher, actually increases fear:

there are depths, depths! The more I go over it, the more I see in it, and the more I see in it, the more I fear. I don't know what I *don't* see — what I *don't* fear! (Felman citation, James's italics, *WM*, 201)

Going over it: that would be a way of thinking about reading. And '[t]he more I go over it (...) the more I fear'. Reading offers no escape from reading. Horror is a ghost effect and an effect of reading not to be taken literally.[15] Escapist reading uncannily turns back on itself. I may read to enjoy feeling invulnerable but still there is an action in reading that is not mine, a movement that is not mine but that I am drawn into, or that happens to me without my being able to appropriate it. The more I ask what is it, what does it mean, where is this taking me, the more fear, the less joy — and the less thinking.

The coracle is very small. There is no room in it for alibis, referees, patrons, makeweights, friends or even a single stranger.

★★★

In 'My First Book', Stevenson describes how *Treasure Island* was written:

I had written it up to the map. The map was the chief part of my plot. For instance I had called an islet 'Skeleton Island', not knowing what I meant, seeking only for the immediate picturesque, and it was to justify this that I broke into the gallery of Mr. Poe and stole Flint's pointer. And in the same way, it was because I had made two harbours that the *Hispaniola* was sent on her wanderings with Israel Hands. (*TI*, 197)

These wanderings of the *Hispaniola* begin where 'The Cruise of the Coracle' ends. Chapter XXIV culminates in a collision and a leap: 'I had scarce time to think — scarce time to act and save myself. I was on the summit of one swell when the schooner came stooping over the next. The bowsprit was over my head. I sprang to my feet, and leaped, stamping the coracle under water' (130). No looking back for Jim, just hearing the 'dull blow' that 'told me that the schooner had charged down upon and struck the coracle, and that I was left without retreat on the *Hispaniola*' (130). The small experimental action of thinking would be meaningless havering without something of this capacity for the thinker to advance alone (to think-without-thinking) when it is necessary in order to keep up with the movement of a thought.

Stevenson had joined his stepson making drawings: the boy 'had no thought of literature' and Stevenson 'would sometimes unbend a little, join the artist (so to speak) at the easel, and pass the afternoon with him in a generous emulation, making coloured drawings' (*TI*, 193). The map is not what a map usually is, a scale representation of somewhere or something that exists:

> I made the map of an island; it was elaborately and (I thought) beautifully coloured; the shape of it took my fancy beyond expression; it contained harbours that pleased me like sonnets; and with the unconsciousness of the predestined I ticketed my performance 'Treasure Island'. I am told there are people who don't care for maps, and find it hard to believe. (*TI*, 193)

The map Stevenson is writing about here is not useful in making the move from seeing to knowing, the move that Felman recognizes in Henry James's governess with her wish to convert 'the fact of seeing into the fact of knowing' (WM, 201–2). Stevenson's map was *for him*. It is the trace of pleasure landing. It registers with him in terms of feeling: to him it was beautiful in colour, shape and form and its colour, shape and form all come from him, while also coming to him in an absolutely fresh way. We don't get to see this map, and if we did, we might not get it. The Treasure is the happy effect of the arrival of the Island on the artist himself, who is very close at that moment to being a child at play. A touch of self-deprecating humour protects him, as Henry James's polite remark about not being able to account for his 'small inventions "after the fact"' protected him, from pirates who always want to get hold of writing, to finally know where it comes from and what it means.

The map in *Treasure Island* itself is for the most part hidden. The map Stevenson drew before he wrote the book was hidden from Stevenson until he drew it. Then it was lost. He sent it to his publishers, Cassell, with the manuscript of the book: 'The proofs came, they were corrected, but I heard nothing of the map. I wrote and asked; was *told it had never been received*, and sat aghast' (*TI*, 197, my italics). Aghast as he was, the loss of the map protects Stevenson's Treasure. In *Treasure Island*, the map exerts its power from inside wrappers and packets or slipped into pockets, for example as part of 'a bundle tied up in oilcloth, and looking like papers' (*TI*, 23). Without knowing what it is, Jim picks it up, concealed in an 'oilskin packet' (24). It is sealed, carried, argued over. The pirates wreck everything looking for it. They want money now and more money later and the map means the latter: '"They might have hid the blessed thing... Take the Georges, Pew, and don't stand here squalling"' (27). There are those who can defer a bit, like Dr Livesey, who took the oilskin packet and 'looked it all over, as if his fingers were itching to open it; but, instead of doing that, he put it quietly in the pocket of his coat' (31). When the map is opened it remains to be read: it shows an island 'shaped, you might say, like a fat dragon standing up' (33). When it is put to use to find the treasure, the pirates find only 'a great excavation, not very recent' (180). Jim does see 'great heaps of coin and quadrilaterals built of bars of gold' but the emphasis doesn't stay there (184). The story of how the gold was moved invites the identification of a pirate and a fool — it 'profoundly interested Silver; and Ben Gunn, the half-idiot maroon, was the hero from beginning to end' (183). 'The map was the chief part of my plot', Stevenson confesses. 'I might almost say it was the whole' (197). The map is a figure for what opens reading, or motivates writing, or starts thinking but does not appear, uncovered, in it or to it.

Freud writes about thinking in 'Anxiety and Instinctual Life' ('Angst und Triebleben', recently retranslated by Helena Ragg-Kirkby as 'Fear and the Drives'): 'Thinking is an experimental action carried out with small amounts of energy [*kleinen Energiemengen*], in the same way as a general shifts small figures [*kleiner Figuren*] about on a map before setting his large bodies of troops [*Truppenmassen*] in motion' (AI, 89).[16] Stevenson's inaugural map was drawn 'at random' and its scale set in the corner 'at a venture' (*TI*, 197). The general is a grown-up with a life-and-death job to do; his map is not just made up. The *kleiner Figuren* must correspond reliably to the *Truppenmassen*. But in Freud's text, where the general and his map is just one more figure for something unimaginable that moves meaning without being reducible to it, there is no such guarantee of cartographical scale. Freud is at pains to indicate that what he is getting up to, or writing up to, has never been received. It remains untranslatable and unreadable, while generating all sorts of meanings and reading-effects.[17] At the close of the paragraph from which I have just quoted, the audience of his imaginary lecture interrupts:

'Stop a moment!' you will exclaim; 'we can't follow you any further there!' You are quite right; I must add a little more before it can seem acceptable to you. First, I must admit that I have tried to translate into the language of our normal thinking what must in fact be a process that is neither conscious nor preconscious, taking place between quotas of energy in some unimaginable substratum. But that is not a strong objection, for it cannot be done in any other way. (AI, 90)

★★★

Sometimes you find yourself hiding, hoping not to be noticed. You slip over the side and curl up in the nearest boat. It is mad. You dream or daydream as an alternative to fear, or despair, or prayer. You make a break for it, as if you were moving a small figure — but secretly, obviously, it's you who moves and is moved. You are Jim Hawkins. Long John Silver calls you back. You are Robert Louis Stevenson. John Addington Symonds would like you to write a book of essays.[18] You don't listen: 'I paid no heed; jumping, ducking and breaking through, I ran straight before my nose, till I could run no longer' (TI, 72). The conditions of emergence of thinking are risky. Who is the general when he moves those figures? What is happening? Who feels the 'joy of exploration' (TI, 74)? Joy frees; fear positions. There is a folly in thinking, as well as in not thinking. No sooner does Jim think of leaving friends and safety, than he's over the stockade: 'I was a fool, if you like, and certainly I was going to do a foolish, over-bold act; but I was determined to do it with all the precautions in my power' (118). He takes some biscuits and a couple of guns.

The maps of writers tend to become invisible. They are described, but they can't be found. Stevenson's gets lost in the post. Sculptor Juan Muñoz's map of the Guarana River 'designed by Yago Levinas around 1550' is also fabulous, with its

> tiny sailboats strolling along the Seadragon. The river sides are covered with exotic plants and the trees, meticulously drawn, are covered with schematic clouds that indicate the direction of the winds. Every time I get bored, or lose myself in thought, I look at that river and follow it, from its beginning to its mouth emptying into the ocean.[19]

It somehow leads Muñoz's text out of boredom or thought, back to Stevenson — but the map no more exists than the one in Jorge Luis Borges's 'On Exactitude and Science'.[20] A general movement of expropriation in writing gives the opportunity to escape, which, according to Muñoz, remembering Stevenson, comes from something that goes under the name of *maps*: 'I remember having read in one of his books that Robert Louis Stevenson [said] (...) that in the room where a writer works, there should always be one table covered with maps, plans and travel books' (SI, 4). That table is, Muñoz says, 'a stage constructed solely for disappearing. As if it were a magic trick. A disappearing act. He who sits there, is no longer there' (4). There is an affinity between writing, reading, unlocatability and a movement without which thinking loses itself in the hesitation and complacency of the known. You climb into the apple barrel but there is 'scarce an apple left' (*TI*, 56). You nearly fall asleep 'sitting down there in the dark, what with the sound of the waters and the rocking of the ship'. You come to surrounded by *pirates*, so that you would not show yourself 'for all the world,' but there you lie, 'trembling and listening, in the extreme of fear and curiosity...'

NOTES

1 Shoshana Felman, *Writing and Madness (Literature / Philosophy / Psychoanalysis)*, translated by Martha Noel Evans and the author, with the assistance of Brian Massumi (Palo Alto: Stanford University Press, 2003), 273. Hereafter abbreviated as *WM*.

2 Sigmund Freud, 'Anxiety and Instinctual Life', translated by James Strachey, *Standard Edition*, vol. XXII (1932–6): *New Introductory Lectures on Psychoanalysis and Other Works* (London: Vintage Books, 2001), 89. Hereafter abbreviated as AI.

3 Shoshana Felman, *What Does a Woman Want? Reading and Sexual Difference* (London and New York: Johns Hopkins University Press, 1991), 4.

4 Jacques Derrida, 'My Chances / *Mes chances*: A Rendezvous with Some Epicurean Stereotomies', translated by Irene Harvey and Avital Ronell, in *Psyche: The Invention of the Other*, vol. I, edited by Peggy Kamuf and Elisabeth Rottenberg (Stanford: Stanford University Press, 2007), 345.

5 Shoshana Felman, *Jacques Lacan and the Adventure of Insight: Psychoanalysis in Contemporary Culture* (Cambridge and London: Harvard University Press, 1987), 5.

6 Robert Louis Stevenson, *Treasure Island*, edited by John Seelye (London: Penguin, 1999), 120–1. Hereafter abbreviated as *TI*.

7 Sigmund Freud, 'The Question of Lay Analysis', *The Standard Edition of the Complete Psychological Works of Sigmund Freud*, vol. XX (1925–6): *An Autobiographical Study, Inhibitions, Symptoms and Anxiety, Lay Analysis and Other Works* (London: Vintage, 2001), 195. See also 'The Ego and the Id', *Standard Edition*, vol. XIX (1923–5): *The Ego and the Id and Other Works* (London: Vintage 2001) 26. Hereafter abbreviated as *EI*.

8   Recently reissued in English: Didier Anzieu, *The Skin-Ego*, translated by Naomi Segal (London: Karnac Books, 2016).
9   Sigmund Freud, 'Creative Writers and Day-dreaming', *Standard Edition*, vol. IX (1906–8): *Jensen's 'Gradiva' and Other Works* (London: Vintage, 2001), 148–9.
10 'Free-floating attention' is one translation of Freud's *gleichschwebende Aufmerksamkeit* (*Gesammelte Werke* VIII, 376). The phrase describes the analyst's contribution to following the free associations of the analysand. See Sigmund Freud, 'Recommendations for Physicians Practicing Psychoanalysis', *Standard Edition*, vol. XII (1911–13): *The Case of Schreber, Papers on Technique and Other Works* (London: Vintage, 2001), 110.
11 Michael Eigen, 'Half and Half', *Fort Da* 8 (2002), 16–17.
12 'My First Book' in *TI*, 193. We should also mention Jim's mother and Silver's wife, not forgetting the *Hispaniola* and Silver's female parrot, Captain Flint.
13 'A Kind of Magic', *Paragraph* 36:2 (2013), 168. I had the pleasure of hearing this keynote lecture in 2007 at 'Hélène Cixous, Jacques Derrida: Their Psychoanalyses' organized by the School of Fine Art, History of Art & Cultural Studies, University of Leeds.
14 Plato, *Timaeus* 52d—53a, translated by Peter Kalkavage (Newburyport, MA: Focus, 2001), 85 quoted and modified by Jacques Derrida, 'Why Peter Eisenmann Writes Such Good Books', *Psyche: Inventions of the Other*, vol. II, edited by Peggy Kamuf and Elizabeth Rottenberg (Stanford: Stanford University Press, 2008), 110–11.
15 See, for example, *WM*, 224–5, n. 52.
16 AI, 89. In German: 'Das Denken ist ein probeweises Handeln mit kleinen Energiemengen, ähnlich wie die Verschiebungen kleiner Figuren auf der Landkarte, ehe der Feldherr seine Truppenmassen in Bewegung setzt'. Sigmund Freud, 'Vorlesung. Angst und Triebleben', *Gesammelte Werke* XV, 95. A passage in 'Negation' emphasizes the difference between thinking and action and the delay involved. It also has thinking feeling its way: 'an experimental action [*Probeaktion*], a motor palpating [*tasten*, to grope or feel], with small expenditure of discharge.' 'Negation', *Standard Edition*, vol. XIX (1923–5): *EI*, 237.
17 This happens by means of *anasemic conversion*. See Elissa Marder, 'Snail Conversions: Derrida's Turns with Ponge', *Oxford Literary Review* 37:2 (2015), 181–96; Jacques Derrida, 'Fors: The Anglish Words of Nicolas Abraham and Maria Torok', translated by Barbara Johnson, *The Wolf Man's Magic Word: A Cryptonymy*, by Nicolas Abraham and Maria Torok (Minneapolis: University of Minnesota Press, 1987) xxxiv–xxxv; and 'Me — Psychoanalysis', translated by Richard Klein, in *Psyche: Inventions of the Other, Volume 1*, edited by Peggy Kamuf and Elizabeth Rottenberg (Stanford: Stanford University Press, 2007), 135.

18 Stevenson recounts Symonds's idea that he 'should write on the "Characters" of Theophrastus' rather than indulging in (Stevenson's words) the 'capitulations of sincerity and solecisms of style' involved in writing a tale of adventure called 'Treasure Island' (*TI*, 196).
19 Juan Muñoz, 'A Standard Introduction to Lectures', *Gagarin* 1 (2000), 4. Hereafter abbreviated as SI.
20 Jorge Luis Borges, 'On Exactitude in Science', *The Aleph, including the Prose Fictions from The Maker*, translated by Andrew Hurley (London: Penguin, 2000), 181.

Dream Treatment: On Sitting Down to Read a Letter from Freud

NICHOLAS ROYLE

I wake up awash in the cries of herring gulls, not yet light, and am thinking what an extraordinary thing, in 2017, to have received a letter from Freud, fresh this morning, written in English. It's the ever-odd of the hypnopompic, how much can be held, recalled, cradled before the great tsunami of oblivion called 'everyday life'. I know that there were several sentences, already receding in a great silent sucking motion, passed all tensions, all tense past, but the only words that survive the experience of being hauled up out of the quicksands of sleep into the not-yet-day of gulls' screeching, squawking, croaking, quacking, clucking rapidly all around the housetop amount to a single verbless sentence: 'Probably not.' These words initially instil a feeling of great calm, as if Freud is reassuring me: it might never happen. *Probably not.* You wonder if the world is coming to an end, on your phone last night you read in the newspaper online that the USA has just 'dropped the largest non-nuclear bomb ever used in combat' somewhere in Afghanistan, you put the phone to charge on a small table beside your desk (only now registering the association of this table with somewhere in the region of Afghanistan — a beautifully carved, if rather battered and cracked little table you bought for five pounds at an auction in Cheam village with your mother one day in the 1970s — and seeing that you actually put the phone down on top of a small volume containing Wilhelm Jensen's *Gradiva* and Freud's 'Delusion and Dream in Wilhelm Jensen's *Gradiva*',[1] in such a way that it concealed the lower half of Freud's face but left his piercing left eye still gazing out above it, his right eye in shadow, and only now puzzling over the fact that it is his face rather than Jensen's that occupies the front cover), you recall pondering as you were leaving the bathroom to ascend the final flight of stairs into the attic what was the difference, what will have been the difference between 'nuclear' and 'non-nuclear' in this context, how long will it be before we hear that a nuclear device, perhaps the smallest ever used by the USA in combat since 1945, was just dropped, dropped earlier today or in the night? What has the US president done now, since I went to sleep? That is the question on your mind these days, every morning when you wake up. Will the world soon come to witness, under the insanity or what other political leaders prefer to call the 'unpredictability' of Donald Trump, nuclear bombs regularly dropped here and there, or will everything remain at the level of dropping the occasional GBU–43/B or Mother Of All Bombs (MOABs)?

All of that, including Freud's eye merely unconsciously noted, at the time, keeping watch from the cover of Jensen's *Gradiva* (only now, thinking of 'Mountains Covered with Cats', does it occur to me that Wallace Stevens's idea — the dear 'I' and dear 'eye' of the idea — that 'Freud's eye was the microscope of potency',[2] must have been inspired by a photograph, perhaps this one), plus so much more, stockpiled anxiety in sleep, exploding in a missive directly from Freud. Like a tweet from Donald Trump. This was another ingredient of the Daily Residue: I had been reading an essay by Howard Jacobson about Trump's tweets. He recalls Hugh Laurie's tweeted query about Trump's language, the tweet messages full of clichéd nouns and adjectives: 'Will there be a separate news conference for the verbs?' Jacobson writes:

> Language has its own power to lead the mind out of smallness. There is a fibrous, organic subtlety in words. They grow connotations. They educate the user of them to want and employ more. They are not the merely outward signs of what we have already made our minds up about; they are the means by which our minds learn to know themselves and discover what else they might come to know. This is what makes the circularity of Trump's speech patterns so telling: the walls he wants to build to keep out unwanted migrants are identical to those that wall him in linguistically. Nothing strange to him is allowed entry.[3]

Imagine Freud's tweets, gathered up from his vast oeuvre, from all the letters as well as essays. Among them might be: 'An author's words are deeds.'[4] Can we expect to see *The Selected Tweets of Sigmund Freud* anytime soon? Probably not.

Trump tweets, Freud treats. I am treated to a letter, treated by a letter from Freud. I now see, as never before, how the thought of the dream as a treat, as a kind of gift, as something 'given without expense to the recipient' (in the rather niggardly phrasing of the *OED*: see *treat* n1, sense I, 4a), might connect, precisely in the element of dreaming, with 'treat' as '[t]he action or an act of treating, or discussing terms; parley, negotiation; agreement; treaty' (sense I, 1), with 'treat' in the obsolete sense of 'trace' (sense II, 9), and finally with the notion of psychoanalytic *treatment*. The dream treats the dreamer. Writing, it seems to me, as well as any other so-called clinical or therapeutic activity, enables the critical and productive encounter of two of the most radical aspects of psychoanalysis: 'free association' and 'deferred effect'. Psychoanalysis begins with the free association to which Freud subjects himself in analysing his own dreams in *The Interpretation of Dreams*, and it ends with the uncanny, inexhaustible demands of acknowledging the workings of *Nachträglichkeit* (deferred meaning, afterwardsness, delayed effect, after-sense and so on). Just as he himself returns, several years later, in his Preface to the Second Edition of *The Interpretation* in 1908, to observe that

> this book has a further subjective significance for me personally — a significance which I only grasped after I had completed it. It was, I found, a portion of my own self-analysis, my reaction to my father's death — that is to say, to the most important event, the most poignant loss, of a man's life.[5]

The dream is a gift, but there is always mourning too, not just in a case of dreaming of someone you love but never knew, could never have known. As Jacques Derrida says in 'Fichus' (also in the context of recalling the death of his father, his dying father):

> dreaming is the element most receptive to mourning, to haunting, to the spectrality of all spirits and the return of the ghosts (...) The dream is also a place that is hospitable to the demand for justice and to the most invincible of messianic hopes.[6]

You receive the dream like a letter from the beyond. 'Dreams await us in a country we can't get tickets to', remarks Hélène Cixous.[7] She stresses what so few notice, the might of the future in relation to dreaming. They wait for us, they are up ahead. There is no bus or taxi, passport or other document enabling entry. And then the dream country lovingly releases you, without your ever having had a proper chance to get your bearings. The dream feels like a treat, but always with some feeling of the unknown and the supernatural. To receive a letter from Freud — it's 'too good to be true', as he might have said.[8] And for this to be 2017, to be the recipient of a letter written nearly eighty years after his death — incredible, it's 'post-truth'! And then, also, it is in English: I still feel, as I did in the dream, a strangely intense gratitude, that he should have been so kind, so generous and courteous as to write the letter in English, knowing that I do not speak German.

I am sitting at my desk and don't know what to do. I already failed to do what I meant to do, what I should have done, namely write the dream down the moment I woke up, but I couldn't because I had no paper or pen or other means of writing by my bedside. I phone Hélène because I'd promised to do so, and we talk about this and that, mostly books, and I mention that I've had this dream, I received a letter from Freud but cannot recall anything of it except: 'Probably not.' She laughs at the other end of the line in Paris, she laughs with that warm, high, childlike laugh I love, a salve, a sleepy oneiric laughter for good, and I remark on the washed-out remains, as if microscopic, just that single sentential trace: *Probably not*. Still there is a feeling of elation of having for the first time in my life received a letter from him. She laughs and says: 'You keep receiving letters from him but you just don't recognize them.' Then she tells me that she has been writing about his essay on Dostoevsky and has been struck by Freud's lack of laughter there, a sense that this man's envy for another man gets in the way.

Of course, she is right, Freud is treating me, treating all of us all the time, and we listen to this and learn, but the dream treatment is something else. As she says in her account of 'The School of Dreams' in 1990:

Like plants, dreams have enemies, plant lice that devour them. The dream's enemy is interpretation. I used to read *The Interpretation of Dreams* with passion, but, though it is a marvelous book, it is a true dream-killer since it *interprets*. It wants to make the dream cough up. The dreams interpreted by Freud in *The Interpretation of Dreams* are all alike: although there is a difference in content, a different nucleus, the writing is the same. The dreams are written by Freud, both his own and those of other people. The flesh of the dream is no longer there. This is the great danger. We must know how to treat the dream as a dream, to leave it free, and to distrust all the exterior and interior demons that destroy dreams. (*Ladder*, 107)

How to treat the dream as a dream: is it possible? Probably not. But this is the driving desire. To treat a dream as dream, to allow ourselves to be *treated* by the dream: this has to do with freedom ('leave it free') and a sense of justice ('the demand for justice', in Derrida's phrase).

The dream continues to recede as the day advances and I sit at my desk. I reread — for the first time in nearly thirty years — Freud's 'A Note on the Unconscious in Psychoanalysis' (1912), a text that he originally wrote in English and that was first published in a special issue of the *Proceedings of the Society for Psychical Research* in London.[9] This calls me back to the fact that, when I tried to write about this text in 1989, it was in the form of a letter ('A Letter on Poetry'), a kind of telepathic letter about literature, dreaming, the hypnopompic and the hypnagogic, which treated Freud's 'Note on the Unconscious' as a letter to the SPR — to which no one, until then, had troubled to respond.[10] What was going on, I wanted to know, and I still ask this question, what is Freud up to in this text when he deploys the word 'foreconscious' instead of 'preconscious', and 'psychical' instead of 'mental'?[11] As I reread 'A Note on the Unconscious' I am struck anew by the clarity of his writing, here perhaps especially given that he is writing it in English. And I see, as so often when rereading Freud, things I didn't see or don't remember from last time I read it. Besides the peculiarities of the 'psychical' and 'foreconscious', for example, there is the intriguing and repeated use of the word 'repulsion' instead of 'defence' or 'fending off' (see 'Note' 264, n1). Is there, I find myself wondering, a *'probably not'* that I have forgotten, a sort of inversion of the *'lapsus linguæ'* (263) of which he speaks? Probably not. But the search for this ghostly phrase (the only words the dead man has ever addressed directly to me) leads to a reflection on that sort of classic Freudian metadiscursive turn, when he stops and says: 'Before continuing my exposition I will refer to two objections which are likely to be raised at this point' (262–3). He outlines the first:

instead of subscribing to the hypothesis of unconscious ideas of which we know nothing, we had better assume that consciousness can be split up, so that certain ideas or other psychical acts may constitute a consciousness apart, which has become detached and estranged from the bulk of conscious psychical activity. (263)

It is difficult not to admire the way in which Freud splits himself up in this gesture, assuming the assumption of another. He goes on to dismiss this imagined objection with brio:

We have no right to extend the meaning of this word ['conscious'] so far as to make it include a consciousness of which its owner himself is not aware. If philosophers find difficulty in accepting the existence of unconscious ideas, the existence of an unconscious consciousness seems to me even more objectionable. (263)

Freud then observes: 'The other objection that may probably be raised would be that we apply to normal psychology conclusions which are drawn chiefly from the study of pathological conditions' (263). The play of the *likely* ('objections which are likely to be raised') and the *probably* ('The other objection that may probably be raised') take on a new strangeness for me. His 'likely' is 'Not likely!'; his 'probably' a resounding '*Probably not.*' They are part of Freud's rhetoric, his lucidity and ingenuity in anticipating counter-arguments, but they are also part of the literary character of his writing, his introduction of other voices, his proliferation of possible or, in his terms, *probable* subject-positions. Psychoanalytic verisimilitude and the laws of probability. Still to be written: *Psychoanalysis and Literature: A Theory of Psychical Realism*.

Against the insanity of Donald Trump (and a few others), Freud offers an insanity far more imaginatively interesting, subtle and promising: 'There is one psychical product to be met with in the most normal persons, which yet presents a very striking analogy to the wildest productions of insanity, and was no more intelligible to philosophers than insanity itself. I refer to dreams. Psychoanalysis is founded upon the analysis of dreams' ('Note', 264–5).

Analysis: untying, literally. And now it has receded so far, grown so dim already, that no longer able to see at all I hear, for the first time, the irrepressible homophone that English gives: *Probably knot*. Everything about psychoanalysis seems to insist on memory and the past, but really it is about the future. Apropos Freud's celebrated remark that every dream has a navel, a 'spot where it reaches down into the unknown',[12] Derrida declares: 'What forever exceeds the analysis of the dream is indeed a knot that cannot be untied.'[13] *Probably knot*: I hear it, washing back once again into the muttering, squabbling, mewing, passionate strains of the cries of seagulls.

Seaford, East Sussex
Good Friday 2017

NOTES

1 Wilhelm Jensen, *Gradiva* / Sigmund Freud, *Delusion and Dream in Wilhelm Jensen's* Gradiva, translated by Helen M. Downey (Los Angeles: Green Integer, 2003).
2 'Mountains Covered with Cats' in Wallace Stevens, *Collected Poetry and Prose* (New York: Library of America, 1997), 319.
3 Howard Jacobson, 'Point of View', *The Guardian*, Review (8 April 2017), 13.
4 Sigmund Freud, 'To Thomas Mann on His Sixtieth Birthday' in *The Standard Edition of the Complete Psychological Works of Sigmund Freud* (hereafter *SE*), 24 vols, translated and edited by James Strachey, in collaboration with Anna Freud, assisted by Alix Strachey and Alan Tyson (London: Vintage, 2001): here *SE* 22, 255.

5 Sigmund Freud, *The Interpretation of Dreams*, SE 4, xxvi.
6 Jacques Derrida, 'Fichus' in *Paper Machine*, translated by Rachel Bowlby (Stanford: Stanford University Press, 2005), 173–4.
7 Hélène Cixous, *Three Steps on the Ladder of Writing*, translated by Sarah Cornell and Susan Sellers (New York: Columbia University Press, 1993), 58. Hereafter abbreviated as *Ladder*.
8 See Sigmund Freud, 'A Disturbance of Memory on the Acropolis: An Open Letter to Romain Rolland on the Occasion of His Seventieth Birthday', *SE* 22, 242.
9 See 'A Note on the Unconscious in Psychoanalysis' in *SE* 12, 255–6. Hereafter abbreviated as 'Note'.
10 Nicholas Royle, 'A Letter on Poetry' in *Telepathy and Literature: Essays on the Reading Mind* (Oxford: Blackwell, 1991), 121–41.
11 See 'A Letter on Poetry', 134.
12 Sigmund Freud, *The Interpretation of Dreams* in *SE* 5, 525.
13 Jacques Derrida, 'Resistances' in *Resistances of Psychoanalysis*, translated by Peggy Kamuf, Pascale-Anne Brault and Michael Naas (Stanford: Stanford University Press, 1998), 11.

Notes on Contributors

Isabelle Alfandary is Professor of American Literature and Critical Theory at the University Sorbonne Nouvelle. She is also President of the Collège international de philosophie. Her programme at the college is on 'Psychoanalysis and Deconstruction'. She has published extensively on American poetry and on the relationships between literature, philosophy and psychoanalysis: *E. E. Cummings ou la minuscule lyrique* (Belin, 2002), *Le Risque de la lettre* (ENS-Editions, 2012) and *Derrida-Lacan: l'écriture entre psychanalyse et déconstruction* (Hermann, 2016). In her current book project, she is addressing the styles of Freud's writings.

Cathy Caruth is Frank H. T. Rhodes Professor of Humane Letters at Cornell University and teaches in the Departments of English and Comparative Literature. She focuses on the languages of trauma and testimony, on literary theory, and on contemporary discourses concerning the annihilation and survival of language. Her most recent books are *Literature in the Ashes of History* (The Johns Hopkins University Press, 2013) and *Listening to Trauma: Conversations with Leaders in the Theory and Treatment of Catastrophic Experience* (Interviews and Photography by Cathy Caruth) (The Johns Hopkins University Press, 2014).

Shoshana Felman is Woodruff Professor of Comparative Literature and French at Emory University, Thomas E. Donnelley Professor Emerita of French and Comparative Literature at Yale University, and an elected member of the American Academy of Arts and Sciences. Her influential work (among other foci) on the intersection of literature and psychoanalysis first found its marked historical expression in the collective volume of *Yale French Studies* she edited in 1977, *Literature and Psychoanalysis: The Question of Reading: Otherwise*. This volume has been foundational in opening up this entire field. Among Felman's key publications (in English and in French) are *The Claims of Literature: A Shoshana Felman Reader* (Fordham University Press, 2007);

The Juridical Unconscious: Trials and Traumas in the Twentieth Century (Harvard University Press, 2002); *What Does a Woman Want? Reading and Sexual Difference* (The Johns Hopkins University Press, 1993); *Testimony: Crises of Witnessing in Literature Psychoanalysis and History* (co-authored with Dori Laub) (Routledge, 1992); *Jacques Lacan and the Adventure of Insight: Psychoanalysis in Contemporary Culture* (Harvard University Press, 1987); *Writing and Madness: Literature/Psychoanalysis/Philosophy* (Stanford University Press, 2003); *The Scandal of the Speaking Body: Don Juan with J. L. Austin, or Seduction in Two Languages* (Stanford University Press, 2003).

Elissa Marder is Professor of French and Comparative Literature at Emory University, Atlanta, where she is also affiliated with the Departments of Philosophy and Women's Studies. She is a founding member of the Emory Psychoanalytic Studies Program and served as its Director from 2001 to 2006. She is the author of *Dead Time: Temporal Disorders in the Wake of Modernity (Baudelaire and Flaubert)* (Stanford University Press, 2001), *The Mother in the Age of Mechanical Reproduction: Psychoanalysis, Photography, Deconstruction* (Fordham University Press, 2012) and co-editor (with E. S. Burt and Kevin Newmark) of *Time for Baudelaire (Poetry, Theory, History)*, special volume of *Yale French Studies* 125/126 (Spring, 2014).

Forbes Morlock teaches in the English Department at Syracuse University London. *Literature and Psychoanalysis* was one of the first academic books he bought that had not been assigned for a course. He took Shoshana Felman's 'Freud and Lacan' seminar twice as an undergraduate, and has been reading and writing on Freud ever since: his publications include *Interpretation*, vol. 1 (with Simon Morris and Liz Dalton) (information as material, 2002), *Freud and the Gift of Flowers* (with Sharon Kivland) (information as material, 2009) and essays in *Angelaki*, *JCFAR* and *Visual Resources*.

Claire Nouvet is Associate Professor in the Department of French and Italian at Emory University. She is the author of *Abélard et Héloïse: la passion de la maîtrise* (Presses universitaires du Septentrion, 2009); *Enfances Narcisse* (Galilée, 2009); editor of *Literature and the Ethical Question, Yale French Studies*, 1991); co-editor (with Zrinka Stahuljak, and Kent Still) of *Minima Memoria: In the Wake of Jean François Lyotard* (Stanford University Press, 2007)); and co-editor (with Julie Gaillard and Mark Stoholski) of *Traversals of Affect: On Jean-François Lyotard* (Bloomsbury Press, 2016).

Avital Ronell teaches at New York University and is the Jacques Derrida Professor of Philosophy and Media at the European Graduate School in Switzerland. Her most recent works include *Loser Sons: Politics and Authority* (University of Illinois Press, 2013) and *Fighting Theory* (University of Illinois Press, 2010), with Anne Dufourmantelle.

Elizabeth Rottenberg teaches philosophy and comparative literature at DePaul University, Chicago. She also has a psychoanalytic practice. She is the editor or translator of numerous works by Jacques Derrida, Jean-François Lyotard and Maurice Blanchot, as well as the author of *Inheriting the Future: Legacies of Kant, Freud and Flaubert* (Stanford University Press, 2005) and *For the Love of Psychoanalysis* (forthcoming).

Nicholas Royle is Professor of English at the University of Sussex, UK. His books include *Telepathy and Literature* (Blackwell, 1991), *After Derrida* (Manchester University Press, 1995), *The Uncanny* (Manchester University Press, 2003), *Jacques Derrida* (Routledge, 2003), *How to Read Shakespeare* (Granta, 2005), *In Memory of Jacques Derrida* (Edinburgh University Press, 2009) and *Veering: A Theory of Literature* (Edinburgh University Press, 2011). He is co-author (with Andrew Bennett) of *Elizabeth Bowen and the Dissolution of the Novel* (Palgrave Macmillan, 1994), *This Thing Called Literature* (Routledge, 2015) and *An Introduction to Literature, Criticism and Theory*, 5th edition (Routledge, 2016). In addition, he has edited a number of issues of the *Oxford Literary Review* focused on psychoanalysis and literature, including *Psychoanalysis and Literature: New Work* (12:1–2, 1990) (co-edited with Ann Wordsworth); *Telepathies* (30:2, 2008) and *Literature, Psychoanalysis, Deconstruction* (38:2, 2016). Royle has also published two novels, *Quilt* (Myriad, 2010) and *An English Guide to Birdwatching* (Myriad, 2017).

Sarah Wood is Reader in English Literature and Literary Theory at the University of Kent, UK. She also works as a psychoanalytic psychotherapist in private practice. Recent publications include *Experiences of Conversion*, a special issue of *Oxford Literary Review* (37: 2, 2015), *Without Mastery: Reading and Other Forces* (Edinburgh University Press, 2014) and 'Swans of Life (External Provocations & Autobiographical Flights That Teach Us How to Read)' in *The Animal Question in Deconstruction*, edited by Lynn Turner (Edinburgh University Press, 2013).